A MILLION A MINUTE

A MILLION A MINUTE

INSIDE THE WORLD OF SECURITIES TRADING—THE MEN, THE WOMEN, THE MONEY THAT MAKE THE MARKETS WORK

HILLARY DAVIS

HarperBusiness
A Division of HarperCollinsPublishers

HarperCollins books may be purchased for educational, business, or sales promotional use. For information please write: Special Markets Department, HarperCollins Publishers, Inc., 10 East 53rd Street, New York, NY 10022.

FIRST EDITION

Designed by Nancy Singer Olaguera

Library of Congress Cataloging-in-Publication Data

Davis, Hillary, 1952–
   A million a minute : inside the world of securites trading ; the men, the women, the money that make the markets work / Hillary Davis.
      p. cm.
   Includes bibliographical references.
   ISBN 0-88730-941-0
   1. Stockbrokers. 2. Floor traders (Finance) I. Title.
HG4621.D295 1998
332.64—DC21   98-28133

98 99 00 01 02 ❖/RRD 10 9 8 7 6 5 4 3 2

CONTENTS

PART III: LOOKING FORWARD

ACKNOWLEDGMENTS

First and foremost, my thanks go to Nicholas Brealey for publishing the original U.K. edition of *A Million a Minute*, as well as to Sally Lansdell for her editing endeavors. My deep appreciation goes to David Conti at HarperCollins, who provided the impetus to bring the book to the U.S. and whose enthusiasm, encouragement, and fresh outlook greatly added to the newly written version.

My attempts to find literature on the topic were supported by the following. In New York: Meg Ventrudo at the Museum of American Financial History; Allison Ramlal at the Federal Reserve Bank of New York; the New York Public Library; the Columbia University Library. In London: the City Business Library, the United Oxford and Cambridge Club Library, and the Cambridge University Library.

I am especially indebted to a loyal group of friends who unselfishly offered their support, hospitality, and comments: Blandine Beaulieu, Anne Tilney Brune, David Conway, Marion Cotrone, Anne Davis, Craig Davis, Ben Eaton, Courtney Hafela, Grove Hafela, Charles Hollander, Heather Pilley, George Sheinberg, and Susan Wood.

The following professionals in the business provided insight, interviews, and contacts. I wish especially to express my gratitude to Joe Stein at Wasserstein Perella. Thanks also go to: Chris Andersen at Andersen Weinroth; M. Belgarde at the Paris Bourse; Frank Bergeot at Cholet Dupont; Michael Bloomberg at Bloomberg Financial; Jeff Chandor at Merrill Lynch; Lou Eisenberg at Granite Capital; Harlan Flint at INSTINET; Gary Goldstein at The Whitney Group; Patti Harris at Bloomberg Financial; John Heiman at Merrill Lynch; Malcolm Herring at Baring Asset Management; Marcus Hooper at Sun Life; Carolyn Jackson; Nachamah Jacobovits at the New York Mercantile Exchange; Peter Jenkins at Scudder, Stevens & Clark; William Johnston at the New York Stock Exchange; Louise Jones at Cassidy, Jones & Co.; Edith Kealey at D.E. Shaw; Chris Keith at Global Trade; Ray Killian at Investment Technology Group; Andy Klein at Wit Capital; Gary Lapayover at the New York Mercantile Exchange; Alan Line at Foreign & Colonial; Herb Lyman at A.G. Edwards; Leo Melamed at the Chicago Mercantile Exchange; Robert Mnuchin at C&M Arts; Phil Nathan at Charles Stanley; Sir Paul Newall at Lehman Brothers; Matthew Newton at Scudder, Stevens & Clark; Susan Ollila at the Ford Foundation; Frank Palameri at Jeffries; Gail Pankey at Gail Pankey & Co.; Ralph Rafaniello at the American Stock Exchange; Peggy Rappaport at INSTINET; Julian Robertson at Tiger Management; Charly Rosenthal at First Manhattan; Stanley Ross; Thomas Ryan Jr. at the American Stock Exchange; Joanne Sage at the Ford Foundation; Professor Robert Schwartz at the Stern School of Management at NYU; James Shapiro at the New York Stock Exchange; David Shaw at D.E. Shaw; Eric Sheinberg at Goldman Sachs; Stanley Shopkorn at Moore Capital Management; Muriel Siebert at Muriel Siebert & Co.; William E. Simon at William Simon & Sons; Peter Stanhope at LIFFE; Holly Stark at Dalton, Greiner, Hartman, Maher & Co.; Ben Steil at the Royal Institute of International Affairs in London; Thomas Strauss at Ramius Capital; Linda Strumpf at the Ford Foundation; Colin Taylor at Merrill Lynch; Foster Thalheimer at Thalheimer Associates; Michael von Clemm, president of Templeton College, Oxford University; Steven Wells at the London Stock Exchange; Steven Wheeler at the New York Stock Exchange; Kimberly Williams at the New York Stock Exchange; Steve Wilson at Tradepoint; Glenn Yago at the Milken Investment Institute; and Stanislas Yassukovich at S.M. Yassukovich & Co.

INTRODUCTION

Almost every aspect of our everyday lives is influenced by traders in the financial markets. Through their collective analysis and reaction to world events and economic developments, they determine the prices of everything from the gold in our jewelry to the steel in our cars to the cost of a summer holiday abroad.

If you are building a home, it is traders haggling in the commodity pits in Chicago that move the price of random-length lumber up or down. Traders working for banks bid on interest rate contracts that influence the price of your mortgage. Pork belly traders influence the price of bacon in the supermarket. Oil traders influence the price of gas at the pump and the heating oil for your home.

If there's one area in the financial markets that hits closest to home, it is the activity of traders; yet all we know about them comes from books that some of them write giving tips on successful investing in the stock market, or from news bulletins when one of them gets into trouble.

I took a different route. I wanted to understand them as people. What they actually do and the motivation behind their actions illuminate why the financial markets behave the way they do. The reason that stocks drop precipitously or currencies are attacked or the price of oil shoots up is that traders are bidding them up or down. Do we blame them when we don't like the results? Going to the source, getting inside their heads, and spending some time with them is an opportunity few have; yet it takes you toward a clearer understanding of what is happening around you and what to make of it. I wanted readers to have that opportunity.

I interviewed the top traders, former traders, the famous and the rising stars. Michael Bloomberg, Leo Melamed, Muriel Siebert, Bill Johnston, Bob Mnuchin, David Shaw, Eric Sheinberg, Gary Lapayover, Stanley Shopkorn, among many others talked candidly about their world.

In the process, the story emerged of a group of heroes—those who rose to the top despite all the odds. They overcame obstacles of race or background or gender, and met the challenge. Most of that group were born with a wooden spoon in their mouth, not a silver one. Some of them went on to create major new markets, and bequeath to those coming up behind them a way to live that will be surprising to some—my word is my bond, and take care of others.

The new generation of traders have the benefit of education, are computer literate if not computer savants, are highly professional, and have honed their skills to face the technological conundrum of today's markets. They are grappling with markets that move faster, and have higher volumes and ever more complex dynamics in politics and world events, than ever before. They have to make sense of these markets in seconds, and react faster and smarter than thousands of other traders around the world in order to keep their jobs.

But what is it that they do? I've let them tell you. You'll meet Gail Pankey and follow her while she trades millions on the floor of the New York Stock Exchange. You'll listen to Muriel Siebert tell how she drove from Cleveland to New York in 1954 in an old Studebaker with $500 in her pocket and ended up having one of the most successful brokerages in the country today—at the age of sixty-five. Leo Melamed describes what it took to become a successful pit trader and what it felt like to switch from trading among the crowds to trading alone on a computer. You'll meet Bob Mnuchin, who started at Goldman Sachs in the early sixties under the legendary Gus Levy, and hear how he came up through the ranks. And you'll meet countless others who discuss their thoughts and experiences.

Why should we care? Companies and governments depend on traders to keep the markets in their securities functioning, and the flow of money between them and the public moving back and forth, which keeps the economy moving. As investors, we depend on them to get us the best price for a stock we are selling, or for getting the bank where we have money out of a currency before it loses value.

They enable the generation of wealth as well as the protection of it, and they enable the creation of jobs.

So how did we come to the point where we view them as greedy and contributing little to society? Perhaps we have been cheated out of a true understanding by sensationalist books and highly entertaining movies about individuals who bear little resemblance to the tens of thousands of traders working around the world. The trading world is wildly competitive and has bigger than life characters who personify in epic proportions what it takes to get to the top. But movies aren't made about them. Instead we are shown the failures.

There's a different story to tell about traders, and you will meet many of them in the following pages. This is not a book about every kind of trader, or even an attempt at a comprehensive history. Rather, it is a book that takes you where you haven't been before, to people you normally wouldn't have access to, which allows you to get to know them and judge for yourself what kind of individuals they are. In the process, you will learn more about the markets than most people would by working in them.

You can dip into almost any chapter at random. The book begins with an exploration of traders' role in the markets, as well as a look back at traders from the 1930s through the 1990s. There are stories of visionaries who changed the world, of women that broke into the traditionally male-oriented trading environment, and chapters dealing with derivatives, currency trading, the buy side, rogues, and quants. The final chapter delves into the future, drawing on the predictions of the people you will meet throughout the book.

There's never been a better time to focus on what is happening within the markets because it is shaping the kind of world we will live in during the years ahead. We are at an epic moment in history, in the midst of a major transitional phase in the financial markets, which reflects the transitional phase in the world of business and geopolitics. And it is happening so fast that even the professionals are surprised.

- A new currency bloc is being born in Europe with the introduction of the euro, which will go head-to-head with the dollar for world supremacy.

- Financial institutions are consolidating into superinstitutions that will span the globe.

- Banking is changing. Who needs to drive to a bank anymore just to stand on line? All you do is call up, bank online, or stop by the ATM machine in the supermarket. This is indicative of a major redefinition of banking as we know it, with some banks breaking into new services and still others shedding their brick-and-mortar structures to develop into virtual banks online.

- Traditional stock exchanges and futures exchanges are linking up electronically. New electronic alternatives are emerging.

- The failure of Asian markets is shaping a new, as yet unknown, Asian experience to deal with.

- The computer and technology revolution is continuing to radically change the way the financial markets look and work.

- People are getting online and questioning politicians, companies, reporting their own news, doing their own share trading. They're breaking away from the way things were done before. That means a challenge for traditional authorities and structures, including the financial markets.

All these events affect traders. They either have to react to them or work within them. And although in the short term traders have to deal with them, in the longer term the rest of us will feel the effects as well. Perceiving these changes through the eyes of the people at the very fulcrum of the markets offers us a way to anticipate what is coming, to avoid the dangers, and to look forward to the benefits.

Hillary Davis
113416.2255@compuserve.com

PART I

THE BIG PICTURE

1 MILLIONS A MINUTE

IT WAS A BIG ADRENALINE RUSH. A HUGE ADRENALINE
RUSH. AND SOMETIMES AT THE END OF THE DAY YOU
WOULD PHYSICALLY CRASH, BECAUSE YOU WERE
PRETTY MUCH HIGH ALL DAY LONG. IT WAS AMAZING.
TIME COULD EITHER STAND STILL OR SPEED ALONG. I
MEAN, YOU'D FIND OUT HOW LONG A MINUTE CAN
TAKE, OR HOW QUICKLY FOUR HOURS COULD GO BY.

GARY LAPAYOVER

Millions of dollars' worth of trades are done every minute around
the world. The sheer speed and volume are due to rapid advances in
computers and communications, as well as to the massive amounts
of money moved into and out of global markets on a daily basis.
These trades are done so fast, and there are so many of them, that
even long-standing market participants find it amazing and at times
unnerving. Because if that's the way decimals of incremental profit
are going to be found, those who don't embrace it will be left
behind—and no one wants to be left behind.

"Financial engineers" with degrees in quantum physics and
mathematics are using their computers to design and trade ever
more complex instruments. Electronic exchanges are emerging,

where trading is done directly, computer to computer. Information technology has brought the financial world together so that what happens in Indonesia can affect the value of a stock in New York within seconds.

The amounts being traded are beyond the imagination. Over $300 trillion—or $300,000,000,000,000—is traded on average in a year in the world currency markets, over $15.6 trillion in stocks on the world's stock exchanges, over $27 trillion in bonds. On the Chicago Mercantile Exchange (CME) alone, nearly three thousand members, traders, and brokers trade futures contracts valued at over $717 billion a day, almost $182 trillion a year. To put that into perspective, it took the United States more than two hundred years to amass a government debt amounting to $1 trillion. These incomprehensible transaction volumes drive products, governments, investments, and many other areas that touch virtually every human being every day.

The development of computers and the speed and data-processing capability they provide have been pivotal in the evolution of trading, allowing more and faster transactions. Traders have become the lightning rod for the huge amounts of money entering the markets. Understanding where they channel it, the reasoning behind their decisions, and how they conduct their transactions is essential in gaining a perspective on the financial markets and world economy.

Tucked away in the canyons of every financial center of the world is a Silicon Valley, where people—or the computers themselves—are quietly trading faster and more efficiently using Sun Microsystem workstations and neural networks. Then there's the vast majority of trading in the markets where the phone is still the most important trading tool, and traders use computers to receive and manipulate instant data and information. Those doing manual trading write out slips of paper and participate in face-to-face auctions, while computers located under the floor relay to the rest of the market the prices the traders arrive at. By the time they drop their hand from agreeing to a trade, the price has been transmitted to computer screens and news services all around the world.

This linkage between computers and capital has democratized the financial markets. It has smashed time barriers, geographical boundaries, and class and gender barriers; and allowed the floodgates of money to open and reach any company, or country, or person. It has freed money to flow easily into currencies, stocks, bonds, futures, and commodities—international democracy at work providing capital for the growth of enterprise.

A TRADE IS a transaction between two parties, each of whom wishes to have what the other has. If you consider that millions of these are done every day around the world, you can begin to imagine the benefits of trading to international economic growth. Traders enable many people or parties to come together who don't know each other, or didn't know the others wanted to transact, allowing transactions to be consummated. The parties could be from opposite sides of the world, speak different languages, and own different currencies, yet through the focal point of traders they have the ability to transact within seconds.

Trading allows investors wanting to buy and sell securities for their portfolios—as well as insurance companies, banks, and corporations that need to invest their surplus cash—to move in and out of the best opportunities. Without traders, investors would have to contact by phone or mail each and every company in which they wanted to buy a stock. Prices would change very slowly, and each company would determine the price of the stock based on supply and demand from the public, rather than the public determining whether one company's stock was worth more or less than another's.

One person may want deutschmarks instead of francs. One may prefer having the stock of IBM, the other would rather have cash. A company may prefer to pay long-term interest rates, while another may want to pay short-term rates. How would they find each other?

With one phone call or keystroke, a trader can switch millions of dollars of currency from one country to the next in seconds. With one trade that may take only minutes, a trader on a commodity exchange can earn a company and its shareholders millions of dollars by locking in an attractive price on a commodity it needs in the future. Traders breathe life into what would otherwise be a very slow activity, making a market that everyone can participate in quickly and efficiently.

By providing the mechanism for exchange, and in the process creating liquidity—or enough activity in a market or security so that it is easy to buy and sell—traders promote economic growth. Through the creativity and product ideas that come from the trading side, they can help create markets and industries.

Michael von Clemm, one of the early contributors to the growth of the Euro market, remembered the creativity of a trader named Oswald Gruebel:

"Ozzie came to a couple of morning meetings and said, 'You know, we are desperate for a five-year triple A Eurodollar bond, preferably from American corporate issuers. There has been so little of it around for so long, and people who have it hold on to it.' This was always the problem in the Euro market because there wasn't enough liquidity. Based on Ozzie Gruebel's firm reading of the market, we decided to buy an entire new issue from GMAC of a five-year U.S. dollar–denominated bond. When GMAC heard our bid they created the issue to meet the demand. This was the Euro market's first "bought" deal."

Not only was GMAC able to raise money from that idea, but issue by issue the Euro market was able to grow, and investors needing the specific type of returns and characteristics that a Eurodollar issue could offer them now had access to an increasing number.

What traders do with their power has become a subject of concern to many market observers. It deserves to be understood, because while vested interests fear them and many don't understand them, traders are integral to the entire capitalist system. They deserve to be understood as people, because it is people who make a market, and their motivations and beliefs extend into how that market is conducted and where it is headed in the future.

GOD, THE PHONE'S ringing.

Bryan fumbled for the receiver as he snapped on the bedside lamp. It was three o'clock in the morning. Tokyo was on the line. Yoichi from the Tokyo office. He was $50 million long on ten-year U.S. Treasuries against a less than perfect hedge in the futures market. The market was now half a point against him.

At three o'clock in the morning he had to start making $50-million-dollar decisions.

He started to feel sick and knew he had to keep his head. He checked the screen beside his bed. I guess this is why I get paid a bonus, he thought. He touched the spacebar on the keyboard to bring alive a six-inch by six-inch screen. The price was now down 22/32nds. Things weren't getting any better!

He got up, had a shower, got into the office at four-thirty in the morning and on to the phone. By seven A.M. he had closed the position down and was having coffee. His first meeting was at seven-thirty in the morning. His day had started.

Welcome to the world of a trader. In another hour's time he knew he would be "loading the gun" against Merrill Lynch, Goldman Sachs, Salomon Brothers, competing with them laying off their positions, getting rid of their inventory in the market the same as he had. All he could think was, thank God he had gotten up at three!

In an environment that would be daunting for the rest of us, traders learn to thrive on apparent chaos. Currencies can rise and fall precipitously, causing a trader to find in the morning that the position he was carrying the previous evening fell 20 percent overnight in markets operating in a different time zone. Stock price swings can be gut-wrenching when a company makes an announcement while a trader is commuting home and other traders working after hours mark the stock down 30 percent or more. If he is trading in many markets around the world at the same time, these often extreme swings can provide a continuously changing, mind-bending new puzzle to solve. The markets themselves, whose cycles once took years to unfold and get used to, are being compressed into mini-cycles of a few months or weeks. It takes flexibility and an open mind when economic history is being thrown out the window.

At times it can seem as if the world has lost its mind. Eric Sheinberg, longest-tenured partner at Goldman Sachs, explained:

"I have to tell you. I have lunch every day with some of my ex-partners, and I tell them I've never seen this before, in thirty-some-odd years. To see a stock go down 50 percent in an hour. There is something crazy going on. Why was it selling at that price to begin with? This is the momentum investor. They just say buy or sell at the market. Why was IBM up today, before the market ever opened? It was trading in the third market. It's great if you owned it."

The seeming chaos can extend to the working environment. The trading floor of a commodities exchange is the ultimate, the most physical and rowdy of trading arenas. It can be as large as an aircraft hangar, big enough for all the different commodity auctions to take place. The minute you walk through the door, a roar from hundreds of people screaming at the top of their lungs hits you like a tidal wave. When you leave, it resounds in your ears.

Organized exchanges that have floors can be massive, meant to accommodate hundreds of people or more. The Chicago Mercantile Exchange (CME) spreads out on two trading floors for a total of 70,000 square feet. The New York Mercantile Exchange (NYMEX) moved in 1997 to two new trading floors spanning 25,000 square feet.

Those are the jumbo floors. Large international money center banks and investment houses like Salomon Brothers or Merrill Lynch also have trading rooms of enormous size, like ones seen in movies or on the news. Rows of traders sit in front of banks of computer screens and telephones, plying their trade in a large open space. Brokerage houses are big, high-powered selling machines, so their activity is as aggressive as the temperament of the people on the floor. There's always a push on to close a sale, to close a trade, to cajole or outsmart, to win business from the competition, to climb the next rung in the league tables. Life becomes dramatic when victory and defeat loom large in your day, where laughter and temper tantrums release tension. It's all played out in the open.

But turn down the volume when you walk into INSTINET, a broker/dealer electronic trading service in midtown Manhattan. You could easily imagine that it looks like the command room at Kennedy Space Center. Set within a steel gray futuristic space, three platforms sharply angle up to resemble bleachers, put together to form a large U-shape. Everyone can see what the others are doing, and all can see down to the flat center square. When meetings are held, traders don't have to leave their screens or phones, they can all see and communicate with the speaker standing in the center. Because this is a high-tech venture where computer power reigns, there is very little movement or noise in the room.

You would feel the hush of a private club if you were shown into the trading room of Scudder, Stevens & Clark, a mutual fund company in New York. It is on a medium-sized, open-plan floor. The long rectangular room that can accommodate about twenty traders is encircled by mahogany paneling and chair rails, cushioned by carpet, and buttressed by state-of-the-art electronic trading paraphernalia. It's subdued; there's almost an elegance to it. Traders look like candidates for the boardroom. Cutting-edge firms peddling high-tech solutions love to come here because the traders on the desk are receptive. One trader has a bank of computer screens in front of him that sits two high and eight across. In this genteel atmosphere, you find traders with advanced degrees, serious involvement in the future of the industry, and a high level of computer literacy.

The most surprising trading room I've seen is located at D.E. Shaw. As small and dark as a womb, the ceilings and walls matte black, with computer screens glowing all the way around. You don't have to, but you feel as if you should duck your head to walk in. There may be only one trader there playing mother, because it's the computers that are trading.

THE ALL-BUSINESS efficiency and sleekness of the new market structures are in stark contrast to the market environments they evolved from. Listen to Colin Taylor in London speaking about the London Stock Exchange in 1960 as he remembers it:

"When I started, it was the old market. The old stock exchange floor. Every Friday afternoon they burnt the place down. It was wonderful really. Just like a load of schoolboys. They'd have fires. You know, they'd set light to somebody's paper, and when he dropped it to the floor, then everybody would throw newspapers on top. Not myself, of course, because you'd have to be senior to do that sort of thing. It was wonderful fun really, the old market."

That was the old, old market. The one thing people still miss the most about it is the sense of camaraderie, something lacking in a computer-driven marketplace where you commune with a computer screen more than with people. Phil Nathan, trader at Charles Stanley in London, reminisced:

"You know, I could talk in the tone and volume that I am talking now with you. You would be talking in the ear of a trader negotiating big money, and you could just quietly say, 'I'll do that.' No paper changed hands. He walked away and perhaps winked or whatever, but you had done your trade. You walked away and got on to the phone and said, 'We've done XYZ.' And the trade was done. Bang. And even though it was a tremendous system, maybe it wasn't big enough to keep up with the world."

A lot of the loyalty for either "screen" (computer) or "scream" (person-to-person trading on a trading floor) can be viewed as a generational bias because it has been in step with advancements in technology. Which is the more efficient for a particular market? They both have their place, they'll probably both survive, although increasingly the "old-school" perceptions and market structures will take on the obvious benefits that the "new school" is bringing to the table.

The people who are doing the trading in this new world and are gaining power are those who have the ability to understand, negotiate, and tame the increasing speed and technology of the financial markets. Rather than belonging to the "old-boy network" that dominated the markets for so long, these traders are rapidly becoming the new driving force, the new school.

Those who went before them and ascended over the years made it despite all the odds. Very few had the privilege of background or money to give them a boost. In fact, even within the financial community, traders have always been thought of as separate from everyone else. Trading drew a different sort of people than the elite group that migrated into other sectors of finance. They have always been accents apart, catechisms apart, and schools apart. Kids with accents from Brooklyn and backroom barrow boys from the East End of London became traders, while talent from the Ivy League or Eton were welcomed as investment bankers and analysts. Most of today's new young traders have had the benefit of education and have an understanding of computers. Both types of traders are at play in the markets.

The new elite doesn't look anything like what went before in the power structure of the world's financial markets. There are no executive office suites. No long boardroom lunches. Very, very rarely are there meetings with clients. None of that happens until they reach the top, and even then they tend to prefer a shirtsleeves environment, and keeping their desk right on the trading floor.

Although many people go so far as to predict a wholesale move toward computer-to-computer trading without human intervention, paradoxically, as the obvious benefits of computerized and electronic trading are ever more clear, the value of the trader as the ultimate tool will increase. You can't program intangibles into a computer, at least not yet. You can program in historical statistics, historical human reaction to a complex blend of events, you can program in probabilities and improbabilities; but only traders have intuition, a "feel" for the market, and above all, the ability to think.

The human art of the trader is to reason, react—and be right. Bob Mnuchin, legendary former trader and partner at Goldman Sachs, told me:

"I pick up the newspaper and I see something and I unconsciously say to myself, 'Well, I wonder if that's oversold here?' I'm not making a judgment about the tobacco case in the Southwest or something in Illinois. But I am a trader, do I think that is oversold? Is it an opportunity?"

Marcus Hooper, the young head trader at Sun Life in London, put a new-school twist to that same thought:

"As a trader, when you talk about the costs of trading, people often forget that the one biggest cost of trading is actually not trading. The minute you don't trade, you are dead. Liquidity is everything. I have to get it done. If I can't get it done, I've just cost the company more than anything else in the world.

"Speed is everything. Don't stop and think about it. Do it now before the chance is gone. Great. Computers. Computers. Get the computers to do it. You can't go faster than the computer."

But even in his enthusiasm for the electronic future, Marcus makes it clear that the benefit of electronic trading is that it allows more time for the trader to think:

"If you take a good trader and ask him what his strategy for an order is, he will say, 'Well, I think maybe it is going to go down a bit so I will wait and buy some if it comes down, and I will sit and wait, and wait again.' That's all strategy in there. The fact that he is saying that's how he feels at the moment is great. That's the human part, the part you can't get rid of. And that's why the computer cannot dispose of that person. When I employ traders, the only thing I want to know is if they can think. As long as they can think, that is fine."

Historically, hearing or learning something a few minutes before the others might have given a trading advantage. That has dissolved in the bright lights of television financial news cameras and instant information feeds from Bloomberg and Reuters terminals sitting on traders' desks. With information being instant, everyone gets it at once. It has leveled the playing field and greatly accelerated the activity and response time.

As money and prices have become information zapped instantly to computer and television screens, they are continuously monitored. Traders all over the world, whether they prefer screen or scream, are absorbing information from the minute they wake up in an effort to anticipate events that might have an effect on what they are trading during the day. Because the world's markets are interrelated and linked electronically, what happens in one has an effect on the others. There are complex correlations between them that you can trade on if you recognize them. So traders will watch the financial news programs on television while dressing, read the papers, make calls on the way to work and once they reach their desk—before the market opens. There is a constant flow of information:

The Nikkei slipped past the key 20,000 level last night while . . . Record low temperatures in the southeast United States hit crops . . . Middle East peace talks were stalled when . . . IBM closed at 98 last night, down a dollar in heavy trading . . . Key jobs figures are out on Friday and traders are waiting . . . Bonds were encouraged by the Gross Domestic Product numbers released . . . Fourth quarter profits of 15 cents a share were above expectations, however . . . the Fed decided to . . .

Traders are constantly registering everything. So when they have to act quickly, it isn't a blind reflex. It all comes together as insight or as a pattern they recognize. They may trade on it then, or a day or week later—but they've been thinking in the background, and at home, and on the way to work. Facts, impressions, previous knowledge, experience and memory, perceptions about people they are dealing with, information coming in from the screen—all are marinating in their head all day. Intellectualizing intangibles and perceptions can be the nuances that make the difference in finding the truth in the noise of the market and in doing profitable trades.

Some successful traders reject absorbing the mass information being fed to others, and go a different route. They select their own "information."

Victor Niederhoffer, in his excellent book *The Education of a Speculator*, provides an example of the mental stretch of a trader. His own contrarian approach to trading?

"The only newspaper I read is the *National Enquirer*. I don't own a television, don't follow the news, don't talk to anyone during the trading day, and don't like to read books less than one hundred years old."

He looks at games like tennis and squash, listens to music, studies the phases of the moon, horse racing, sex, the behavior of ants, world wind patterns, relationships with his family and friends—an odd blend.

Trading takes a certain mind-set. One famous trader in New York who wanted to remain anonymous put it bluntly:

"I hate to tell you this, but people that are successful in this business work twice as much as everybody else. They have more drive, and they have a group of assets that other people don't have. And there's nothing you can do about that, because it is totally genetic. You're not going to make yourself 150 IQ when you are born with 100."

He went on to give his opinion that most people don't understand how difficult it is to reach the top in the trading world.

"This is harder than being a sports star; it's tougher to make it than in the NBA. Everyone in the mediocre jobs here makes less than in other professions. In this business, there is a higher percentage of losers than winners. Of all of the people I started with in my age group—and I'm forty-seven years old—I am the most successful. That means everyone else was a loser. Half of them left the business by the time they were forty."

Trading is definitely not a field for mediocrity. Many drop out either because they can't take the pressure past a certain age, or they came into the business dreaming of making it big and not realizing that it took a blend of talents and intellect that they didn't have. If it were easy to win at trading, traders wouldn't be paid so well to do it.

It was a hard lesson for me to learn that while trading and investing other people's money, I was taking the risk of losing part of it. Some traders and money managers eventually leave the business because of this same feeling of not wanting to lose someone else's money. They care too much. But caring is good. Being humble and cautious in the face of a market exerts a discipline on your approach to trading. Despite the best of intentions, the reality is that there is little statistical chance that you will win every time, even if you are good.

The great misconception about trading is that it is being done by young, inexperienced people transacting at the speed of light, who exhibit the attention span of a gnat while moving huge sums of other people's money. Rest assured, any major firm with a reputation to preserve and a bottom line to protect would not knowingly let an inexperienced or unproven person trade in any great amount. The likelihood of that happening is remote. There's just too much good talent out there to be had. Most young traders start out with a small amount that they are able to trade, and work up gradually. Of course, there are some rogue traders, and we'll be meeting some of them in these pages.

There are no tricks of the trade or secrets that will ensure success. It takes special people to make a lot of money consistently. And because each and every market and each and every trader does and needs something different, it is really what makes them tick, how smart they are, how competitive they are, what motivates them, how good they are at seeing things others don't, how much risk they are willing to take, that make a good trader. You can be taught rudimentary truths—accept losses, don't add to a losing position, know the amount you are willing to lose, utilize discipline and hard work—but it takes more to succeed. It takes incredible mental gymnastics, excellent timing and feel for the market, being able to withstand high levels of stress, excellence on every level, and even then some.

TRADERS' COLLECTIVE DECISIONS determine the prices of everything that touches our daily life. The process of "price discovery" that results from trading (one trader is bidding to buy, another trader is selling, and the price they agree on is "discovered") influences everything from the cost of orange juice or a loaf of bread to the price of the oil you'll be using in the winter to heat your home. Trading in the currency markets determines what the exchange rate will be when you travel on holiday, what the Japanese car you want to buy will cost, and what income your company can expect for the products it exports.

The process of traders bidding and selling that allows prices to be discovered is driven by a chain of causation that begins with world events. This is precisely why news and information is so important to traders, and why they are intensely alert and focused on it. If traders hear or read that there's a war brewing in the Middle East, they may reason that the oil supplies the world needs from the region will be severely restricted. They may decide immediately to buy oil contracts, because either they think they can make some money for their own account if they buy low and sell high later, or they want to buy the oil contract for their clients now before the price is bid up by the rest of the market. With everyone else thinking the same thing, the price of oil rises. Something that happened across the world set the traders in motion and resulted in their collective appraisal and determination of the value or price of oil.

While investing is considered a worthy activity, however, trading is seen as speculation. But there's good speculation and bad speculation—good speculators and bad speculators. The last thing you want is some dumb or irrational guy taking your firm's money and speculating with it, or assuming three hundred times more risk than there is capital to lose and taking you down with him. Luckily, dumb guys don't last long.

The word *speculate* comes from the Latin "to spy or watch," and implies observing or thinking about a topic and then making a judgment or taking an action based on that observation. The process of using the information you have at hand before making a decision can diminish the element of chance if your judgment is reasonable and sound. That intellectual process allows you the conviction to make a decision and the possibility of making a profit.

The distinction between good and bad speculation is not only having a shrewd trading strategy in place, but also having a realistic appraisal of how much you can afford to lose. By assessing the state of the market, doing your homework on the security before you buy it, understanding the odds, and exerting emotional discipline to sell when you reach your target or before you lose too much, you introduce intelligence into the decision-making process. You've thought about it. And a certain amount of risk has been limited.

Good speculators also take into account the chance of something unexpected happening. Human nature and acts of nature are probabilities. Political upheaval, unexpected shifts in monetary policy, or hurricanes and earthquakes may be factored in. You can't predict them, so you have to consider them. In the same way that a life insurance company must factor in the uncertainty of how long its policyholders are going to live or when or how much the company will have to pay out, traders must consider probability, knowledge, risk, and the unforeseen.

Good speculation can be great for business. There are whole departments of multinational corporations and banks that speculate in the financial markets, hoping that the stocks and bonds and currencies they buy will go up. They are motivated by profits, not losses, which if accomplished will benefit their shareholders. Small businesses speculate in real estate and risky ventures that, if they are right, can grow into substantial and respected businesses that provide jobs. Consumer products are introduced on supermarket shelves every year. The companies have done their market research and surveys beforehand, but they have no guarantee that consumers will buy the products they introduce. If they do, the business will grow.

That's speculating: making an educated guess, or thinking about it and then making a calculated bet. Risk is always involved. Without the willingness to take a chance, there would be little progress. But the act of speculating can help manage risk, because an assessment is being made based on a combination of information, intuition, and experience.

Is trading like gambling in a casino? Sure. But if traders are playing games of blind chance rather than ones that involve an intelligent guess of the odds, then it is to be hoped they are doing it with their own money and not mine. The majority are taking calculated risks that they have absorbed enough information and are sufficiently smarter than the next person to take advantage of a situation and make a profit. Risk is at the very heart of trading; there is no guarantee, for example, that a stock you buy will go up.

Tom Strauss, former president of Salomon Brothers, sees it from a different perspective:

"When you gamble, you have no control over your destiny at all; it is whatever cards you are dealt, whatever dice you throw. Clearly, good risk takers feel they have the knowledge or information flow to give them some opportunistic benefit to make money for their shareholders or the firm they work for."

My perception is narrower. I view trading as a form of gambling, not as in using dice or craps or slot machines, but as in games that incorporate reasoning. It's more like blackjack or bridge, where probability and statistics help you decide how much risk to take. It's not a coincidence that many traders are devotees of those games.

If currency traders see a government act in a way they think will be detrimental to the health of its economy, especially compared to what other governments are doing, they will reason that bad government will choke off business and hurt prosperity. They'll *speculate* that sooner or later the country will suffer, and armed with that reasoning, they'll sell the currency, or "trade out." The biggest rationale for trading out would be to preserve their clients' or their own capital from the anticipated fall in the value of the currency.

People who invest entrust their money under certain terms and conditions: that there will be a rational environment, a government that is accountable and doing its best, and transparency, or information that is aboveboard and available to everyone. If any of those conditions change for the worse, it's rational to expect that investors would want to find a safer place to put their money. A trader at a bank is expected at the very least to preserve the clients' or bank's capital, and ideally to make money with it. When investors and traders come to the same conclusion at the same time, the wayward government is faced with a problem it is forced to deal with right away, rather than later.

When a stock gets hammered on the stock market, traders may be speculating again. If numbers are released showing that profits are down, sales are slipping, or management is moving slowly or in the wrong direction or is enmeshed in bureaucracy, traders will speculate that the company's stock is not worth as much as that of a company that is performing well, where management is in tune and hard-working. They'll sell the stock. That puts pressure on management to perform, if for no other reason than its shareholders will be unhappy that their stock isn't performing either. That's good for the economy as well as the company.

FOR MOST PEOPLE, the maneuverings of traders in the financial markets are a total mystery. Yet the majority of the trading community remains resolutely protective of its anonymity. It rests willingly in the shade of incomprehension. Traders shun publicity, having been burned by articles and books and movies that they feel harm their image. Rather than be diverted by the attention, they get on with the trading. This book will shed some light on their world and the effects it has on the rest of us.

It is increasingly less of a male world. Women are making inroads, slowly but surely. Muriel Siebert began trading and overcame the gender bias of the financial community of the 1960s to become the first woman ever to own a seat on the New York Stock Exchange. She used it as a springboard to build what is now one of the most visible and successful discount brokerages in the United States. There are others right behind her, and you'll meet some of them in the following pages.

Some traders are visionaries, like Michael Bloomberg, once a trader at Salomon Brothers. He saw the need for traders to have access to information, and founded a media empire based on providing financial news and data right to their desks.

Some have become legends but stay quietly in the background, relatively anonymous but continuing to trade.

Consider Leo Melamed, a Holocaust survivor who traded pork bellies in the teeming commodity pits in Chicago. He became incensed when he learned that individuals were not able to trade currencies. Only commercial interests were accommodated by banks. He went on to create the first successful foreign exchange futures market, spawning other currency and derivatives markets around the globe.

In the 1970s certain small or risky companies were being denied access to capital by Wall Street firms. In response, Michael Milken, then a trader at Drexel Burnham Lambert, developed the high-yield bond market, which democratized the activity of raising money and was instrumental in the growth of such formidable companies as CNN and MCI.

Gus Levy, a legendary trader at Goldman Sachs, fathered block trading, when the trader takes one or the other side of the trade, rather than acting as a go-between. Robert Dall and Lewis Ranieri at Salomon Brothers developed the idea of mortgage-backed securities, which generated development of other asset-backed securities and all kinds of structures that became big, profitable industries.

Some traders are postmodern statesmen on the world stage, like George Soros, who regularly offers his opinion on philosophy and on economic and regulatory policy.

Others are world-champion bridge players and blackjack junkies. And some are in jail.

Getting to know traders as people—how they view life, how they reason and react, what their motivations are—and taking a look inside their world gives you an insight into the financial markets that you normally wouldn't have unless you worked in them. There are lessons to be learned from the best, and from the leaders that provide role models for other traders. They also provide clues as to the future.

2 MY WORD IS MY BOND

THIS BUSINESS OPERATES ON TRUST AND GOODWILL. BECAUSE WHEN YOU DO A TRADE, EVERYTHING IS VERBAL. YOU ARE TALKING TO SOMEBODY AND SAY DO THIS AND DO THAT. AND YOU DON'T WANT THEM TO CALL YOU BACK AN HOUR LATER AND SAY, WELL, YOU REALLY DIDN'T DO THAT TRADE, AND THAT'S NOT WHAT YOU SAID, AND I DID IT THIS WAY. IT IS A BUSINESS THAT OPERATES ON TRUST AND SOMEBODY'S WORD AND AN ORGANIZATION'S REPUTATION.

LINDA STRUMPF

The people who grew up in the trading culture from the late 1940s onward developed a code of ethics that persists today, and that all traders have in common: "my word is my bond." It is a key reason that trading can occur with such ease and in such great volume.

Alan Greenberg, chairman of Bear Stearns, explains the code of conduct this way:

"Traders exist in a world where one's word truly is one's bond. The fundamental nature of the business is one of honesty and integrity. In what other industry can individuals call each other up on the telephone, quickly agree to a transaction valued at millions of dollars, and hang up, knowing in full confidence that the bargain will be kept—without contracts, witnesses, or even lawyers? The hundreds of millions of shares traded all over the United States each day are an affirmation of the character and honor of those who allow this system to succeed."

In contrast, a big real estate transaction wouldn't be a deal until fourteen lawyers got together and wrote up a piece of paper.

The code of conduct based on trust developed from two sources: economic necessity, and the type of people doing business.

In the 1950s and 1960s, the vast majority of people who worked Wall Street in the trading area came up from clerical positions, where everybody was Jewish, Irish, or Italian. Those were the kinds of jobs that people of those ethnic backgrounds could get on Wall Street then. Those who wanted to become traders had to fight their way to the top. Many of them went on from the hurly-burly of the trading desk to overseeing it, managing other traders, and creating new business for their firms. They overcame the prejudice of the financial community to gain a foothold in the establishment. They were the heroes because they grew, they evolved.

Outsiders in many respects on Wall Street, traders had to depend on one another within their community. Depending on one another meant trusting one another's word.

Before the 1930s there had been few if any rules. Economic necessity—in the interest of fair markets and the pursuit of profits in an equitable manner—spawned a host of regulations in that decade that clearly delineated what the government considered right and wrong.

Before stock exchanges were formally organized, trading used to take place on the curb, in the street, and in coffeehouses. It was like the Wild West before regulatory bodies began to define behavior. Congress passed legislation in 1933 and 1934, creating the Securities and Exchange Commission and crafting regulations to ensure proper registration and public information on securities, among other things. Before that time it was a free-for-all. There were no personal income taxes. There were no barriers to becoming a participant in the markets other than having money. It was legal to use inside information to manipulate stocks and to put together pools of investors to corner a market.

Arthur Levitt, chairman of the U.S. Securities and Exchange

Commission, discussed that time in a speech he gave at the University of Virginia in 1995:

"John Maynard Keynes, a masterful investor as well as a great economist, described the stock market he knew as a 'casino.' Before the [1929] crash, stock prices often had little to do with the fundamentals, because most of the fundamentals were never disclosed.

"Not only was the market a casino—it was a casino in which the games were rigged. Cash was paid to reporters at the *New York Times* and the *Wall Street Journal* to plant false information on companies and false tips on stocks."

After Jay Gould and Jim Fisk had precipitated a financial panic on "Black Friday" in 1869 with their attempt to corner the gold market, the U.S. House of Representatives determined that they couldn't be punished, as many had called for, because what they had done was not illegal then. Many of the famous pre-1930s traders made fortunes that couldn't have been made after that time—people like Gould; Bernard Baruch; Joe Kennedy, the father of President Kennedy; Billy Durant, the founder of General Motors; and Daniel Drew. They were masters of psychology and masters at manipulation.

These characters were bigger than life, and their every move, collusion, and counterplot was avidly followed by the popular press. Their personal dealings were enormous in size and spectacular, even by today's standards. William Crapo Durant, having resigned from GM at the age of sixty, descended on Wall Street like bird after prey. By 1928 he was speculating with a kitty of over $1 billion. With a further $2 billion under his wing from the members of his pool, he directed them where to put their money.

But these people were of their time. The chaos that they generated in the markets served an economic purpose in the end. With their aggressive brand of trading, they stoked a speculative fever over the years that ultimately built up enough opposition to spawn serious legislation to protect the small investor and company shareholders from the fallout of their maneuverings.

The necessity to have a fair and orderly way to raise money for our expanding industrial economy planted the seeds for the philosophy behind the trading of financial securities that has been in place from 1934 until today. Your word is your bond, and trust is everything.

That philosophy is even behind the way trading floors are designed. You can see it by comparing the physical layout of a traditional corporation with that of a trading floor.

Corporate environments are made up of offices with doors to shut. Partitions and compartments separate people rather than bringing them together. They offer room for office politics and private meetings, and a peaceful environment for the thoughtful production of reports, studies, planning, and memos. I have seen trading floors of all different sizes and types, and they have all shared the attribute of openness, a metaphorical extension of the openness and trust needed to deal with each other in order to do business.

I WAS STANDING in the observation booth above the New York Mercantile Commodity Exchange. It was quite dark and I thought I was the only one there. Then I noticed a young woman staring down at the trading floor, her hands holding tightly on to the rail in front of her.

We began to talk, and she confided that her husband, who was a trader down on the floor, had lost $400,000 over the last few days and he was trying to earn it back.

He was what they call a "local" or "day trader," who trades his own money. A $400,000 hit would break him. He'd be finished.

Just before we spoke, he apparently had looked up to where he knew she was standing and made the thumbs-up sign with a big grin, waving her to go home.

"He had been making $50,000 a day and was on a roll. Last Friday he made $87,000. Everything looked great, and then it just turned. I guess I'm overreacting. I'm just not used to this yet. He doesn't get fazed by it at all."

We looked back down to the trading floor and could hear the roar below. It was colorful, yet it seemed black and white and gritty. A tangle of waving arms, a screaming mob of heated, pushing bodies thriving on the rush of adrenaline provided by the market's volatility. There was nothing glamorous about it.

Yet down there, dreams were within reach. Fortunes could be made and lost, and so many people were there because they shared a sense of certainty about destiny. That woman's husband dove back in and fought for it. And he'd do it again tomorrow and the next day. You've got to believe and you've got to have the guts to be willing to take risks.

There's no way you could ever be bored. Trading is high-pressured and thrilling, whether you are on the floor of an exchange with everyone else or sitting in front of a computer. You are reacting to and are part of a constantly changing world picture. That's what traders love about it. Most of them can't wait for Monday morning, accepting pressure and tension that would put most of us out of commission. If we lost $100,000 one day, the next day earning back $50,000 in the morning, maybe losing it in the afternoon, we'd crash.

Some liken it to having the toughness of a marine—being able to handle tremendous stress with minimal emotional distraction, while at the same time making split-second decisions in a fast-paced environment. In fact, in 1996 a group from the U.S. Marines came to traders to learn the secrets of making decisions under pressure. Invading the trading floor of the New York Mercantile Exchange, one of the generals explained why they were there: "On a daily basis, the traders are at war." By engaging in mock trading sessions in natural gas futures contracts, the marines tried to figure out exactly what it takes to operate in seeming confusion and chaos so they could translate those skills for use in combat operations.

Not all trading is similar to the "hand-to-hand combat" on the floor of a commodity exchange. That is the ultimate stress test. But all traders, if they are going to do well, learn how to handle emotions that are the result of being under pressure, and channel them into positive results—turning them into money.

THE MAJORITY OF traders I have talked to said they love their work. They have a passion for it. Even after they've earned millions they still trade. The ones that don't have a passion drop out.

Their belief in themselves and what they are doing or what they can achieve may come off as arrogance, but that confidence in their convictions gives them strength to act in difficult circumstances. I've rarely heard self-doubt.

What about risk? Every transaction has inherent risk, and the more transactions you do and the bigger the money, the more willing you have to be to take risk. In this most risk-taking of cultures, the best traders skillfully take on and manage it to their benefit.

They learn to handle stress from the very beginning of their training. When they are first learning to trade, one of the hardest obstacles to face is simply understanding what the hell people are talking about. Traders have a jargon all their own. When markets are moving quickly, seconds can be vital. They are dealing in incremental price movements on very large amounts of money, and absolute precision is needed in communication. Every minute counts. In order to disseminate information very rapidly, a shorthand method of communicating has developed.

Holly Stark, a buy-side trader at Dalton, Greiner, Hartman, Maher & Company, trades by phone and computer from an office in midtown Manhattan. She explained what it was like when she was first learning how to trade:

"There's a whole nomenclature of trading that is almost indecipherable to the layman. If you listen to a phone call you would wonder what those people are saying. They're talking at the speed of light.

"I remember when I first started, I would madly write down what people were saying and say, 'Okay, I'll call you back,' and hang up. And then sit there and say, 'Okay, he said this is bid an eighth, five up, and twenty-five up,' and that meant, and what did this mean. It was tough. I made mistakes, everybody does."

That was in New York. For Colin Taylor in London, entering the London Stock Exchange floor "as a young lad" for the first time produced the same reaction:

"The first day you walked in it was all total confusion. You didn't understand anything anybody was saying. Whereas now we make prices in pence: they are one four, they are three six. In the old system, with the old money, they had names called 'closer with the figure'—which meant threepence three farthings.

"And there was penny hapence prices. If it was threepence, you didn't say twopence farthing to threepence three farthings. You said threepence 'close to close.' But of course, you didn't say 'close to close,' you said 'threepence clo clo.'

"There was no mercy at all. If you didn't understand, and said, 'I'm sorry, I missed that,' they'd say, 'Give it to me! I won't bother to ask you again, boy!'"

As trading has become international, misunderstanding cultural differences can be a stress in and of itself—even when you are both speaking English. Michael Paull, former head of commercial paper business at Union Bank of Switzerland, related an incident he saw that stayed in his mind and illustrated the U.S. way of doing business that had invaded London when he was working at Security Pacific of California. Security Pacific had bought 25 percent of Hoare Govett and threw the traders from both firms together on one floor to work it out among themselves. This was on a large trading floor of the bank.

"I can well remember one trader called Michael Flanagan, who was trading on the U.S. Treasuries desk doing a gilts trade with the Hoare Govett gilts desk on the other side of our dealing room.

"The gilt trader moved his price in response to the market halfway through the trade, which is right to do. The trade wasn't closed. The price was off, and Flanagan was about to close with the investor. And there was an enormous shouting match across the floor. But where the culture clash came in was the language that was used.

"Flanagan was a New Yorker. He had red suspenders on, standing up, waving the phone in his hand, swearing loudly, saying, 'Don't you ever do that to me again!'

"And the gilt response was more polite: 'I say, old boy, you are a bit out of line there!' That was the cultural difference: 'Take it easy, old boy, you are a bit out of line!'"

The trading world would be shocking to some. There's profanity; words aren't minced, they're to the point. If you are in a conversation and the person turns and walks away, you can't be offended. It means there is business to do and he had to go. There's always that sense of urgency. If someone loses their temper, you can't waste time thinking about it. The pressure on the floor can be overwhelming sometimes when a trade worth tens of millions of dollars blows up. Since there are no offices to go have an argument in, and since everything is out in the open, arguments will happen in the open.

The rate of change in a market can be so rapid that if you stop to think about how you are addressing someone and their feelings, the trade could move away from you. So you learn to put up with a lack of social graces. Then if people think you are tough, smart, work hard, and are developing a reputation that you can be trusted, they'll take care of you. Inexperienced traders are usually put next to mentors, or tormentors, so that they learn the drill. Sometimes they let you hang yourself because that will be a lesson well remembered and could protect you in the future.

There's no doubt about it, a Darwinian attitude permeates trading and is an aspect of the free-market philosophy that most of the financial world embraces. Competition is considered a wonderful thing. Change for the better is believed to come from those who are smarter and stronger and quicker, rather than from those who are slower and not too smart.

Competition among themselves and competition from trying to beat the market force traders to draw on every talent at their disposal to survive. If they don't perform as well or better than others, they won't last. Someone who yearns for the comfort of a calm office with a secretary, job security, and a steady paycheck wouldn't like trading. The type of people drawn to it tend to be hyperactive, type A personalities who thrive on challenge and pressure, to whom winning is everything and money is very important.

Stanley Shopkorn, managing director of Moore Capital and former head of equity trading, sales, and arbitrage at Salomon Brothers, explained:

"Most of the good traders that I know are A personalities. I think you have to be. Because A personalities want to win. A personalities have to teach themselves, however, that they can lose. And then when they do, that is just the end of an episode, and you can go back to doing well. The A person's psyche challenges him to do well and be right. And I think that is very important."

Winning builds confidence, which is vital to being able to move quickly and make instant decisions. Pondering and doubting don't work. You have to have the belief in your judgment, as well as the wisdom and the courage to know when you are wrong. If that crosses the line to a lack of humility and reason, it becomes something else. The best have learned the difference.

If traders lose, they can't really blame anyone but themselves. So it becomes a highly personalized, ego-driven job compared to one where you can blame the company you are working for or the boss. At the end of every day you know what your score is, whether you did bad trades or good ones. Every morning you start at zero.

What seems unique is an ability to rein in a type A personality with left-brain thinking. Traders blend right-brain intuition—the ability to remember patterns, to feel strong emotions, to be comfortable with abstract thought—with cool, left-brain logic and an understanding of probability and statistics. It is a rare mix. Being able to take that kind of thinking into a market that is complex and always changing, and do something with it, is what sets good traders apart. It is particularly suited to an environment where you are expected to quantify, or anticipate, or speculate on the unexpected.

TAKING INTO ACCOUNT all of the above, succeeding in the trading world takes even more. You have to be consistently a winner—consistently make money and consistently not lose. The business doesn't suffer people who don't make money. When people work in a business so focused on making money, they inevitably take on that same focus in their own lives, especially when the amounts of money they are capable of making for their firms can be so large. No one is more aware of their own worth than the trader. Money is a strong incentive in and of itself to win and be competitive.

I asked Gary Goldstein at the Whitney Group in New York about compensation over the years he has been recruiting traders:

"When CMOs [collateralized mortgage obligations] were developed in the seventies, it created a whole superstar status for traders. Mortgage traders had become the highest-paid traders on the street. This was before proprietary trading. Before people were creating internal hedge funds for their firms.

"The mortgage trader ruled for many years. In fact, I could argue today that they are still the highest-paid traders, in terms of pure product traders. Back then, a really good trader was making $1 million to $1.5 million, including bonus. Most others at that time barely saw a salary of $100,000—even $75,000 was high. I would bet John Gutfreund, former head of Salomon Brothers, didn't make much more than $2 million back then, so his top traders were making a million or a million and a half dollars.

"Now a top trader at Bear Stearns is making $12 million. A top trader at Salomon Brothers on the proprietary side is making $25 and $35 million a year. There are guys at hedge funds who are making $100 million plus."

But those are at the very pinnacle, and not everybody gets there. It is more normal to see a good trader in New York making up to a million dollars a year including bonus. If you are a trader in London you are making a lot less than traders in New York, and if you are a trader in Paris you are getting half of what they earn in London.

One of the highest-compensated financiers ever locked in his pay structure when he was still a trader at Drexel Burnham Lambert in the early 1970s, Michael Milken was trading high-yield bonds then. "Tubby" Burnham recalled:

"Mike worked away trading securities nobody else was interested in. I offered him $28,000 a year and increased the position that he could handle [trade] from $500,000 to $2 million. I allowed him to keep a dollar for every three he made. He doubled the position's value in a year. Our deal never changed."

In 1987 Michael Milken earned $550 million.

Gary Goldstein added this observation:

"Look at a baseball player. Look at the cost of a ticket today versus what it was five years ago or ten years ago. And why is that? Because the salaries have gone way up. It is supply and demand. If people are still going to the games and still want to pay the dollars, then I guess the market has a way of correcting itself and finding what the tolerance level is. If people stop going, and protest because it was too much money, then salaries would come down, because they would have to."

For most, money is a way of keeping score. How much you have made for the firm tells you how successful you are at what you do compared to others. That creates peer-group pressure to be paid as much as the next guy. No one wants to see someone making a lot more money than they do.

If you hear that another trader got a million-dollar signing bonus to change firms, you end up always looking for the next job. There can't be a clearer indication that the partnership ethos that ruled Wall Street and London for so long has disappeared. It was a tribal, sociological thing that bound people together and defined a certain behavior that made firms strong, that made people want to stay and grow within their firms. Michael Bloomberg in his book *Bloomberg by Bloomberg* talks about having been proud to be a "Salomon man." Old-school traders still talk about missing that special something that inspired loyalty to and bonding with their firm—an esprit de corps.

Most firms in the past were composed of partners who had equity stakes in the company, resulting in a team spirit hard to duplicate in a public company. Since the partners' own money was at stake, it created a common cause. The partnership culture began to fade on Wall Street in the 1970s, when the volume of business began to expand and firms needed cash to grow and add more people. The culture for the most part dissolved in London after Big Bang in 1986, which altered the shape of the market in terms of the types of firms participating in it. As U.S.-style investment banking became the vogue, it eliminated the remaining partnerships that were stock-broking firms, combining merchant banking activity with stock-broking.

Goldman Sachs experienced the same breakdown in esprit de corps in the 1980s as those firms that were not partnerships at the time, simply because the growth in its business required it to bring in people from other firms.

Eric Sheinberg, who had been at Goldman for over forty years, points out that a change in the culture happened when the firm grew very rapidly:

"We had to hire people who were all from the outside, because there was so much business, we didn't have enough people.

"Where we always used to hire on our own and train them right out of college, we just couldn't do it anymore because there was too much business. So we hired people from other firms. And you really didn't know what habits they were coming in with.

"We wound up hiring a guy who injected politics into the firm where we never had it before. It is a sad story. He used to take people out, take their wives out, promise them he would make their husband a partner, only trying to find out all about their personal lives. Which I could never understand. Why was that his business anyway? Horrible."

Loyalty died with escalating compensation and the disintegration of partnerships, introducing an environment that, more than ever, was "me-oriented."

Should there be loyalty to the firm, or is a wish for loyalty just nostalgia for the old days? For traders in particular it is an interesting point. On the one hand you want a competitive environment, a fluid labor force, but on the other hand you want some consideration from that labor force not to bring the firm down with them by taking inordinate risk in order to get higher personal compensation.

An argument can be made that Nick Leeson, the trader who brought down Barings in London, felt no special ties to the firm, no identification with it. His loyalty instead rested firmly with how much money he could make as his year-end bonus, and because of that he took astronomical risks. The question becomes more problematic as the competition is increasing for jobs at firms that offer monetary rewards greater than psychological rewards. Large international banks looking for larger market share are invading New York and London—paying whatever it takes to lure away the best.

The other result of escalating compensation and the battle for hot talent has been that they have at times drawn in people with the attitude that they are there just to trade, just to make as much money as they can as soon as they can.

Stanislas Yassukovich used to interview university graduates when he was chairman of Merrill Lynch in Europe in the 1980s. He was struck by their focus on "making a lot of money" compared to the reasons his generation went into the business:

"I would be told there are these four or five unbelievable stars, and we absolutely had to have them. Say whatever it takes to get them because Goldman or someone else wants them. So, I would say to them, 'What is it that you would like to do?'

"I would say, 'I imagine you would first of all want to get an understanding of everything we do at Merrill Lynch and you would like to spend a year or two moving around, getting a feel of the total business.'

"'Not at all,' they would say. 'I want to be a Turkish lira dealer.'

"Why? 'Well, somebody told me you make a lot of money there.' And then they would say to me, 'Unless you can promise me that I will be immediately assigned to this particularly specialized area, I am not interested, and somebody else out there will assign me to that.'

"Then I would say, 'Well, what about your long-term ambitions? Would you like to ultimately be head of the firm?' No. They couldn't care less. No interest or ambition at all to get to the top. They wanted to be in the hot seat."

I would like to think that the pursuit of profit for personal gain, in effect the American dream, serves the common good. If there were no incentive to make money, or to make a lot of it, we wouldn't be where we are. Although it is a constant source of debate, specialization may be exactly what is needed for traders to be able to focus when confronted with the increasing complexities of today's markets.

This is quite different than what the old school experienced. Bob Mnuchin, at one time a famous trader and partner at Goldman Sachs, told me:

"You know, the world has changed immensely. Today you have a very, very high degree of specialization. When you talk about the fifties and sixties, when I was learning and serving my informal apprenticeship, this kind of very, very rigid specialization just didn't exist. Some of the things that I was involved in had an over-the-counter stock, had a convertible and common stock, and everything all entwined. So you ended up actually having been a practitioner in each of those fields."

Yassukovich concurs that there has been a tremendous shift:

"We were generalists, and the international capital markets are now, if you like, maintained by specialists. My generation, people like Michael von Clemm and others, were generalists with a feel for all aspects of the business. We understood how bonds were traded, sold, who bought them, why. We understood the corporate structures that were funded through the international capital market, and we engaged in a certain amount of financial engineering without having the very specialized skills which are much more necessary today."

Compensation is important, but so is a reputation. For some, over time, it becomes their identity. Gary Lapayover, former vice chairman of the New York Mercantile Exchange, told me what happened to him as a trader over his years on the exchange:

"I have been here so long that my trading badge has become my persona. Because I've been this Zero guy for about sixteen years now, I don't know who I'd be if I wasn't Zero."

I asked him what he meant by saying he was Zero.

"That's my trading badge. My trading name. But it is me. Zero is the personality that is here. Zero is a much tougher guy than Gary Lapayover. But how do you separate that after sixteen years? It's like, how can I just be me?

"That guy is known all over, in a lot of places around the country and in spots around the world. There are people that don't necessarily know who Gary Lapayover is, who I've met not realizing they know me or have heard of me, and they'll say, 'Oh, you're Gary Zero!' So how do you leave that person who is somewhat notorious, to be just Gary Lapayover? It's a tough thing."

It's a bit like being a sports star. You can make a lot of money, your pay is bid up depending on how good you are, and as you go up the scale you earn a reputation and status that become important to you.

The sports connection seems a uniquely parallel comparison in a tribal and male kind of way—despite the inroads being made by women. Tom Ryan, the president of the American Stock Exchange, made the connection this way:

"When the market is open, you have to make decisions and they are going to be right or wrong. And you are going to be a winner or a loser. It is very easily quantifiable.

"And so it is much akin to playing sports. We're going to have a game today and we are in it and we are going to make some mistakes, and hopefully do some good things. You have to understand what the competition is and what's going on in the marketplace. What supply and demand is. What customers want. And there's a whole host of variables that determine how the day goes."

But it is harder than being a sports star. If you win, you win big. And if you win big, how do you go back? Gary Lapayover enthused like a kid at a baseball game:

"As you started getting more successful and started making some money, it was very much like sports. It was like playing center field for the Yankees.

"When we started to make more money, we used to talk and compare ourselves to tennis stars in the paper, and say, look at this, we are number four on the tour! You could sit there and say, I make as much as Mickey Mantle! And that became a tremendous thrill. It was fascinating."

Like sports stars, traders know that they have a relatively limited high-earning period in their lives. You don't see many gray hairs on a trading floor. With pressure to perform in nanoseconds, every day, you can only take it for so long. So very few of them experience their top earning power beyond ten years. Like markets that move in cycles, they don't last forever.

3 FREE-MARKET WARRIORS

ANYTIME YOU LOSE YOUR HUMILITY IN THIS BUSINESS, AND ANYTIME YOU THINK YOU ARE IN CONTROL OF ANYTHING, IT IS GENERALLY THE TOP OF THAT MOVE, AND YOU USUALLY GET BELTED IN THE NOSE.

STANLEY SHOPKORN

He thought it was the strangest thing he had ever seen. It was a big, sweaty room filled with people pushing each other.

One person whizzed by him, and he followed with his eyes to see him squeeze into a circle of traders frantically waving their hands in the air, as if either throwing a baseball or catching one. Everybody was shouting. How could one person be heard in that bedlam?

He moved closer to the group of traders, and he could hear words. They sounded like barking dogs, sharp and insistent. At a peak in the activity everything sounded like it was prefixed with "fucking," as in "Fucking sell three thousand!" and "Fucking buy three thousand!" There was a lot of fucking going on.

And what were they doing? They looked a bit like ex-football players and were wearing multicolored cotton jackets, some with tropical fish or flags on them. His training as a teacher hadn't prepared him for this or for the intensity he could palpably feel, sometimes emanating from a mood of urgency, sometimes from everyone standing around just waiting for something to happen, as if they wanted to be the first off the mark, ahead of the others around them.

It was 1973 and Gary Lapayover was out of work, with no prospects and a new wife. A relative who was involved in commodity trading had convinced him at a Sunday barbecue about the opportunities and the possibility to make good money. He just wanted a job. So he came down on the train from New Haven every day, starting out as a runner at very low pay, believing at the very least he would have nothing to lose. He would later become vice chairman of the New York Mercantile Exchange.

But at the time the odd thing was going home at night and hanging out with the college kids he knew from Yale, talking about the capitalist running dogs. Capitalism wasn't big on college campuses then. They'd ask him what he was doing and he wasn't able to describe it. It looked to him like everyone was buying stuff they didn't want, that wasn't for them, and that everyone acted really thrilled when something bad happened to somebody else.

After four months he felt he was starting to get an idea of what was happening, but what he had known with certainty from his very first day was that he loved being there. There was an electricity, as if things really mattered. He also liked the way you could talk or socialize to whatever extent you wanted with millionaires or clerks. If they thought you were smart and decent it didn't matter if you were living in an apartment in Queens and they were living in a big town house on the Upper East Side.

Years later, when he was wiser and understood the ramifications of what was happening in that room and how it affected normal people in his neighborhood, he developed a caring beyond the rush of excitement. When he first started out on the commodity exchange, which was when the first energy crisis hit, he could only get gas for his car a couple of days a week. Even then he and his wife had to take turns lining up for an hour or more early in the morning. Then the puzzle started to come together for him. Because of the fear of high oil prices, people on the commodity exchange were trading in the oil pit to lock in prices and protect themselves from the craziness in the outside world.

He was starting to understand what it all had to do with the economy, the implications it had for every consumable. He didn't trade oil, but he watched it because he learned it was a good indicator. Crude oil was not just heating oil and gasoline, it was also everyday stuff. The polyester he was wearing was an oil-based product. His wife used Vaseline—a petroleum product. If the price of crude oil rocketed, then his home heating costs would go up. His electricity bill would also go up because oil drives the turbines that create it. Clothing and food costs would go up because the cost to the manufacturer of getting goods from one spot to another by truck would go up and be passed on to the consumer.

The interesting thing was that people in New Haven could look up the wholesale price of gasoline in the newspaper every day. They would know that if the price was up, it would translate into higher prices at the pump a week later.

He trained his neighbors to ask their heating oil distributors to tell them what they would be paying in the winter so they could budget. As a homeowner you are not going to get into the commodity markets, but you want a distributor who does. Because if the guy that delivers your heating oil has hedged the summer before, then he should be able to guarantee you that he won't charge you more than a certain amount a gallon, no matter what happens. In order to do this he buys what's called an options contract, which will lock in what he will have to pay for the oil when it is delivered to him. If you do business with an oil distributor who doesn't go to the commodity market to lock in his costs, he may have to charge you more because he'll never know what tomorrow is going to bring.

The oil trading pit could become wild when there was a major world event that might affect it. Gary remembered:

"Leading up to the Gulf War, when Iraq moved into Kuwait, everyone was starting to become frightened about a potential shutoff of oil to the outside world, potential boycotts, and disruptions. The perception was that the price of oil was going to skyrocket. The market started moving rapidly higher, and it was experiencing a lot of drastic price swings. You had certain analysts and experts predicting that oil was going to $100 per barrel. All sorts of wild things.

"In fact, they announced that U.S. troops had started the invasion after the market had closed, New York time. U.S. troops had invaded sometime in the late evening. The initial reaction when our market opened in the morning was that the market price for oil went up a little. Then the price plunged, because essentially the war was over and all those fears about dislocated oil deliveries were no longer valid. And the market price dropped right down to the level that you'd assumed it would have been without any possible interruptions. The prices at the pump were down in a week."

He also learned that if there was a disease hitting pigs in the Midwest that resulted in a shortage of pork bellies to be traded on a commodities exchange, fewer pork bellies for the same amount of people wanting them meant higher prices, and that meant the price of bacon in the supermarket would be up. It could also turn the other way. Something like the no-fat, low-fat diet trend could affect the price of pork bellies, because slab bacon would not be in as great demand in the supermarket.

IT USED TO be that if you mentioned that you worked in commodities, most people would think you worked at a produce market— flowers and fruits and vegetables. You would end up just saying that you worked on Wall Street to move past the subject quickly. Now almost everybody has at least heard about commodities futures. A big jump in public awareness came with the release of the movie *Trading Places*, and when First Lady Hillary Clinton made profits in trading commodities that received a lot of press attention.

But what happens on a commodities exchange trading floor? And what is all the yelling and screaming about?

There used to be more than 1,600 commodity exchanges in the United States trading butter, cheese, eggs, onions, and cattle. Even cat pelts were traded in St. Louis. Today only nine financial and commodity futures exchanges are left in the United States and three in the U.K., out of forty in the entire world. In New York on the mercantile exchange they trade strategic materials like platinum, gold, silver, copper, crude oil, heating oil, natural gas, and electricity. The trading that is done by the floor brokers represents business people all over the country trying to lock in the price for which they sell or buy their goods.

Someone with a gold mine will sell a futures contract on the commodity exchange to set the price they will receive for their gold when they deliver it. That will not only allow them to know exactly what their income will be, but it will protect them if the value of gold falls in the meantime. This ability to *hedge* enables commodity producers to stabilize their revenues and costs, and helps them do business with less risk of losses.

It's basically the same function with exchanges that specialize in financial commodities, rather than agricultural or energy commodities. In that case companies want to buy or sell financial instruments to lock in interest rates or currencies at a cost that they then know for certain and can budget for, to protect themselves from uncertainties in currencies or interest rates that could hurt the bottom line, and as a result hurt the consumer and the shareholders in their company. Banks, for instance, by fixing their costs in this way, can then offer their customers fixed-rate loans and mortgages. It's the traders who enable that to happen, and the benefits trickle down to the consumer.

If you are a trader, these clients come to you to do the buying and selling for them on the floor and to get the best possible price and execution of the transaction that can be achieved at that point in time. They are asking you to trade for them in *futures contracts*.

To trade, you stand in the "pit," usually a circular area, and shout and throw your hands in the air—beckoning toward you if you want to buy, away from you if you want to sell. The louder you can yell, and the bigger you are in order to be seen, the better. Your trade, the price you bought or sold for, is recorded by a person in the pit punching the information into a small handheld computer terminal that transmits the price arrived at to the main computer system of the exchange.

Instantaneously the main computer sends the prices from the pit to the news wires and information providers like Bloomberg and Reuters. What you do in the pit will be read around the world just seconds after you drop your hand. The beauty of this is immediate, total dissemination of prices. Everyone knows the same information at the same time and can place a value on what they are buying or selling—in sync and efficiently and with confidence that there are no secret deals.

The other type of trading on the commodity exchange floors is done by independent traders. Their function is vital to the working of the markets because they provide *liquidity*. The markets would not function without their wanting to speculate with their own money for their own accounts. Gary Lapayover describes it this way:

"Speculators provide the ability for somebody who is a producer of, let's say, oil, and that producer feels he would like to protect the profit he needs on his oil production and may need to sell it at $20 to make a profit.

"But the customer says, 'I don't think it's worth more than $19.' A speculator might step in and say, you know what? I think it might be worth $20. And he will buy it. So they provide the ability to shift risk. The speculator could be dead wrong, but he is taking that risk on himself. It frees up a market and makes it work, providing liquidity."

Speculators are probably the least understood of all traders in the financial markets, yet their function is vital and has an important economic purpose. Leo Melamed, chairman emeritus of the Chicago Mercantile Exchange, explained it to me this way:

"If it was just commercial users trading with commercial users, it wouldn't work, because most commercial users are going in the same direction at the same time. They all want to be buyers or they all want to be sellers. Too often they are moving in the same direction.

"So you need a countervailing force that will take off their desire to sell, or take off their desire to buy. And that countervailing force is a speculator. Without that speculation you wouldn't be able to have an efficient market. You have to have the speculator, and most of the time, the more there is in terms of speculation, actually the more efficient the market becomes, because then the market becomes very, very competitive.

"So it is only a combination between the commercial and speculative forces that produces a very liquid and a very efficient market."

On the New York Mercantile Exchange, speculators, referred to as "locals" or "day traders," can account for up to 50 percent of the volume. Their skill in making money for themselves comes from understanding the commodities that they are trading, as well as being able to read the other traders, watching their faces, getting a feel for the people they are doing business with, and developing relationships built on trust.

Their function in other markets is much the same, a mechanism for shifting risk from the person who is trying to get rid of something to the person willing to take it on, in the belief they can profit from the transaction. The benefit is the creation of a transaction, or business, where none would have occurred before. And it determines a price for something where one wasn't evident before.

THE TRADER WHO fits the image of flailing arms and screaming that is so amazingly set in our minds is normally found only on financial and commodity futures exchanges, and to a lesser degree on stock exchanges. Those are the two major financial markets that take place on formal exchange floors.

But the function and purpose of traders are the same in all of the financial markets, whether the trading is in currencies or derivatives or bonds—and whether it is done on exchange floors or in big banks or corporations or investment firms.

There are always two sides to a trade, and two types of traders—one buying (the buy side) and one selling (the sell side).

Imagine the buy side's frame of mind. For the most part, buy-side traders don't make investment decisions and aren't risk takers. They are navigators in a sea of alternatives. A portfolio manager at a fund will decide to buy Intel, for instance; then it is up to the trader to buy that stock most effectively. Facing several computers and a bank of phone lines offering an array of choices, he constantly jockeys among those sources searching for the best price and the deepest market.

He's thoughtful and hyper-alert to the markets, constantly refining his trading strategy to fit the vagaries of perpetually changing variables. At the bigger firms he may have hundreds of millions of dollars worth of securities to move at one time. Imagine a trader no one hates. He's got business and commissions to hand out, and today the numbers can be seriously large.

Now imagine the sell side's frame of mind. He wants the buy side's business and he's competing with everyone else in the world to get it. Knowing that he'll either bag a huge fund trade and make millions for his firm in one go, or he'll have to execute tons of trades all day where he's earning a small fraction in order to make a decent contribution to the firm, he's under tremendous stress to perform. Most sell-side traders at brokerage firms like Merrill Lynch facilitate buy-side customers.

There's another kind of trader on the sell side: proprietary traders who trade the firm's own money. They are the risk takers, the high-wire acts, and they operate on a vertical enough risk/reward curve to be compensated extremely well if they are good.

Once you get past the most basic buy-side/sell-side distinction, traders work in vastly different jobs and environments.

The day I met, let's say his name is John, he was just zipping up his sleeping bag. He had worked through most of the night and after only a couple of hours' sleep felt anxious to get up and work at his computer again. He loved working at D.E. Shaw. It was like being in a college dorm. You'd never know it was one of the most successful hedge funds in the United States and its traders and programmers some of the best paid in the industry.

They were young and laid-back. I didn't see anyone wearing a suit except David Shaw. There is no vacation policy, no regular hours, as long as you are productive, and above all creative. Shaw skims the cream of the best technical and mathematical minds in the world and brings them to work for him. Many of their offices resemble the rooms at school they recently vacated, with posters on the walls and scruffy soft toys sitting atop their terminals. The place has a fuzzy feeling. John thought there was nothing wrong with this. He had never stepped inside the door of another investment bank on Wall Street, so he didn't know.

Trading at D.E. Shaw is very quiet, done by computers that have been programmed. A large number of traders working in the financial markets are "quants" like John—quantitative analysts, what we used to call computer nerds. They read *Wired* as well as the *Wall Street Journal*. A new generation has arrived with advanced engineering degrees and Ph.D.s in computer science or mathematics or physics.

Quants are new-school traders, who believe in pure mathematical manipulation using computers. Being a good programmer is a priority. They exemplify the groundswell toward specialists in the markets who know little about the areas of finance that they are not active in. They don't always care about research, sales, new products or the inner workings of a company whose stock they are trading.

It's trading without emotion. Pulling a quant's attention away from the computer is almost like pulling a child away from the television. It takes their eyes and minds time to unglaze and refocus on the reality away from the screen. Like watching violence on television, they become inured to the millions and millions of dollars they are trading, or the computers are trading. It's just more TV. Their conversations and surroundings are so low-key, you could hear a fly buzzing.

That's at the extreme other end of the spectrum from the high-voltage trading environment where personal contact is so important, where elbows and a strong voice and good interpersonal skills are needed.

Other than on an exchange floor, the vast majority of traders work side by side at long rows of desks, like chickens in a coop, initiating trades over the phone or through their computers. The decibel level is a few notches lower than on an exchange floor, but the electricity, tension, and adrenaline rush are still there. Brains and intuition and guts are engaged in the actual function of trading. Their primary trading tool is a bank of phone lines and computers that they use for manipulation of data and for monitoring the changing prices on the world's markets. They're somewhere in between the old-school, seat-of-the-pants traders and the new-school quants.

There are as many different kinds of traders and trading styles as there are instruments to trade. Some stock traders "go with the flow"—trade with their instincts. If they think a stock is going up, they buy it. And they sell it when they think it has topped out.

Another kind of trader will be found at Merrill Lynch, facilitating customer business. He may be trading when he really doesn't want to be in the market, just to help the customer relationship and provide a service.

Hedge fund traders are triathlon types. They do everything. They find values in trading currencies, fixed income products, equities, derivatives, whatever—and they tend to have a macroeconomic approach to looking at the world, viewing the big picture. They may make the investment and trading decisions or do the trading for a hedge fund manager.

Even a hedge fund manager can be considered a trader, or to have a trading mentality. He may hand the actual trade to someone else to execute for him, but his mind-set could be that of a relentlessly aggressive trader. Michael Steinhardt, who ran a private investment firm, started out as an analyst, then became a trader, then took his trading mentality with him when he managed his own fund.

George Soros began as a trader for small firms in New York before he opened his own investment fund. Most would agree that Soros has a trading mentality: he can be in and out of huge positions in one day. Some of the best-known hedge fund managers in New York can be found at the trading desk in front of their screens, trading as well as giving orders to the traders who work around them.

Some people trade in markets where there are no publicly disseminated prices, so they have to call around to get a feel for what something should cost. Ali, as we agreed to call her, works in merger arbitrage, buying a stock if she thinks a company will be taken over in the future, and in high-yield bond trading:

"There is no tape or any place you can see prices. You just have to trust that the person that is telling you something isn't lying, not taking a point out of you when he trades with you.

"It is very intensive as far as the phone calling when you do a trade. Because there is nowhere to look. You can phone around for an hour trying to establish your marketplace before you get to trade."

Pure program traders watch their computer screens, and when they see a market get out of line, they *arbitrage*. If they see that the stock market is selling off, for example, they will buy a basket of stocks and sell futures, or buy futures contracts and sell a basket of stocks. They trade back and forth between markets in the hope of earning a profit.

Specialists on the New York Stock Exchange are traders. They are the traders' traders, in that they stand at their trading post and provide an auction for the other traders, and they trade for their own account.

Block traders working at investment firms buy and sell "size." They commit their firm's capital and facilitate their institutional customers by buying a big block of stock from an institution that wants to sell. Then they hope that they can sell it, or hold on to it because they think it might go up in value.

There are traders at banks that have twenty-four-hour trading operations at play. They'll trade currencies, bonds, stocks, futures, derivatives.

Some people trade corporate or government bonds. Bond traders primarily watch the economy, interest rates, and government fiscal policy as a basis for their trading.

Some earn their living trading from home. Marty Schwartz manages investors' money as well as his own, and actively trades. He has been called one of the world's best traders.

THEY ALL HAVE their own trading styles, some preferring to trade face to face, some over the phone, some letting their computer trade for them. But traders are a like-minded group when it comes to viewing the world: they have a shared belief in openness, free markets, meritocracy, "your word is your bond."

All you have to do is watch the reaction of traders in the markets to observe that, when they perceive that a government is acting irresponsibly and in a way they think will be detrimental to the health of the economy, when they see taxes levied to make up for the shortfall, when they suspect company management of being weak and ineffectual, they'll turn thumbs down.

They will be the first to applaud privatization. They will be the first to cheer a free-trade agreement or an entrepreneurial high-tech company. Tax burdens, slow growth, high budget deficits, rising interest rates, individuals feeling stretched—these do not make happy traders. They believe in performance in their own lives, and they're hard on others they don't think are performing. Traders have been called the ultimate optimists, but at the same time they are ultimately skeptical—especially of politicians and corporate management.

How do they exert their influence? They sell a security or currency when they lose faith. They buy when they think there is a reason to be hopeful or opportunistic. They have a vested interest in seeing an economy or company grow because it is good for their business. Most of them would tell you that the less government is involved in regulating the economy or companies, the more prosperity there will be.

These free-market warriors are at the front lines of the economy, making their collective opinions felt in a variety of ways. Where they came from, and how they evolved from a relatively innocuous base to achieve this power to influence, is what we will look at next.

4 FROM ANALOG TO ALGORITHM

WHEN I STARTED IN THIS BUSINESS, FOUR MILLION
SHARES WAS A BIG DAY. IN 1997 WE WERE AVERAGING
527 MILLION SHARES PER DAY. TECHNOLOGY HAS BEEN
A BIG, BIG SAVING GRACE.

BILL JOHNSTON

"Will you come up?"

I couldn't see a thing, but let my hand guide me up the stair rail until I saw towering above me what looked to be an English professorial type with tweeds and rumpled hair. In this old brownstone just off Park Avenue, I met Bob Mnuchin, one of the legendary traders whose career began in the 1960s. He is well known for developing the market for institutional block trading—huge blocks of stocks to be bought or sold at one clip for institutional investors.

Now he is making a name for himself in the art world. He runs an art investment fund called C&M Arts, dealing in some of the most sought-after abstract expressionist art in the world: paintings by Mark Rothko, Willem de Kooning, and Jackson Pollock. And he and his wife have restored a beautiful old country hotel, the Mayflower Inn, which sits amid the rolling hills of Connecticut.

It was very dark when I entered. Only starlight halogens picked out the canvases on the wall that individuals would come to view by appointment and perhaps buy. It felt like a chapel.

Having arrived at the second floor, we walked in and sat in the midst of more priceless art. The room was so quiet. The ceilings were high, which made our voices acoustically interesting. And I remember reflecting on the difference between this refined and peaceful atmosphere and the atmosphere of a trading desk, where Bob had spent over thirty years of his life. He had begun right out of school:

"I was looking for a job in the trading community on Wall Street, but it was not a sought-after area. Most people who were traders on Wall Street then had been Teletype operators or wire carriers or people who worked their way up and were around the process. I had gone to an Ivy League school and I had foreign language skills. So I did not find it hard to get a job, albeit that I started at $52 a week [in 1957] and was a little bit of a gopher."

One of the most significant developments in the history of the securities markets was block trading. The technique had existed in the bond market, but there had been no such thing before in equities. A block trade is when the trader doesn't act as the go-between, but actually takes the other side of the trade, either buying or selling. What seemed to spark the advent of block trading was the "Kennedy Crash" in 1962, when President Kennedy tried to persuade steel companies not to raise prices. The market didn't like it. The Dow acted like a yo-yo, shedding 100 points over eight days, then adding 40 points over three hours—very significant moves at the time. That day the New York Stock Exchange experienced the second-highest volume of trading in its history, and the tape ran two or three hours late. That day it was noticed that it was the institutions, not the individual investors, doing the majority of the buying. Firms like Goldman Sachs, Oppenheimer, Smith Barney, and Salomon Brothers paid attention.

Mnuchin was at Goldman Sachs and was in on the very beginning of institutional block trading, when the evolution in the business in terms of complexity, size, and range was incredible. He went from trading a block of 5,000 shares, which was big then, to huge program trades in securities. Gus Levy and Bob Mnuchin were traders who not only enabled Goldman Sachs to build a business reputation for trading securities with institutions, but also propelled the birth of a market. Mnuchin apprenticed under Levy, who sat behind a glass window on the trading floor:

"Gus Levy was an extraordinary man. An extraordinary man. Today I understand the impatience. But I learned somewhat by watching him, and largely by being criticized when I was wrong. I think many would say that Gus Levy, who was 'Mr. Trader' at Goldman Sachs, gave birth to the original concept of institutional trading. And where it really came out was, Gus was a very serious, if not the biggest, arbitrageur on the Street. Government regulation had broken up utilities and railroads into different pieces. You'd have your debentures and warrants and there were different prices. You could buy the underlying stock and sell off those pieces. That was around 1945.

"Gus said, this is great, but who am I going to sell these debentures to? He'd call a few institutions and say, listen, you ought to take a look at these Mach 5s, they're cheap as hell."

Something is cheap only if there is someone who wants to buy it. Gus Levy would talk firms into selling something else they held in order to pay for what he wanted to sell them. He came up with the idea of buying from them whatever they wanted to sell, to fund their buying his debentures.

Bob continued, "And that's sort of how block trading was born. That was really the very, very first seed of block trading."

Gus refined his pitch to calling institutions and offering to buy anything when they needed to sell it, providing them with an immediate sale and cash rather than the more normal month or six months it used to take to move a position. It created *liquidity*, or an easy environment in which to buy and sell. When liquidity dries up, there is a thin market with few able to find a buyer or seller. Liquidity is good for business.

"We did it as part of a service in creating liquidity. And in some of those many transactions we were able to get buyers for some or all of what they were going to sell. Or sellers for what they were going to buy, and got small positions on either side. We built up a big pile of commissions and hoped that we could handle the positions we ended up taking from these people—where they were on our books when we couldn't get somebody to buy it or sell it—well enough so that it wouldn't erode all of those commissions."

One day Gus Levy was at lunch, and the partner who worked directly under Gus was also at lunch. There was no one left at the desk but Mnuchin. A young institutional salesman came over and told him that one of his accounts was indicating that it would sell a certain amount of a stock. Both men were perplexed; neither had done anything so big. Mnuchin's response was:

"Well, you know what we do now, Larry? We go around and tell the other guys, hey everybody, Boston, Philadelphia—we had a loud-speaker then—listen up! We've got somebody that is willing to sell a block. Good size. Really good size. Some RCA. Anybody out there want to buy some?"

Gus Levy had a few accounts that he had been calling for years, which Mnuchin proceeded to call because his boss wasn't there:

"The trader on the other end said to me, 'How many shares do you have?' And I told him. And he said, 'We could be very interested. But we are never allowed to make a bid. We have to have it offered to us.' I said, 'Oh, okay. Let me make a phone call and I'll get right back to you.'"

He called Larry, his salesman, and explained the situation and asked what price the stock was offered at. Larry came back a few minutes later and told Mnuchin what his client had said:

"'We are not allowed to offer a stock. I shouldn't have even told you we had it for sale, but I am certainly not allowed to put a price on it.'"

Mnuchin sat and thought about this for a few minutes, and came to the conclusion that it was the most ridiculous thing he had ever heard in his life. On one side there was this institution saying that it wasn't supposed to tell him it was selling, although it was, but it was not allowed to put a price on the sale. On the other side there was an institution saying it could have an interest in what was being sold, but what was the price? Bob continued:

"What the devil do I do? Well, it really didn't take me very long to figure it out, because it was simply a question of, was I authorized, and did I have the courage to do what needed to be done?

"The last sale was at 52 and 5/8ths. And I went to the seller and said, 'The last sale was at 52 and 5/8ths, I'll pay you down a 1/2 point from the last sale, less commission—52 and 1/8th for your 50,000-odd shares of stock.' I was making that bid. I was praying to God that the other institution would then say that they would buy it. And he came right back and said, 'Sold you 52,400 at 52 and 1/8th.'

"Now I picked up the phone and I called the other institution and I said, 'Alice, I have good news for you. The last sale is at 52 and 5/8ths, I have 52,400 shares firm at 52 and 1/4.' She said to me, 'Hold on.' I said, 'Do you think it will be very long?' She said, 'Not very long.'

"Well, it seemed like an eternity. She came back and said, 'Yes, we will buy 52,400 shares at 52 and 1/4.' So now I went back to the seller, and I said, 'Listen, I've got good news for you. You know that 52,400 shares that you were going to sell at 52 and 1/8? You're not selling it at 52 and 1/8. I got you an 1/8th of a point more. I got you 52 and 1/4.'

"Well, he was ecstatic. We put the trade on the tape, everybody roared. People from all over the firm came around—I mean, it was a major event."

Gus came back from lunch and called Mnuchin into his office. He told him that he had heard about the RCA trade and congratulated him on it. Mnuchin thanked him and walked out. Then he turned on his heel and walked back into Gus's office and said:

"Gus, I'm wondering . . . was I allowed to do this? You know, I didn't have a bid or a customer. And I bid for this. And we might have bought it all if the customer hadn't come through for us. Am I allowed to do this sort of thing?"

Gus said, "You just use good judgment, but yeah, I guess so."

Mnuchin concluded with:

"And that's how I became a trader, because up until then, I was just another rookie."

From the mid-1960s onward, the size of the orders grew as insurance companies and pension funds started to switch from buying bonds to buying equities. They were deemed the "go-go" years, when block trading grew as money managers became more aggressive in their outlook. The Dow rose 45 percent from 1963 to 1967. Which came first: the money managers' change in style and needs, or the realization by firms that here was a new type of customer? From all accounts they happened concurrently. Firms on Wall Street could earn 30 cents a share, so a few strong ones joined the trend of committing their capital to try to buy market share. That was when traders began to earn their salt.

Prior to the days of capital commitment, there wasn't much skill required in being a trader. It had basically been a clerical function. From the market collapse in 1929 there had been a stigma attached to Wall Street that was to continue through the 1930s into the 1940s and 1950s. As the 1960s began, volume on the NYSE started to pick up, and block trading took off. Institutions began actively to look at the stock market and study industry groups to determine what were the best stocks to own, once they recognized the fact that this handful of firms were willing to provide them with liquidity, or to buy big blocks of their stock from them for instant cash. By the late 1960s trading volume on the NYSE approached 10 million shares.

Traders were still working with pretty rudimentary tools. To the rest of us, the decade of the 1960s means the Kennedy assassination and flower children. But to traders, the significant event was that direct telephone dialing came in. Stanley Ross was working in London then:

"I learned firsthand what new technology can do when direct telephone dialing came in 1967 and wiped out overnight the entire method of international trading we used during the fifties and much of the sixties, when our trading room arbitraged its way around the world by cable. Can you imagine such a thing? And by telex, often at quarter to half speed. We did this between all capitals of the world, in all manner of securities, calculating different currencies on heavy circular steel slide rules."

Mnuchin remembers that in New York they had little else to trade with other than a telephone and a ticker tape:

"There was this big roll of paper around a machine. And that paper tape ran across your desk, and you sat there and looked at this little tape. As transactions were reported, they were transmitted to the machine, which then printed it out onto this paper tape.

"And the old timers used to say that they could tell when the market was changing by the sound of the ticker tape. When it sped up, it went across your desk faster, it had a different sound, the market was turning. They knew the market was turning by the sound of the tape. I came out of that era. I used to look at the tape, and the tape used to talk to me."

Businesses were just learning in the 1960s how to use computers that had been created to do arithmetic, and they were massively expensive and as big as a room. In 1962 Burnham & Company installed its first computer for back-office accounting; its first huge IBM mainframe came in 1966. During the stock market boom of the 1960s the sudden increase in business resulted in huge backlogs at brokerage houses, and those without a computer facility to handle the sudden increase went out of business. By the late 1960s over two hundred firms had gone down or merged because they didn't have the data-processing capability or people in operations who understood how to handle the mountains of paper. By the late 1960s the NYSE, in order to cope as well as compete with the block traders, had developed BAS, Block Automation System, an automated trading system for large blocks of stocks, and in 1969 it opened another trading room named the "Blue Room."

In the days before computers, working had been sensory. Traders from the 1960s talk about the magic of the marketplace, the sounds and atmosphere, and the intangibles. They talk about touching and feeling the market. Without the shower of nonstop information that traders benefit from today, they were in effect blind, responding to different stimuli—or manufacturing their own stimuli to move the market. Their trading style was seat-of-the-pants, reliant on intuition. The total dependence on the telephone meant that it was a crucial skill to flush out the trader on the other end of the phone to find out what cards he held, to see how far you could push or intimidate or cajole him. It was crucial that you were mentally agile and street-smart.

Mailroom clerks or runners or people who were sweeping the floors at night—anyone who could quickly figure out a 16-point spread in their head and could add fractions swiftly—were given a chance on the trading desk to learn and apprentice up. They became respected if they were good at riding the markets; but although many would inspire awe in those immediately around them, few made it into the power structure of the firm.

It was through the part they played in the birth of a market that traders broke through and eventually rose to run their desks and then their firms. Bob Mnuchin went on to become head trader, then became the head of the department, rose to managing partner, and was on the management committee at Goldman Sachs. And he didn't have to give up being a trader to do it.

* * *

As the 1970s rolled around, survival was foremost in everyone's mind. Oil shocks had us sitting on gas lines. The Consumer Price Index doubled over the decade, and inflation soared. Vietnam War spending added to the inflationary pressure. Bond prices were volatile, and interest rates hit levels never seen before, climbing up to about 20 percent by the end of the decade. Then there was the less-developed nations' debt crisis. From 1969 to 1970 stocks fell 35 percent. Fixed currency rates were done away with, and currencies began to float. Business dried up in 1972, and the United States went into a recession in 1973 and 1974. There was Watergate, and Nixon resigned. Inflation took off again in 1978 and 1979, and the markets suffered. Cynicism marked everyone's face.

As a result, between 1972 and 1978 there was tremendous consolidation in the industry. Business dwindled, and firms merged to survive or bulk up—or simply out of panic. The major upheaval in the financial markets turned out to be a gift for traders. At the time, they might not have chosen that word to express it, but in hindsight, the gut-wrenching changes opened doors and the best walked through.

The genesis of their ascendancy was in this decade. Three major developments allowed it to happen.

The first in the United States was that, after May Day in 1975, commissions became negotiable, whereas prior to that date, commissions paid by buyers to sellers of securities had been fixed. *Negotiable* is a crucial word; it implies trading skills.

Muriel Siebert, founder of the discount brokerage that bears her name, saw it happen:

"ERISA [Employee Retirement Income Security Act] came in, which is what we called at that time 'everything ridiculous invented since Adam.' That was the part that said you had to get the lowest cost, the best executions at the lowest cost. At that point, the profession started to emerge as a profession."

What happened was predictable. Once the fat, guaranteed commissions were gone, income dropped precipitously, and firms that couldn't quickly adapt went out of business. With lower income due to commissions that were spiraling downward, trading activity was suddenly stepped up and relied on to compensate for the lost revenue.

Donald Marron, chairman of Paine Webber, commented in an oral history he gave to *Institutional Investor*:

"The biggest thing at work in bringing down commissions was the growth of the industry; there really was an awful lot of business, and more coming, and when it was freed up from this artificial structure, it just encouraged more people to do more trading. Things changed very, very fast."

A transactional, capital-intensive trading environment took over. As competition grew, the ability to take risk and to manage risk determined which firms were successful and which weren't. A lot of people on equity desks on Wall Street lost their jobs, from firms going out of business but also from not knowing how, and not wanting, to handle large block transactions because they didn't want to take on the risk involved. The traders who were able to do that and do it well became very valuable to the firms they worked for.

Stanley Shopkorn was another who took to the challenge. Now managing director at Moore Capital in New York, Stanley was at Loeb Rhodes in the late 1960s and early 1970s, and has poignant memories of what it was like trading before and during the changeover:

"We had a Quotron, we had a paper tape, and your position on the tape was your position of seniority in the trading room, because the tape would run from where it came out to where the spool wound it out. There were four or five traders who sat in a row, and the most senior person sat closest to the tape. Your access to news was a Dow Jones machine which stood right by the ticker, and when important news was breaking it would ring once, twice, or three times—three times being very important.

"Lionel Smith, who was the number one person on the desk, would sit right by the machine and by the tape; and effectively, if you were down at the end of the line, you had to be a better trader. Because once you saw things on the tape, people were clearly seeing it ten or fifteen seconds before you were.

"The key was to move closest to the right to be closer to the machine so you had better positioning. I don't know if you've seen those old Dow Jones machines, but the ink used to spit out, and I used to lose a shirt every other week because, being the last person in, I was supposed to change the paper in the machine.

"Before 1973 you got a weekly chart delivered to you in a book, and you had to update that chart yourself, but then you wouldn't see a chart again until Friday. You would die to get the charts on Friday night or Saturday morning, when they were delivered special delivery to your house."

What traders had to rely on then was luck, persistence, and being smart. Shopkorn had originally wanted to be a lawyer. He went to Brooklyn Law School, passed the bar, and clerked for a lawyer for a while. It was boredom with that experience that turned his head toward Wall Street:

"I decided that I didn't want to practice law. But I couldn't get a job on Wall Street. It was tough, because people said to me, why do you want to be a trader? You're a lawyer, lawyers don't want to be traders. In those days, you know, they didn't look for a lot of education, and I didn't go to the right schools to be an investment banker."

He worked under Charly Black and Lionel Smith at Loeb Rhodes, who put him through panic drills and repeatedly questioned him—if this happened, what would you do? And if that happened, what would you do? They taught him to watch out for the pitfalls. The lessons began to sink in:

"Lionel went on vacation and it was a deal between World Airways and INA Insurance. My broker was on the phone with me from the floor of the exchange when I saw on the tape 'I'—remember this is a paper tape that prints out 'N . . . A . . . T . . . E . . . R . . .' and that's all I had to see. I was sure that the word was 'TERMINATES.' I said to my broker, 'Buy 300,000 shares of INA at market.' And I'm watching the tape go by and I see 100,000 at 43 and 1/4, 200,000 go by at 43 and 1/2 . . . Just at that point Charly came walking into the room and said to me, 'What's going on?'

"I said, 'Well, here's the story. INA terminates merger.' And Charly asked, 'What did you do?' INA was now trading at $47 dollars. I called the broker and found out we had bought 300,000 shares back at a price $4 or $5 dollars below where they stopped trading. Charly looked at me and said, 'That was great, but why didn't you buy more?' But I had learned you never want to be a pig in this business.

"What we used at Loeb Rhodes for convertible bond trading were conversion cards, which you would print up yourself and which told you at what price in the stock the convertible bond was worth. You always had it in front of you on the desk. If you traded convertible bonds, you had as many cards, if you will, as convertible bonds you traded. And you could line them up in a row right in front of you along the way under the tape so that you could see the tape, see the price, then translate the value of the bond to that value.

"So no computers, everything was done by hand. There was one point where American Telephone did a huge rights deal, where we had cards coming out of our ears so that we knew what each eighth was, and you had to compute by hand. You had a calculator. Trading then was a bit different because you had fewer tools available to you. You didn't have updating charts as you do today, so you had to be able to stock a lot in your head. I was able to do that, so I moved up rather quickly, and after four years ran both the convertible area and the risk arbitrage area."

In 1975 Stanley moved over to run the block trading area at Salomon Brothers. Salomon had been fighting to be thought of as an investment bank, so Stanley's mission as head equity trader was to build up the block trading capability, to give it credibility in handling big blocks of stock in order for its investment banking side to win mandates. He epitomized the risk-taking trader. On the desk they devised debt-for-equity swaps, where corporations could call in their debt and issue equity against it, and Stanley would place the equity on a block trading basis. These were very big trades for that time.

That kind of trading and the ability to take on huge risk were important in Salomon's growth characteristics. Tom Strauss, former president of Salomon Brothers, explained that they became part of its culture:

"It was a culture that intellectualized risk taking. We understood it. We understood taking losses. We had all grown up in that environment. It is something that takes years and years to develop. John Gutfreund was an important part of it. John more than anyone was responsible for inventing the modern-day syndicate business and taking it into a real risk-taking business. That culture spread throughout the firm. He was prepared to risk the firm's capital."

This was when monitoring block trades and the size of trades on plus ticks or minus ticks to see if there was accumulation or distribution was just beginning. Today the computer gives that to traders. It wasn't until the early 1980s that screens began to give traders an edge. By the mid-1980s hand calculation had completely disappeared and everything was finally on screen.

The second major development was a new focus on products. As products became more sophisticated—financial futures, derivatives, options, mortgage-backed securities—they required a higher level of math and statistics.

In April 1973 listed equity options came into being on the Chicago Board of Options Exchange. Computer-oriented traders began looking at them and calculating them with Hewlett-Packard handheld slides. The old HPs used to have a card that you put in when you had to go to another function. They would take more than sixty seconds to calculate one option by hand, figuring it all out according to what was called the Black-Scholes formula. And if you wanted to calculate and trade lots of them, it became problematical.

It wasn't until years later that traders had PCs to help them. Options were complex, and required an understanding of Black-Scholes models and elaborate pricing structures that the traditional traders didn't possess. Traders who could negotiate these new products became the hub of the wheel. By 1977 tremendous volume had developed in options.

A third major breakthrough came for traders in the mortgage-backed securities area, a product developed at Salomon Brothers by Robert Dall and Lewis Ranieri. Dall and Ranieri grouped mortgages together to make up a security that could be sold, and the product took off. Mortgage traders became "stars" and the highest-paid traders on the street.

Computers began to be used more and more in every part of the business. In 1971 the over-the-counter NASDAQ exchange began, and traders could now trade stocks using information on a computer terminal. Bond traders had government bond broker screens to use, and back-office operations began to be wired and automated in a way that supported whatever dreams they had in the front office. Computer nerds were tinkering at the fringes of the trading floor by the mid-1970s, fascinated by what they could do with the new technology. The synergy between mind and computer power produced new products for them to trade, and the ability to trade faster.

The new breed of trader began to write computer programs for merger arbitrage strategies, among other lucrative ideas, and they became very sought after. By the end of the 1970s some were viewed as superstars, and with superstar status came huge paychecks and power, at least within the firm and within Wall Street. Names emerged like Lewis Ranieri, John Mulheren, Larry Fink, Howie Rubin, Michael Milken, and Stanley Shopkorn, among others.

Looking back, it's hard to imagine that Apple Computer was founded only in 1977. But Apples caught on quickly and by 1979 traders were carrying them under their arms, particularly because of a software program that could run on them called VisiCalc, which could do number crunching faster and in more complex ways than a calculator. Buy-side traders previously had kept track of their orders on a pad of paper, and at the end of the day they would use their calculator to work out their average price and divide it up among accounts. Now they had help.

LARGER-THAN-LIFE personalities emerged in the 1980s, partly because of tremendous growth in the markets and the opportunities that afforded, partly because of a change in the U.S. business environment, and partly because the press began to take more interest in what was going on in the financial markets. Ivan Boesky emerged, as did Dennis Levine. But while the press brought us the villains, the financial community benefited from the likes of John Gutfreund, Lewis Glucksman, Peter Buchanan, and Richard Fisher, who had risen to the top of their firms and were relentlessly pushing them forward.

Big changes—not only economic, but technological—affected the markets and participants. The spirit of unbridled capitalism reached its zenith in the Reagan years. Tax rates, interest rates, and inflation rates began to come down in the United States after 1982, and the stock market surged for the next five years. The New York Stock Exchange poured over $24 million dollars into a technological overhaul to accommodate the burgeoning market volume.

Real-time information in the marketplace became more important, and filing times for debt and equity offerings that the corporation finance side did were shortened in 1982 by the Securities and Exchange Commission, in its shelf registration ruling 415. It became imperative for corporate finance to be more in sync with and rely more heavily on the traders on the floor. Time frames were being dramatically compressed. A shelf registration meant a corporate client could register in advance with the SEC all the issues it wanted to do over the following two years. Issues could then be done within the day, according to market conditions. It meant the client could also choose at the last minute who they wanted to do the issue. Investment firms had to be capable of launching an issue quickly, whereas before, filing registration statements and other paperwork could take several months.

The speed that shelf registration afforded meant more than ever that the investment banking side and the trading side had to work together. If they didn't want to, or didn't get along, forget it. This was for the most part what happened, because historically the two sides came from different backgrounds and cultures.

Trying to adjust from an elitist, corporate finance orientation over to the new trader orientation caused severe cultural problems within many firms. Goldman Sachs had internal difficulties trying to assimilate the traders who were now being listened to and were important to the firm. Morgan Stanley had the same problem of internal conflict and went on to grow because it managed to embrace trading. Dillon Read never did. Lehman Brothers strangled itself trying. It was all part of evolution.

Another reason behind a growing trading mentality was that by 1983 the boom in the new personal computer business had saturated Wall Street. IBM introduced its own PC in 1981. Another was that the new people coming into the market were computer friendly. In London a cannon went off with Big Bang in 1986, with the deregulation of a market that would change the face of the City forever. These were golden years for traders, who now generated a large part of the profits for brokerage firms. And the once maligned trading area that had been spurned by past MBAs became a hot target for those newly minted.

The 1980s were also marked by the huge amounts of money that entered the markets in great waves, each wave bigger than the one before it. By the late 1980s the mutual fund industry had truly taken off. The size of the funds became enormous, as were the orders. The crash of 1987 only multiplied the amount of money pouring in to be managed by the mutual funds, as people began to perceive that they couldn't handle investing by themselves anymore. Highly publicized leveraged buyouts and mergers stoked stock market fever as people chased rumors. It was also the era of a boom in the high-yield junk bond market. All of this added to global awareness of the action in the markets.

In 1982 John Gutfreund and Stanley Shopkorn made a call on the price of oil. The price had gone up with a sharp surge, and oil stocks around the world were trading at over $100. Stanley related the rest:

"We just believed it was overdone, and established some very large short positions in oil companies. We were right. There was massive liquidation in 1983 of oil positions and, having had so many short positions set up, we basically were the clearinghouse for oil stocks in the United States market for close to a year. It was one of the more profitable calls that we made at Salomon Brothers.

"Some of the really big blocks we moved were for the Basses; we took Carl Icahn out of a very large piece of Texaco, along with Lehman Brothers and Goldman Sachs. We took the Fisher brothers and others out of a very large piece of Avon. On a historical basis, we took ourselves into the business with the notion that we were willing to take risks on block trades.

"Both Salomon Brothers and John Gutfreund were fabulous when it came to putting on a print and saying, 'Look, we are long this, we need to walk away for three or four weeks,' or 'We need to take this into the investment account,' as we did with the Texaco transaction and a Lockheed transaction. It was a very important part of Salomon's growth characteristics, not only in trading but in investment banking, to do that kind of trading."

A new kind of person began arriving on Wall Street, one that was cerebral in an entirely different way than before. While the world was captivated by the more flamboyant traders and personalities, there was an influx of technically oriented, computer-literate traders who labored under less glamorous visions of themselves and used the latest technology to solve back-room operations problems, to build new specific software solutions, and to leverage their skills to excel in such lucrative areas as risk arbitrage. Although one trader told me that even in 1986 when she was working at Chase, there was only one PC for six traders on the swap desk, computers were increasingly present and computer power had increased enough by the second half of the decade to run elaborate programs. A sudden rise in the technology curve enabled globalization and the liberation of markets from their geographic boundaries, which propelled all markets forward.

Now for the first time, the buy-side traders at the mutual funds and pension funds, who previously had been in the background, started getting together to talk about market issues. Not at golf outings or dinners, but at meetings to talk about how to become a force in directing changes in their markets. These weren't the typical order clerks that many buy-side traders had been in the 1970s. They started to look at their jobs seriously and they were politically active. The pay gap between the sell side at the brokerages and the buy side at the pension and mutual funds was still large, and they were asking why this should be so, especially since they increasingly had the big money on their side of the desk.

Of course, the big event of the decade was the 1987 stock market crash, which still echoes in the minds of people who work in the markets. We all have our stories to tell—of getting goose bumps staring at the screen, of everyone gathering in the trading room saying that they had never seen anything like this, and "Oh my God, oh my God, can you believe it?!" It was stultifying. People who had worked in the markets for twenty years were having a hard time believing what they were seeing and experiencing. The losses were enormous, and it shook the confidence of people within the markets as well as outside them. Stanley Shopkorn remembered that the market "shook, it rumbled. There were days during the process where people were on such emotional highs and lows, sheer survival, that it's very hard to get it out of your head.

"I am sure that Billy Johnston had a time of it, because there were specialist firms during the course of a couple of days who were on the brink of going out. The system did hold. There was massive cooperation from John Gutfreund, who was the head of Salomon, to the trading partners that were on the floor, to the specialists on the floor of the stock exchange, to the administrators of the stock exchange. And the government itself was monitoring what was going on."

Perhaps some of the hardest hit as traders were the "specialists" on the floor of the New York Stock Exchange. Bill Johnston was a specialist then; now he is president and chief executive of the New York Stock Exchange. The day of the crash, Bill didn't feel fear until he went home. How was he going to pay for everything the next day? Would the banks lend to him?

That was the night of October 19, 1987, and Bill had just come off the trading floor after the chaos of the stock market crash. All day, people had milled around in the streets outside the exchange as word spread of the carnage inside. Television vans topped with large satellite dishes were parked along the curb, their anchors pushing each other out of the way to get hold of anyone who looked like they knew what was happening or had a story to tell. Doomsayers were parading along the street with signs that warned of the end.

The specialists inside on the floor of the exchange just couldn't keep up with the pace of the trading, there were so many sell orders coming through. By exchange rules, a specialist has to provide a "fair and orderly market" for the stocks he represents, which means buying if the stock is plummeting and there are no other buyers. So after the debacle was all over, specialists were left with huge positions of stock on their own account for which they had to come up with the money. Bill relates:

"On Monday, October 19, 1987 the inventory that I owned at the end of that night I had to pay for on Monday 26, one week later. In those days we had five business days' settlement. And I couldn't have paid for it without the banks loaning me the money. Even though I had liquidated the inventory, I still had to pay for it.

"I made some phone calls to some people in London that I knew because I thought I could borrow some money, and in fact they would underwrite me if I needed it, which I never did. John Phelan, chairman of the exchange then, went to the Federal Reserve and the Fed opened up the spigots. They got the banks to make some money available. We had been that far away from going out of business. Thank God for rallies."

There are circuit breakers in place now to slow down such a collapse. Could it happen again? Perhaps. But it shook the foundations enough that post-crash investigations, reports, and books exploring the topic, as well as new regulations and safeguards, mean that it is at least better planned for.

Some blamed program traders for the crash. There are about fifteen program traders who are big and active today in the New York market. They don't have any portfolios. All they do is arbitrage between markets. When the markets get out of line, they put them back in line. If futures are higher or expensive in relation to the underlying stocks, the stocks will be bought and a short position taken in the futures index. If the futures look low or inexpensive in relation to the underlying stocks, the futures are bought and the stocks are sold. The program traders' profit is the price difference minus their trading costs. This arbitraging has been done forever, and is a simple and straightforward kind of trading.

Program trading, on the other hand, is a style or method of trading used by big institutions like mutual funds. They make a decision, usually moving in the same direction at once—for instance, to sell stocks. If, say, three or four fund managers decide to sell portfolios carrying 400 stocks, they push them through their computers linked to the order-taking systems at the New York Stock Exchange and sell everything within minutes. It makes sense. For one trader to sit and divvy up $10 million or $40 million worth of different individual trades would take too long and not be terribly efficient. Program trading accounted for almost 16.8 percent of the share volume every day in 1997. Advances in technology made this style of trading possible. The sheer weight of money and its slamming into the market at the same time are what move it.

Bill Johnston began his career on the floor in 1962 when he was twenty-three years old:

"I opened a brokerage account when I was fifteen, collateralized by Treasury bills that my mother loaned me. I bought and sold stocks. Dad talked about the market at dinner. I think that I knew before I ever got out of college that I wanted to work on Wall Street."

He became a member of the exchange in 1964, and by 1967 was responsible as a specialist for five stocks: Atlantic City Electric, Orange and Rockland Utilities, San Francisco and St. Louis Railroad, Chicago and Eastern Illinois, and Kroger. Of those today, two railroads are gone, one utility still exists, and Atlantic City Electric merged in 1997 with Delmarva Power.

Most of his career was spent as a specialist on the floor, making a two-way market in stocks. He was at the fulcrum of the live auction market that swirled around him—the anchor point where buyers and sellers come together to meet at a price for stocks that he specialized in. He actively traded while keeping constant watch on the computer screens to monitor changes in all the markets so that he might be as much as twenty seconds ahead of the others.

If you walk around the floor of the exchange, you can pick out the specialists standing in front of their posts with a "crowd" of traders in front of them actively buying and selling the stocks they are auctioning. During that time they may be using their own money to smooth out the volatility that could be occurring during the trading. A specialist knows his stocks like a bird knows the sky. He knows how changes in the market or economy will affect them, how they tend to move at certain times of the day, and when demand could heat up for them. In the old days, the post was a tall, round kiosk. Today it is a kiosk structure threaded with advanced communication lines and topped with computer screens and televisions displaying the major business television channels.

I wondered whether Bill missed the noise and frenzy and camaraderie of the rather rough-and-ready stock exchange floor, with its old floorboards littered with slips of paper, compared to his current immaculate perch on the executive floor under tight security. Everything is cream there: deep cream carpets, heavy cream walls, high ceilings, and long expanses that seemed to take forever to walk across. When you walk into his office of presidential proportions, you pass a large mahogany table with a foot-high crystal jar filled with red, green, and yellow peanut M&Ms. To your left is a long desk that is backed by an equally long credenza topped with two computer screens and televisions tuned into the financial networks. There are large sofas for meetings, and the walls are hung with traditional prints.

A diplomat for the most influential market in the world, an ambassador of sorts for U.S. capitalism, cosseted in this eyrie he has the peace needed to study the stacks of reading material that cross his desk every day, to prepare speeches to be given to the business community, and to court the heads of foreign governments and companies keen on becoming part of the biggest stock market in the world. It is an incredible change from his lifestyle as a trader. He has made it to the top.

Every day a car picks him up to take him to his five A.M. workout at the gym. Then he slips back into the car to be taken to a breakfast meeting with customers and companies before being dropped off at work. Previously he would have gone to his specialist post to see what the accumulation of buy and sell orders was, and to look for news on his stocks that he might not have seen earlier. Now he goes to the RAMP, the command center that monitors all the systems, and checks to make sure that they are working.

The rest of his day is a continuous flow of meetings, seeing companies, unlisted and listed, but spending most of the time with unlisted. Lunch is entertaining again, usually upstairs in the old

Stock Exchange Luncheon Club, where members eat together or with customers over a cuisine completely in tune with the gentleman's club feel of the place. Little has changed. The ceilings are high and the dark, wood-paneled walls are decorated with gold leaf. You can't really grasp the importance of Bill's work for the exchange until you walk behind him going into lunch. It's like the parting of the Red Sea. From the minute he passes the antique post with its brass plates and enters the hall, people make way for him or hurry over to shake his hand. People look up from their tables to catch his eye, and call out. Despite his down-to-earth demeanor and good humor, he is learning to act the part for those who look to him for leadership.

The end of the day means being back on the floor at four P.M. for the closing gavel. His bushy white beard is a familiar sight up on the podium at the closing bell. He likes to stay visible. There are more meetings, and then he is out to dinner every night with members and customers, listening to their concerns. Summer weekends he puts on his driving cap, puts the top down, and tools out of Manhattan to a slower life at the beach, making remarkable time for someone who never goes over the speed limit.

What was his biggest obstacle coming up through the ranks?

"Fighting off what I considered an ancient culture, people that were doing business in a less progressive manner than I perceived it to be. It's the young forcing out the old with young ideas, and I was seeing that even here in my own firm a year ago, with the younger guys taking a much more active role, trading bigger and better than I ever dreamt of. Taking more risk, but better risk. They were less emotional about it and less apt to fall in love with a stock, so that if they bought something and it went against them, they were quicker to sell out. That was something that was encouraged in our firm.

"I don't know how much of trading can be taught. It's instinctive to a degree. If you like it and are good at it and you can go with it and take a loss and live to trade another day, then you are fine. You do that by taking losses and getting back into the flow again when things look better for you."

IN THE 1990s everything speeded up. Computers did one thing that was very important and used to be very time-consuming: they gathered and collated information faster than you could ever hope to do as a trader or as a group of traders. Without a computer, a trader would be able to manage only a finite number of trades; with one, he could manage exponentially more at one time, increasing the amount of money he could make for his firm. Multiply that one trader by thousands in the markets, and you see how quickly the volumes of business and the speed with which it was done grew. Technology raised to the third power what traders and the markets could achieve.

While the New York Stock Exchange went from strength to strength in the 1990s, the stock exchange in London experienced problems. More international companies listed on the exchange and there was merger mania and flotation fever, but market participants drifted away. Many think the decline began with the rapidity with which the changeover from a physical trading floor to a computer screen system took place after Big Bang in 1986. The old outcry system on the floor changed within a week and a half to one of computers and phones for remote trading. There were also problems following the much publicized and costly failure the next year of the exchange's new Taurus share-trading system.

Even now, although the exchange has a screen trading system, alternatives exist and pose a challenge. Tradepoint screens, for example, immediately show traders the best quote on the London Stock Exchange as well as their own best quote. So you can choose whether to send your order to the London Stock Exchange, where it will probably be put through more quickly because of the depth of its market, or to put your order through Tradepoint, where it will cost you less but where there is a possibility that it won't be consummated until there is a matching order for yours. It depends on how much of a hurry you're in.

Eric Sheinberg found the tumult in London very much to his liking. He must have taken the City by surprise, because you would never guess that this man, with his cultured exterior and devotion to fine wine and antiques, would be such a fierce competitor underneath. But he had trained in the early days, when guts were as important as the computer is today.

Eric told me that he had been hired by the legendary Gus Levy after having worked summers for Goldman Sachs in New York since 1956:

"Just before I went back for my senior year in college, Gus called me into his office and wanted to know what I was going to do after college. And I said, 'I'd like to come back here and trade.' And he said,

'Well, you'd better.' People like him don't exist today because, when people tell you that today, unless you get it in writing, it doesn't mean anything. But his word was his bond."

Eric went back to Goldman Sachs and slipped into the only empty seat, right next to the convertible bond trader who was seventy-one and had been with the firm for fifty years. Eric was twenty-one. There were no training programs then, only OJT—on-the-job training. So he traded convertibles until 1975, when Levy asked him to take over the corporate bond desk. In 1984 he switched to non-U.S. trading, and more recently traded foreign exchange, bonds, equities, and futures.

So here we had an American trader with a wealth of experience arriving in London. And the thing he found amazing was that they had never done block trading the way they did it in New York. He introduced it to them U.S.-style, with his very own little Big Bang:

"What they called block trading was if somebody wanted to sell a block of securities, they would take a 10 percent discount. I thought they were kidding. Mnuchin and I worked together at the time, and I used to say, this is insanity. Because if somebody wanted to sell a block of stock in New York, anything less than the last sale or an eighth below the last sale, you wouldn't do the transaction. This was late 1989 through 1991.

"We, as an American firm, could not understand why a client, whether it was for 1 percent of a company or 5 percent, would take a 10 percent discount to the market price. I was always asking, 'How could the guy make money?' The firm that dominated that business at the time was Smith Newcourt. And they were good at it, they had it to themselves. But we went in there, and to buy a block of securities at a 3 percent or 5 percent discount to the market for us was like Santa Claus arriving at your door every day. Now of course, you took risk if you couldn't sell it."

He looked like he was enjoying the memory:

"One day Lazard approached us with a block of Elsevier. It was a competitive situation, which I wasn't really aware of at the time. I assumed we had an exclusive, which we didn't. Anyway, everyone was shooting against us. This was 1991. The clients knew the stock was for sale. But we didn't tell anybody. We were told that we weren't allowed to tell anybody or preshop it. But I didn't know our competitors were out shopping the damn thing.

"We couldn't understand what was happening in the market, because the market went down from 77 guilders to 71 or something in a period of a day and a half. And I couldn't understand. And I said to myself, well, somebody knows something.

"I bought the block at a premium to the last sale. I bought the block thinking I wasn't in competition. I only found out afterward, what happened was that everybody else was shorting the stock, because what they used to do is short the shares figuring that they would buy the block and buy it cheaper. We never operated that way. In the United States you couldn't do that, you'd go to jail. But outside of the United States I guess it was evidently legal. In any event, I bought the block, it was 10 percent of the company.

"I called one of my traders, because it was traded in London and I was in New York, and I told him, 'Now, I'm going to show you what CBOT is.' Most people think that is the Chicago Board of Trade. I said, 'Now, I'm going to show you what chopped balls on toast is.'

"I said, 'Buy X number of shares at the market.' And the next thing you know, the stock went up from 71 to 77, because everybody was short. But I had all the shares. All those guys had shorted against it. The Elsevier was about a $600 million transaction, which at that time was probably one of the bigger transactions."

Now he was really warming up:

"The other one was a French one, for Louis Vuitton. The Vuitton family wanted out from Arnaud, why I don't know. I think he was a pretty bright guy. But they were just fed up and they weren't running the company anymore. And I did the same thing, but I knew I was in competition.

"I paid the market price for the shares. And I know that the person that was advising the Louis Vuitton family told them they would be literally leaving $20 million on the table. Because the competing bid was down 10 percent. It was absolutely insane. It was a very big transaction.

"I not only bought almost 5 percent of the company, but then I had to buy another 1 or 2 percent in the marketplace because everybody was shorting. Once again, what had happened was that all of our competitors had presold the shares. They went out and shopped the thing all over the world. It went down. I bought it at the last sale. They bid down 10 percent from the last sale after already knocking it down 10 percent. It was crazy. And then they were all short again.

"And they had developed the interest. Everybody wanted to buy it, and we were the only ones with the shares. So then they figured, well, if I paid that price, then I must be crazy, because we were out of money. One thing we had was capital. And in the trading business, capital is the most important thing, if you use it effectively. If you don't use it effectively, you are a fool. That transaction was even bigger than the Elsevier one.

"I'll tell you what was great about it. The profitability. We took the risk. And if we were wrong, it was going to cost us a lot of money, but it was worth the risk. I've always looked at a transaction this way: I never worry how much am I going to make, I worry about how much am I going to lose if I am wrong. Because we were all brought up that way, one thing you don't want to do is bury the house if you make a mistake.

"In London, the difference I think was that when they did these deals, they would always have them presold. It would look like they were doing a very big risk transaction, but you would get two or three major institutions that would commit to at least half the deal. So they never really had that much of a risk. It was already half sold. To me, committing capital is having no buyers, no shopping, you make a judgment, and then you go out and market it after you have committed. But they were used to an agency business prior to 1986, so there was no such thing as having to take a risk. It's almost like what we used to have before we had negotiated commissions."

For Eric, it must have been like feeling for the walls in a dark room. Anyone else would have just done okay in an unfamiliar market, not knowing how the game is played, or at least had a learning curve. He did spectacular trades in a period of six months, and the numbers were huge. And no one had ever done it that way. The other aspect that he brought to the table was the creation of a more liquid market. If a piece of business came in, he didn't have to wait three days. If it was a very large deal, he'd talk to another one of his partners, Bob Mnuchin being one. But he would be able to come to a decision very quickly and come back with an answer within half an hour. This meant a deal would get done and an institution would get cash more quickly.

"You know the difference between London and New York, the real key in terms of block trading—in trading and dealing where the commission wasn't going to pay for the trade? In London, if you took the risk, the rewards were potentially huge. Just figure it out. If you bought $60 million of stock at a 3 percent discount, and had an organization that worked and could blanket the world in twenty-four hours, and if you bought at the right price . . . even if you bought it at a 3 percent discount and could sell it at a 1 percent discount, you're still going to make $1.2 million on that trade. That's still a lot of money."

"The Eagle Has Landed." That was the ad he used to put on the back page of the *Institutional Investor*. It had a big eagle and offered his home phone number, advertising "Yankee Bond Trader—24 hours a day." He was probably one of the first to do twenty-four-hour global trading. That's Eric, a totally unique personality. Understandably, he thinks traders today rely too much on the computer compared to using their own understanding of the markets:

"Because the machine is telling them what to do. I used to kid people and say, 'What would happen if the electricity went off? You'd all be dead.' Which is really true.

"Look at the program traders. Or the momentum traders. They use computers to alert them either that the volume is up a lot on a stock, or the stock is trending down, and all of a sudden, they just buy stocks or sell stocks. And they don't know what the company does. It's crazy. Trading by a machine and doing something because the machine says to do it is the equivalent of charts. Because the computer says, this is what is happening, join the party. There's a party at this house. You're invited for ten minutes. Get in."

The funny thing is, Sheinberg is pretty damn good with a computer.

5 BIG CIGARS AND RED SUSPENDERS

THE PRESS COVERS WALL STREET FOR ONE THING, SENSATIONALISM. WHETHER IT IS THE *WALL STREET JOURNAL* OR THE *FINANCIAL TIMES*, SENSATIONALISM SELLS. WHY WRITE SOMETHING NICE ABOUT A GUY WHEN YOU CAN WRITE SOMETHING BAD?

ERIC SHEINBERG

It was in the 1980s, when business swelled and compensation became generous, that young traders acted out in real life the roles that the press envisioned them playing. Cigars and red suspenders and conspicuous consumption became part of that image. Journalists began to take an interest in the subject of investment banking, and when the excitement wasn't there, they invented it. As the journalists wrote, so the traders increasingly behaved.

There's no doubt about it, the 1980s were wild. People lurched into new money in a clumsy way. Young traders I knew overdid and overconsumed. Even London was not immune. The Ferrari Boys were talked about derisively. Phil Nathan of Charles Stanley observed:

"The City, I think, went through a bad time when the term *yuppie* was brought in. That damaged the image of traders, and some started to act like the trader with the loud mouth, in the bar drinking champagne, with a mobile phone sticking out of his ear."

The impact on the historical imagination of that cultlike image lingered for many years after the 1980s, when the image was honed to perfection. It was a game of mirrors. It nourished a certain macho instinct that had previously been contained within certain bounds. A speechwriter for President Reagan, Peg Noonan, once remarked that we as a society are increasingly becoming like actors, taking our cues on how to behave from the media. As the financial media grew in size and influence in the nation as a whole, it had a similar influence in shaping the self-image of Wall Street and its traders. By the end of the 1980s it was playing a pivotal role in roasting people in the financial community. The press depicted Michael Milken, for example, as a criminal before he was proven guilty, according to Milken supporters such as Glenn Yago.

Stanley Shopkorn, then working at Salomon Brothers, remembers that the press had a major impact on the image of Wall Street, and agreed that some traders came to think of themselves as Masters of the Universe:

"There are always people in any epic period in any business that lose fact and create what movie producers and reporters want to write about. The other side of the coin is, anytime you have an industry that is successful, or people earn a lot more money than either a reporter or writer can fathom, there is an iota of jealousy. Or an iota of, well, he must be doing something wrong, or, he must be arrogant—so that those people are tainted immediately.

"I spent very little of my time talking to reporters because there were so few reporters that would give a fair view to what you were saying. They wanted to write the story they walked in with. And it never changes. That person in the movie *Wall Street* was a minority, or a microcosm, of what the business is about. Anybody can create any movie that they want on a microcosm of life, but that doesn't mean the people are like that."

This is not to imply that press attention wasn't courted. Ivan Boesky was skilled at eliciting attention for what he thought were his greatest exploits. His speech on the premise that greed is good made great copy. Newspapers like the *Wall Street Journal* brought his exploits to public view. But the newspapers that are normally read to gain an understanding of what is going on in the markets are not always right.

Stanislas Yassukovich, chairman of EASDAQ, told me what he thinks:

"The quality of the financial press [in London] has deteriorated because it is not a career that is attracting the best people. I think the quality of the Lex column has gone way down, I mean, they just get things completely wrong, they fail to understand some transactions. Now, this may be because the volume of business is that much greater and they have less resources to cope with it."

Privacy and unwillingness to talk to members of the newspaper press corps or writers of books have become a code of behavior in the financial community. Firms now have professional press relations departments with big budgets and defensive postures toward the media. As one famous trader told me off the record:

"We don't need the publicity. What for? We have an important job to do. No one wants to talk to the press other than if they think it will increase business for the firm."

Bill Simon, at one time the senior partner in charge of the government and municipal bond departments at Salomon Brothers, who went on to become U.S. secretary of the treasury, once wrote:

"You are fair game if a lifetime of private sector work has made you wealthy and successful, because the majority of the press seem to believe that you must have done something shockingly wrong to arrive at that happy condition. To today's news media, a good story is one that brings down some prominent victim."

He went on to add:

"Too often the media seem driven by the dark side of their nature. They have a fixation on failure, a delight in defeat, an enthusiasm for embarrassment."

Traders were treated to another version of what the media thinks they are like in a sitcom based on their world that airs on Lifetime television. Listen to the review given in *Traders* magazine:

"The capital-raising process never had such a stinking bunch of demons as those that come together in *Traders*, a one-hour drama series. Keep a sense of humor. This foul concoction produced in Canada is part insult, and part an outrage to the art and science of trading. According to Sandra Macdonald, head of equity trading at Sun Life of

Canada in Toronto, 'I watched the first episode and was torn between embarrassment and horror. More than twenty Securities Commission and Exchange rules were broken but hey, never mind, this is just a drama.'"

The coverage that financial news television gives the markets and the people in them, however, is completely different. They have almost become part of the establishment. Financial television is turning business leaders into celebrities, and is fueling retail interest in trading and investing. This brand of business TV began in 1981 with the launch of Financial News Network. Now CNBC, which started up in 1989, is the dominant player, beamed or cabled into over 65 million homes in the United States and shown in millions more around the world. CNN Financial News reaches about 8.7 million. You often see stocks move after the CEO of a company has been interviewed on one of the financial networks. Sometimes they don't—but no one wants to miss it if they do. So it can have a direct effect on the market in its own way.

Most traders start their day by flipping on CNBC or CNN or Bloomberg Business News to check what has happened overnight. To accommodate the television stations, special studios have been constructed at the New York Stock Exchange. Like Russian icons, they are perched up in the corners of the room to peer down at the floor activity below. Television screens are omnipresent over every trading post on the floor, are prominent in executive offices upstairs, and are already part of daily life in the homes of individuals everywhere around the globe where satellites can beam down.

The watershed event that seemed to lead everyone in the financial world to keep a television turned on during the working day was the Gulf War. In the old days, retail investors would call their broker a couple of times a day; now they can have the television ticker running across the bottom of their TV screen while the markets are open. This seems to be a uniquely U.S. product. Business news doesn't appear to have found a large audience in Europe yet, where traders are content to glean the news they want from Bloomberg and Reuters.

Because television news is flashed around the world with simultaneous access for everyone, its effect on the world's markets is almost instantaneous. Traders are forced to decide much more quickly than ever before if what they are watching is pushing the market one way or the other, and whether it is something they should act on immediately, or project out to what could happen in fifteen minutes?

The question becomes, do the financial news channels editorialize the news they transmit? Assuming that there is some editorialization, then aren't they interpreting the news? It's not always straight news. When it isn't, they could be reaching a conclusion or communicating an implication that may not be the conclusion a trader would have reached had he heard the news without their slant on it.

And if that is true, then they must have an influence on investment behavior. Holly Stark, a buy-side trader, finds the impact that the financial television programs have on the market remarkable:

"I watch it to get the quick and dirty of what a market is doing. With sound bites though, how much can you really go into depth in three minutes? I think it has made people aware of the markets. Although sometimes I go home and watch TV and listen to them describe what happened in the market; and I sit there and go, wait a minute, were we watching the same market? I would hope that the reporters that are covering the financial markets are doing so in an educated way."

Major events like the Kobe earthquake in Japan or a bombing of oil resources in the Middle East are relatively straightforward, and professional traders would come to their own conclusions on the effects such incidents might have on the markets. But they still monitor the financial news channels in order to hear and see what everyone else in the market is hearing and seeing.

Traders thrive on information. And it comes not only from television, newspapers, and radio, but bombards them nonstop through their computer screens. They can tap into data banks on financial events that happened ten years ago as well as into what took place ten minutes ago. Where financial news television offers programs with commentary and only breaks in with important stories, the screens on a trader's desk are an immediate banquet of everything.

Obviously, this has been the major change of our time. In the 1920s, 1930s, and 1940s people had very little information to trade with. Rumor was important, but it would take a day or so for a rumor to be substantiated. Now it is immediate. And that has taken away any advantage that traders previously had over others. Today everyone has the same information at the same time. It is public, not hidden.

* * *

GREED ALSO BECAME part of the trader's image in the 1980s. It was something that was manifested not only in the financial world, but in a variety of ways in the popular culture of the time. Reaganomics and Thatcherism may have contributed to the feeling of exuberance, the idea that wealth was indeed attainable. When it all went wrong was when it became excessive. Both New York and the City of London experienced it, as the two markets exchanged personnel in a kind of cross-pollination. The private reality was that many people working in the industry made unheard-of amounts of money, but they also gave a lot of it away. They always have and they still do.

Fund-raising in New York for institutions that the public enjoys, like the New York Public Library, the Metropolitan Museum of Art, the Museum of Modern Art, and others, is aggressively supported by Wall Street. The only difference from London that I could discern is that in New York there tends to be more money for philanthropy. Most of the hedge funds run charitable foundations. Julian Robertson's Tiger Fund runs such a foundation to benefit the inner city. Paul Tudor Jones does fund-raising for the inner city as well.

George Soros, who is based in New York, is famous for his philanthropy. He has given away over $1 billion of his own money in Eastern Europe to train teachers, aid intellectuals, start a new university, and provide aid to Bosnia. Much of it has been to promote the free flow of information by providing photocopiers, typewriters, printing presses, TV cameras, and computers to those who need them—all since 1991. Soros's foundations gave away $360 million in 1996 alone. Soros family members actively give their time and money to support various charities and cultural institutions in New York City.

Charity has a long tradition there. Gus Levy, legendary trader and former head of Goldman Sachs, was well known as a philanthropist on Wall Street. Eric Sheinberg remembers that "when Gus Levy would call you up and say, 'Will you do me a favor?' there were no questions." As a director of the Police Athletic League of New York, Sheinberg claims he experiences the same kind of generous support in his philanthropic endeavors from his partners and former partners that Gus did when he was alive.

At the age of thirty-six, Michael Milken cofounded the Foundations of the Milken Families, one of the largest private foundations in the United States. It funds education and health care, with a particular focus on the inner cities and minorities. In 1965 he talked about hitting a personal wall and realizing that he wanted to become involved in giving to others. It had happened when he attended a football game with his father in Los Angeles:

"It was right after the Watts riots. There were armed personnel carriers, with machine guns mounted, patrolling familiar streets. It was obvious to me that something was very wrong. If we do not have a strong society and a strong civilization, in the end we cannot have a strong private enterprise system."

After that game he dedicated his time and money toward helping people who live in those neighborhoods. Without the public being aware of it until recently, he has been giving math classes to poor inner-city kids for the past twenty years. More recently he added cancer to the list of his concerns, dedicating $25 million to fund and found the Association for the Cure of Cancer of the Prostate, which brings together top researchers, thinkers, doctors, pharmaceutical companies, and lab technicians from all over the world in an effort to find a cure.

Bill Simon takes his philosophy about philanthropy to the street— not only giving money away, but personally committing his time. He and his wife worked regularly in a number of shelters, and for several years on Christmas Day took their children to a soup kitchen to prepare and serve food for the needy and to distribute presents to poor children in New York.

A devout Catholic, Simon has worked as a Eucharistic minister, giving communion to patients in hospitals in the New York area. He devotes hours of his time to AIDS patients at the Cardinal Cooke Center in East Harlem. In an interview in 1993 he explained his belief about giving:

"I've always strived to follow Andrew Carnegie's admonition in his 'Gospel of Wealth,' that those who have been blessed with wealth must consider themselves trustees of that wealth and use it for the well-being of society. We must use our resources to create new opportunities and jobs, and try to place within reach of every child of God a ladder that he or she may climb."

Michael Bloomberg, who began as a trader at Salomon Brothers, is the Colin Powell of the financial world. He unashamedly inserted a chapter-long plea in his book *Bloomberg by Bloomberg* for the business world to give in their own way, but at all costs to give. As chairman of the board of Johns Hopkins University, he has personally donated well over $65 million for research in medicine, public health, nursing, clinics, and hospitals. He gives to educational endeavors like the United Negro Fund. In 1994 he donated eighty-three terminals worth $2.6 million to the United Negro College Fund to launch students on the information highway and to give them a boost in learning the techniques that might help them get jobs on Wall Street, where African Americans are still few and far between. When I asked him about his philosophy of giving, he responded:

"I think those people that have a lot of money would find, as I do, that you get enormous value, enormous pleasure, out of buying a picture for a museum, a classroom for a school, a laboratory for medical research, a scholarship for a kid. And those are things that you buy just like other things. The question you have to ask yourself is, will you get more pleasure out of a new Mercedes or out of helping to cure cancer? It is a very simple thing.

"Unfortunately, I don't think people give enough that have money. Most people talk about it. They pay lip service, but they tend not to be very generous. Keep in mind, you always have these people like Newt Gingrich or Bill Clinton or Ronald Reagan, all of whom lecture us about private philanthropy, and to the best of my knowledge, none of them have given anything material whatsoever. Clinton deducted the cost of underwear he gave to Goodwill."

Stanley Shopkorn was one of the original group of people raising money for St. Jude's Hospital. In their first year they raised a couple of hundred thousand dollars. In 1996 they raised $2 million, which built new labs. Stanley donates time to various charities as well as St. Jude's; and his girlfriend, a former trader, has for years spent her Saturday mornings working with disadvantaged children. His personal philosophy echoes what others told me:

"You always want to give something back because whether you are religious or not religious, it's good karma to give something away. And if you give it away you will always get it back. I learned that from a very dear friend of mine. If you don't share it, you don't get to keep it as much. So we're happy to give it away."

"Ace" Greenberg, a trader who became chief executive of Bear Stearns, has been noted as one of New York's largest individual donors to the United Jewish Appeal. He put a rule into effect at Bear

Stearns, that each managing director has to give away 4 percent of his salary and bonus to charity.

Muriel Siebert chose a different method, by establishing the Siebert Entrepreneurial Philanthropic Plan to give to charities half of her company's profits from new securities underwritings. In its first year it gave away $310,000. Since then it has donated well over $4 million. "It is our way of giving back and helping to make the 1990s the decade of decency."

In the old days on the floor of the London Stock Exchange, raising money for charity was a regular part of the ritual. Phil Nathan, head dealer at Charles Stanley, was there, and remembered that a gallon of whiskey would be sitting regularly up on the counter for bidding and auctioning. Today fund-raising is more of an independent activity. Nathan is one of the leaders of the Lions in England, and spends a part of each day working the phone to raise money for worthy causes. Traders are good at working the phones. In 1996 he raised money from the City to take emergency aid to Croatia. He and his wife and a team of forty other individuals drove a caravan of trucks to Croatia filled with 100,000 parcels for the refugee camps. In 1997 his group brought over eighteen children to the U.K. for emergency operations. He also traveled to Bosnia in 1997, and supervised financial aid to build a pediatric hospital for children there. Trading during the week and organizing charity work on the weekends, Nathan told me that his firm is fully supportive and understanding when he is raising money. For the rest of the financial community, charity dinners and charity sports events, while being enjoyable, are taken seriously in London.

These are but a few examples. Their giving could easily be explained away as tax advantages to offset their wealth, except for the fact that most of them go millions beyond the bounds of tax tables. And the hours they spend every week on planning, meetings, phone calls for fund-raising, as well as personally spending time as volunteers in their communities, can't be written off to taxes either. It is more a way of life. Perhaps it derives from the binary way they view their work: you win or you lose. And having experienced that for so great a part of their life, maybe they are especially tuned in to the fact that the balance could easily have tipped the other way for them. It also could have something to do with where some of them came from.

PART II

UP CLOSE

6 THREE VISIONARIES

This chapter tells the stories of three visionaries who began as traders, chosen because they share one vision: they put their free-market philosophies into action by democratizing markets. Bloomberg: by opening up the world of information to all traders who wanted it. He was a major force in creating the present environment, where everyone can get the same information at the same time. Melamed: being frustrated that trading in foreign exchange was the exclusive realm of companies, he created the foreign exchange futures market. Now everyone has access to foreign exchange trading. And Milken: by opening up the capital markets for emerging companies that were denied access before, or to companies that previously were not considered creditworthy.

MICHAEL BLOOMBERG, FORMERLY a trader at Salomon Brothers, has achieved great significance as an innovator in the 1990s. He is reinventing the environment traders deal in. He is a man driven by a vision. After having been let go from Salomon Brothers in 1981 when the firm merged with Phibro Corporation, Michael took his $10 million share of the profits. He then was not lured by retirement, but went on to found a company that markets computerized financial information to traders, sends out business news over the electronic highway, owns a radio station, and broadcasts Bloomberg Business News for television.

He also invented the omnipresent Bloomberg Box, a small terminal that sits on almost every trader's desk and brings electronic data to the financial community around the world. Bloomberg represents a huge transfer in power that has taken place from the old boys to the new boys in finance. He leveraged his knowledge of the markets to grow beyond the scope of the trading world and build a media empire that spans the globe. Bloomberg the Trader became Bloomberg the Terminal Man became Bloomberg the Media Mogul. Where would he go next?

With an engineering degree from Johns Hopkins and an MBA from Harvard Business School, he began his career at Salomon Brothers in 1966 as a clerk for a salary of $9,000 a year. He made his way up from being a trader to being chief of the Salomon equity trading department by thirty-two. And by fifty-five he was a successful entrepreneur with a private company that had grown to $1.3 billion in revenues. It now employs over 4,500 people around the world and has over 89,000 of its Bloomberg terminals on clients' desks.

As I walked into the waiting area of his Park Avenue headquarters in New York City, and later walked around two of the six large floors connected by spiral staircases that Bloomberg Financial occupies, I came to realize that, although it was an information news business, he had set it up along the lines of a trading floor. It was an open plan with no offices and no secretaries. Conference rooms were lined with glass and were available to everyone. You just sign up for a time slot. Everyone could see everyone else, and Bloomberg could see everyone.

I mentioned to him that it felt as if it were bursting at the seams because it was very crowded, with people running back and forth, standing in groups, and visitors spilling out of the waiting area into the hall. Not at all, Michael responded. That was his intent. I could see what he meant. There was a buzz and an energy there. People were constantly communicating and interacting, unable to hide away in an office behind a door. Yet everywhere were large aquariums filled with sapphire blue and yellow fish, a counterpoint to the frenzied atmosphere, a sight you could look at during the day and unwind.

Beyond the reception desk you enter another world, something like a country store where everything is free. Coolers of soda and bottled water, constantly refilled urns of coffee, display counters crowded with baskets overflowing with snacks, popcorn, bowls of fruit—and comfortable sofas where you can sit and watch Bloomberg News. This is an informal common area where staff congregate, although I doubt socializing would be the intent as much as that office politics probably dissipate in this kind of atmosphere. It also makes sense to service the reporters and staff who work long hours. Bloomberg himself is at work at six-thirty, and leaves late.

I asked him why he is still so driven. He laughed and said he worried because he had two teenage daughters who had their hearts set on new ponies.

Bloomberg still exhibits the rapid-fire speech and impatience typical of so many traders. But once you get his attention, the conversation is riveting and all business, revealing the complexity of his thinking and the reasons behind his phenomenal success. He's a variegated character. Tough and curt on the outside, opinionated and stubborn, he can make you laugh at will. It's easy to find his heart: his philanthropic activities take up at least two days of his week.

Bloomberg's management style in many ways is a throwback to what he learned in his trading days at Salomon Brothers. He believes in setting an example and in inspiring loyalty from the people who work for him, which was part of the culture of Salomon when he worked there. In his book *Bloomberg by Bloomberg*, he writes:

"I owe a great debt to William Salomon and John Gutfreund. They were my mentors. They taught me ethics, philanthropy, hard work, and to take care of others."

As it happened, a year into his career at Salomon Brothers he became a clerk on the trading floor. Then he was moved to the block trading desk to work at the side of Jay Perry. It must have been an incredible time to be at Salomon. While he and Perry were working the new market, their counterparts were legends like Cy Lewis at Bear Stearns and Gus Levy at Goldman. Competition kept them on their toes. In 1973 Bloomberg was made a partner and was put in charge of all stocks, arbitrage, and convertible bonds.

Fate has had a strong hand in his life. What seemed to be an odd reassignment to the computer area by 1979, well away from the trading desk, was the beginning of the beginning. There he put his head down and worked on information systems and computer development. And he developed a product. Stanley Shopkorn confessed:

"Bloomberg is an inspiration to watch. He was a visionary. He had a product at Salomon Brothers that the traders didn't quite understand. And when Michael left when the firm merged, they didn't care whether he took his product or not. He took his product and had a vision. What he has done has changed the business dramatically. There were days where people that had an advantage on information were the people that did well. Today everybody has the same information at the same time. He made an important contribution."

Bloomberg began with the concept of providing financial institutions with information. Computer software would allow the manipulation and analysis of that information. His initial investment to start the company was $300,000, with an additional $4 million to develop the terminals and software that his first client, Merrill Lynch, had ordered. By the end of his first year in business there were five employees, including Bloomberg. Four of the original five are still part of the team. What can a customer do with a Bloomberg terminal on their desk?

"We give our clients the ability to select investments, do 'what if' scenario analysis on their securities portfolios, and communicate over a private, secure e-mail system with their customers, suppliers and associates. We allow them to study markets and securities in absolute terms and relative to alternative investments. They can research companies, buy and sell stocks and bonds, even create new financial instruments."

For a man so into technology, Bloomberg is a strong believer in person-to-person contact. The electronic systems that he offers the financial markets increasingly take the wind out of traditional systems, but he emphasizes that they are execution systems. Automation will never take the place of people. People are needed to think, based on the information he provides. Marcus Hooper, head dealer at Sun Life in London, explains what's happening:

"The stock exchanges globally are starting to lose control of the markets. That's what it comes down to. People like Bloomberg, people like Reuters—we have dozens of computer systems. They are the people that are gaining from the traditional market structure. They are gaining because they are providing things electronically, which is not the nature of the stock exchanges."

In ten years' time will they replace stock exchanges? Hooper replies:

"Who knows? They effectively provide a market structure.

Which is something that the stock exchanges used to do. Who actually controls the exchange anymore? Who controls the marketplace? Is it the exchange, or is it the information providers and the service providers and the computer companies?

"The exchanges may have the regulatory controls, but you don't need an enormous exchange just to control the regulatory side of things. You'd need an office, wouldn't you? But is an office the same as an exchange? That's the way I see it. The marketplace is now moving to the information providers like Bloomberg.

"What we are seeing in some ways is something very, very similar to the way the Internet began. It began as pockets of information held in minicomputer networks, small intranets, eventually getting linked up over time, to form the Internet. And that is what we are seeing in the financial markets. It is just the internal structure that hasn't become linked together yet."

Does that mean that the traditional stock exchanges will cease to exist in the future, or is it just that their role will change?

Most probably, their role will change, because traditionally they provided a place to go in order to trade. But with the proliferation of electronic trading systems, it could well become more of a computer network linking all the alternative ways to trade together.

As Bloomberg drew a distinction between his system and that of Reuters, I could appreciate why traders are enjoying an increasing array of alternatives. He explained:

"If you buy data from Reuters, you pay for a fundamental product of news stories. If you were to buy it, you can write some software on your computer to access it and look at it. What we have is very different. In many senses we don't compete with Reuters at all. They do one thing and we do another.

"We give you prices and the derivation of those prices, which you take and, for example, compute yields. We give an awful lot of added value. We are also going toward flat-panel technology, which is a screen you just plug into your PC. It generates less heat, generates a lot less radiation, and it comes with a keyboard that is connected to the computer via infrared, so you don't have this cable on your desk that takes a lot of space and knocks over your coffee all the time."

There is a certain sense of inevitability that the future will go toward electronic trading. Bloomberg is aggressive in his aim to be the premium means of communication between the institutional buyer and seller. His computerized information system, which provides real-time information to a larger audience than ever before, has had its impact on prompting new methods of trading. Systems like Bloomberg's are a motivating factor in the developing securities markets.

Already Bloomberg embraces equities, money markets, fixed income, foreign exchange, Eurobonds. You can trade on it. You can access the Internet. It has a deep database to dip into, which you can load onto your spreadsheets and manipulate for your own needs. You can listen to Bloomberg Business News on it and watch video reports and press conferences with CEOs. It offers music, movie, and book reviews, and allows you to order flowers and read sports scores and horoscopes. You can even buy a mattress through Dial-A-Mattress on the Bloomberg network. So will a catalog online be next? Basically the system is feeling its way toward becoming a broader and wider information provider.

Michael told me, "We are up to 89,000 customers, and we are growing very fast."

No wonder there is constant speculation that he might sell the company. But somehow I think Bloomberg relishes the thought of going head-to-head with people like Reuters in a war of the screens, more than he does selling out. Bloomberg News billboards dominate train stations in New York and the Bloomberg name appears in magazines and newspapers in London, building up brand name recognition with the public as well as with the financial community.

"News gets our name out there, and the news that's on our television is also on our Web site and is also on our terminal.

"The people who come in to see us because we're going to get them on television are people we want to have for interviews on our terminal. It all fits together. Remember, we have, I think, the largest group of business and financial news reporters of any news organization in the world."

Launched in 1993, Bloomberg AM 1130 produces twenty-four-hour news, reaching over 11 million people a week. Bloomberg also produces business news television programming and Bloomberg Information TV, beamed out by satellite and through cable systems. He publishes *Bloomberg* magazine, a personal finance magazine, and books. As well as the Bloomberg professional service, there is a Bloomberg Web site that individuals can access on the Internet, and Bloomberg is the news provider for AOL.

My guess? He will offer his own version of news and programming, packaged in a new way and channeled in a new way to a larger consumer audience. In simple terms, it will be something like CNN, only better and different. I can envision that once the telephone and PC are folded into television, the evolving Bloomberg output could then be offered to a wider public, available on demand, brought to you at your choice of times, including online in real time and tailored to your liking.

I can't help but feel that with his book and the omnipresent Bloomberg billboards, the brand name is being brought to the public in anticipation of a launch into the mass market. He's already partway there, although he presently is providing content aimed at upscale financial and business people. He continued to explain:

"We have twenty-four-hour-a-day English language for North America on Direct TV. In New York you can see it on Liberty Cable, on USA network nationwide, both twenty-four hours a day, and on every cable system from five to seven in the morning. We have twenty-four-hour-a-day English language programs for all Asia Pacific. We have twenty-four-hour-a-day European English language television coming out of all of our European bureaus, put together in England. We have twenty-four-hour-a-day Japanese.

"We have twenty-four-hour-a-day French on Canal Plus. We do French news with Agence France Presse. They do the domestic, we do the international business and finance. They do sports. We both do lifestyles. All done by French people speaking French, with a French focus. Stop me when you get bored. We have twenty-four-hour-a-day Italian. The summer of 1997 we started Dutch, Spanish, Portuguese, and German. I want the same format in each country. I want the stories that transcend countries, like financial markets, to be the same worldwide. They will be in different languages. If we film World War Three outside, we will use that film, just different voices, on every network.

"I think that in television we can build a worldwide network for upscale seriousness."

So television, radio, intranet, Internet, books, magazines, and what next—newspapers? It looks as if the floor is being laid for a new-age, new-definition multimedia empire. In the meantime the former trader is contentedly reshaping the way the world trades.

A SMALL MAN with glasses showed me into his hotel room.

I had been phoning from the lobby for half an hour and I was told by the hotel operator that all three of Mr. Melamed's lines were engaged—the entire time. I gave up and got into the elevator. But as I walked behind Melamed into the room, it all became clear.

A laptop alive with color and blinking numbers was set up on a desk by the window and was hooked into one telephone line. The voice of a woman reeling off changing prices and market shifts was in the background, obviously tying up another telephone line. That loudspeaker was on for the rest of my visit and probably for the rest of the day. It was his assistant right on the floor of the Chicago Mercantile Exchange, relaying a continuous stream of prices on yen and the Dow and S&P contracts.

I could imagine her there. You could hear all the background screaming in the pits near where she was standing. Her intense voice was hoarse from yelling out orders to a clerk she obviously had eye contact with. She was listening for Leo Melamed's instructions to her over the speakerphone from this hotel room in midtown Manhattan—a world and a half away. Every now and then he literally had to scream back into the speakerphone for her to hear him above the din around her.

Indicating with a quick nod of his head toward his makeshift desk, he said:

"I travel with more electronic equipment than most engineers. And I tie in, whether I am in Singapore or Czechoslovakia or China or New York. It's not always easy, because sometimes it is in the middle of the night. I tie into a modem anywhere I go."

Leo Melamed, the legendary leader of the Chicago Mercantile Exchange. He reminded me of a windup toy that just never stops. I couldn't believe mental alertness like this was possible. He was trading constantly. He had one ear cocked to the voice talking to him in the background and the other focusing on what I was asking. He spent time speaking about the markets with me and then would jump up all of a sudden to yell into the phone to his assistant to ask where something was trading: "Buy! No! Did you buy? Tell him to wait a minute! Okay, now buy! Did you hear me? Buy now! Did you buy? Did you buy? Talk to me, I can't hear you!!!"

I felt the undertow every time he jumped up. My heart beat faster. I could hear the assistant's frustration in getting the trade done immediately. She got tired and had to eat, and another assistant came on shift. I worried about every trade. I wouldn't have made a good pit trader, I decided, as I watched Leo use his emotions for generating action on demand, yet remain so cool while deciding what he wanted to do and when. He wore them out. He never stopped for a minute.

Time travel, I thought. One minute he was standing up, straining toward the phone, shouting, waving his hands as if he were right there in the pits with her. The next minute he would be sitting in front of me completely composed, hands at rest in his lap, his face at peace. Leo writes science fiction in his spare time; he's in the middle of his second book. When he's not trading he is in space. I smiled at the thought. He's perfect for this double life. It suits him. It must be why he is open to the future, why he is an avid electronic trader, why he can see the major shifts before others can. It's why he's invented markets where there were none before.

"I love writing, and besides trading, I would say the writing is probably my next favorite thing. I'd like to be writing more science fiction.

"But you have very little time in this life, and trading takes a great deal of your time. And then the administrative function of my life takes even more. I love trading. You are never at rest. Your mind is always being challenged. Which direction, basically, is the market going. Is it up or down? And how you can figure out that direction, and capture a portion of the potential profit that would give you, is a most exciting venture. And so, if you learn the tools of trading and you treat it like a business, then you have an opportunity that is very, very worthwhile."

If you talk to anyone in the business, the name Leo Melamed is repeated in awed tones. Gary Lapayover was fascinated by a move that Melamed made in January 1997:

"He staged a coup of nontrading members that own seats. He positioned himself in this major political battle out in the Chicago Mercantile Exchange against his former protégé. In an election, he got six of his ten candidates elected. He started to combat what he perceived as a lack of direction and vision and not following through with the achievements that were accomplished during his tenure. They appointed Leo as permanent adviser to the board and permanent adviser to the executive committee. He is an amazing person."

A Holocaust survivor, Melamed started his young life in a new country at the age of nine, in the inner city of Chicago. From that inauspicious beginning, he carved a place for himself in the history of the international financial markets, and became a personage so powerful that the markets he imagined in his mind became a reality. A survivor of death who turned to trading pork bellies in the teeming commodity pits on the Chicago Mercantile Exchange, he created the first successful currency futures market, the International Monetary Market, which was launched on the exchange in 1972.

The New York Mercantile Exchange had offered the first currency futures contracts, but they didn't work. They didn't have the support of the outside financial community. It was due to Leo's will and determination to make it happen that the IMM succeeded. He worked relentlessly to win over the financial community, and to convince traders at his exchange who had been used to trading tangible products that these new financial futures would take off, and that traders could make money in them.

In 1986 Merton Miller, Distinguished Service Professor of Finance at the University of Chicago, later a Nobel laureate in economics, called financial futures "the most significant financial innovation of the last twenty years." From 1976 to 1986 the annual volume of financial futures contracts grew from 37 million to 216 million. By 1996 about $12 billion in currency contracts was traded on average every day on the Chicago Mercantile Exchange.

The idea for financial futures developed in Melamed's mind when he began casting around for ways to make the exchange grow. Before 1972, when financial futures began trading, the exchange traded only physical commodities. Melamed had been watching currencies and had come to the conclusion that the pound sterling was overvalued. He formed the opinion that something had to happen, either devaluation or severe strain on the British government defending it.

And he was surprised when he heard that you couldn't short the pound. The average person could not walk into a bank and trade the pound. Banks would deal only with businesses doing currency exchange in the forward markets, not individuals. Melamed had been talking about this with the economist Milton Friedman, who himself had tried to trade pounds and was told that he couldn't. Friedman confirmed Melamed's suspicion that the current system of fixed exchange rates was probably going to unravel. Bingo. If it were to unravel, Melamed wanted to be there with a product based on currencies. And it would be a currency market for everyone: a futures currency market.

It was a revolutionary idea for the Merc. To gain the credibility he would need to launch such a novel product and make it work, Melamed asked Milton Friedman to back him up with a feasibility study.

World events were fortuitous. In 1971 Japan and West Germany uncoupled from the dollar and let their currencies float. Later in 1971 U.S. President Nixon closed the gold window, no longer willing to exchange gold for dollars held abroad. He did it primarily because the government had a high deficit in the balance of payments, which was equal to its gold reserves.

By that December the Bretton Woods system of fixed exchange rates had begun to unwind enough for Melamed to believe that it would continue to break down. He made an announcement that the CME would be offering a new futures market in seven foreign currencies. The International Money Market was officially opened for business in 1972. Leo's selling point to the international community was that the financial futures market would be a tool to reduce foreign exchange risk and would be valuable to anyone whose business involved international trade and foreign exchange.

The birth of this new market was the genesis of the modern futures industry. Its first major test came in 1976 when the Mexican government devalued the peso by 50 percent. It became impossible to find a forward price for the peso. The only place you could go was to the IMM, which continued to trade and quote prices. Leo believes that this was an important turning point:

"I think from that day forward, it really started to move fast. Our market represented a viable force in currency forwards, so we often led the direction of market change. And that is still true today."

The next market Leo championed was an index based on the difference between the yield on 90-day Treasury bills—which are the benchmark for the short end of the yield curve—and 100 percent. The index could be used to protect against interest rate volatility risk. The IMM T-bill contract began trading in January 1976. Now the CME had both a currency future contract and an interest rate future contract to offer. That was followed by a Eurodollar future contract in 1981. It could be argued that the advent of financial futures propelled the growth in international trade, making it more secure for multinational companies to expand abroad and generate more income. The S&P 500 stock index future came into being in 1982.

As the technology developed to allow for electronic trading, Leo Melamed became convinced that this would also be an added value to trading on his exchange. So in 1987 the Merc launched GLOBEX (Global Exchange), the first futures exchange in the world to allow for after-hours trading through a computer screen, a trade-matching system allowing you to buy contracts twenty-four hours a day. The announcement of this electronic trading facility led other exchanges to follow and initiate similar electronic systems of their own, firmly entrenching the acceptance and practice of electronic trading around the world. Guided by Leo's twenty-five years of leadership, the Chicago Mercantile Exchange became one of the world's leading futures markets.

But a growing number of critics claimed that trading financial futures was too much like gambling in a casino, where huge amounts of money can be made or lost in a day. Melamed obviously disagrees, and explained to me why he thinks trading in financial futures is important to the economy:

"The same mechanism that was always true for agricultural products and nonfinancial products, that allowed the producer an ability to hedge his risk and protect his profit flow so that he could continue to use his capital efficiently and wisely and expand his operation, is equally true, if not more true, in finance.

"These instruments provide corporate treasurers, institutions, and financial managers a means of protecting their constant exposure in business to changes in interest rates, changes in currency values, and changes in a variety of financial matters that eventually affect the bottom line of their entities The only way they can protect themselves is through use of financial instruments of trade, whether they be in the futures market or in the over-the-counter market.

"All of that is to the benefit of the public at large because it reduces the need for taxation, for instance, because if you can produce more income flow for the business community, ultimately it translates to wages and jobs and less dependency on government for the daily economic needs of life."

Leo Melamed's evolution as a trader went through three stages that he likes to call sea changes:

"I started life as a pit trader. All I knew was that I could react to order flow coming into the pit. I could watch the eyeballs of the other guys around me and see their fear or their greed and try to beat them. Sure, I had ideas about the market generally, but those were usually overtaken by the immediacy of the situation in the pit, the orders coming in and getting out. And I was trying to trade, in small increments, as the bids and offers came in, the ebbs and flows of the market. I was a very good pit trader. And I made good money.

"Then, later, when I took over the administration of the exchange, I was drawn away from the pit. That was my first major sea change. I couldn't be in the pit anymore. Now I had to learn to trade, sometimes off the floor of the exchange, upstairs in an office, somewhere in a meeting room, or even on the floor of the exchange, but outside of the pit. And I had to learn to trade in different ways. I had to now have a much stronger opinion about the direction of the market rather than its immediate little ebb and flow. I couldn't participate in the ebbs and flows as a pit trader can. I had to trade the larger movements, based on fundamentals or major technical developments. But in a larger sense. So I became more of a position player than a day-to-day player. That was in 1971. I began trading in the early sixties, so about ten years later I had to change because I had taken over the running of the exchange.

"Well, that was a very difficult change. I couldn't rely on the feel in the pit. I couldn't rely on the eyeball-to-eyeball confrontation of the traders. It was quite difficult. In fact, it took about a year, as I recall, for me to learn how to trade away from the pit.

"Then about ten or twelve years later came another sea change. That was about when screen-based technology came in. Now I was very, very busy. The exchange had grown far beyond anything I could have ever imagined. We were a world-class exchange. And my day was almost always off the floor. So I had to learn to trade off numbers and information coming at me from a screen. This was a very difficult change.

"I no longer heard any noise. It was the sterile environment of a screen with price changes and information flow. After about a year, I started to get the kind of feel from the screen that I could depend on.

I wasn't dependent on noise anymore, I was dependent on information. I was more dependent upon changes in prices, screen-based ticks coming at you. Today I am living in that kind of world and I am still trading. I was able to make the change. I think traders can transfer their capabilities."

Melamed used to lecture about the meaning of financial futures by relating the story from the Bible in which Joseph talked the Egyptian pharaoh into buying grain and storing it during the seven years of plenty, so that there would be grain for the seven years of lean. In the United States, farmers have always, in effect, done the same thing. They'd use futures contracts to protect themselves against things like falling prices in years of abundance or against ruined crops. Now we can look at the future and imagine what it will hold. How about futures contracts on electricity? Housing starts? Catastrophe insurance? Potable water?

Less than a year into Melamed's renewed involvement at the Chicago Mercantile Exchange, in September 1997, a new E-mini S&P futures and options contract was introduced. The new contract, priced at $50,000, requires only a $2,500 margin to participate and is available to investors on the Internet. The E-mini proved to be an inspired move, the first time the small investor could access the trading floor in Chicago through technology. It became the fastest-growing index ever launched on the exchange.

"With the E-mini S&P contract, we are again at the threshold of leading the futures industry into exciting, uncharted territory. This CME innovation of combining the most sophisticated electronic trading systems with the global reach of the Internet, while retaining the large order efficiencies of 'open outcry,' will bring the best of many worlds to the equity futures marketplace."

A new investment vehicle like this is not only democratizing the marketplace, but at the same time bringing electronic trading to the floor. A whole new breed of economically literate financial investors who use e-mail rather than paper mail are expected to be the biggest retail users of the electronic trading medium that the Internet provides. They can access an online simulated trading program to practice trading the new contract before entering the process, and the CME's Web site provides live quotes and educational materials. Traders on the floor who prefer computerized trading can enter the

E-mini trading pit to do electronic trading of the contract. It is expected that the two groups will create the liquidity base.

Leo Melamed hasn't written the last chapter for us yet. His story is still in progress. He was recently appointed to the ultimate position in terms of power to influence the direction of not only the Chicago Mercantile Exchange, but also that of the markets in which he loves to trade. As permanent adviser to the board, Leo will be involved in developing new ideas for the exchange, as he always has. Remember, he loves to write—not only science fiction, but history.

MICHAEL MILKEN BY Tom Strauss:

"Milken was found guilty. I think that is bad, although I do think that in modern financial times, he, probably more than anybody else, had the greatest impact on modern finance as it is perceived today. He was in a funny way the ultimate risk taker. He understood that it was in his client's best interests to borrow money at debt rates with equity risk. That was the junk bond business as it existed at that time."

Michael Milken by Chris Andersen:

"So what Michael had done, starting in the late sixties and seventies, when he started trading this paper, was that he found out that the people who were the buyers were some of the big wealthy families, and very smart guys in America. So he was trading it, coming to be the focal point of what had already existed. Because if you think about it, there have always been high-yield credits. Since the days of Mesopotamia. The problem is, who understood it? Who did their homework? Who had the risk tolerance? It was very wealthy people and private pools of capital. It wasn't the big funds, and it wasn't the insurance companies."

Michael Milken by Stanley Shopkorn:

"I don't agree with the way that Michael does business, but that does not take away from the fact that he created some brilliant products. He showed companies that it is possible to concentrate on winning and giving the people that own them the ability to win big. He was an important part of the business, but I don't think his approach was the right approach. When you try to control a market, you get yourself in trouble. He was a creator . . . and we need them."

Michael Milken by, let's call her Ann:

"I wasn't operating in his universe of trading at that time. I worked with someone who was, and I was actually questioned. It's a shame. What the government did when they were investigating, it was really like scare tactics. I was on vacation, and they showed up at my house, an IRS and SEC agent. And I had no clue about anything. And they just left a business card and said I should call them. You go down. They say they want to ask you some questions about trading at a firm I'd left, so I didn't think anything of it. I showed up. All of a sudden I could see where the questioning is going. It is threatening. They used a scare tactic on everyone. They would call you down over a three-year period, they never told you it was over. After a year and a half, they'd show up again. And I didn't do anything wrong, so it was weird. After Milken's probation is over, he'll be back again in some form. He can't be a broker/dealer, but so what. He's a smart man. Some of the shrewdest business people court him, and they are smart enough on their own."

Time and time again, if you talk to people in the business, they refer to Milken as a visionary, a builder, a genius, a dreamer of dreams—and if you talk to anyone outside of the business you hear references of a completely different nature. We've all read the articles and seen the television documentaries. So who is this man, really?

When I was researching this book, I was told I would be unable to interview Milken due to the terms of his probation and various other restrictions. During that time, no business. He could talk about his pet projects, cancer research, and technology in education, but not business. He'd love nothing more than to talk about business, I was told—but not yet.

Milken was never macho, not in the usual sense of the word. Jesse Kornbluth says in his book *Highly Confident*:

"Milken had a sense of decorum that was novel and refreshing and he never oversold; if you asked him about a bond, he told you about its attractions, pointed out any negatives, and then, like a gentlemen, left it to you to make your own decision."

He wasn't really liked in the beginning by the other traders. He was Jewish in a Wasp firm, and somehow didn't fit in until Drexel merged with Burnham and Company. He sat in a corner of a back room and traded bonds no one wanted. He saw things no one else saw. He was studious. He wasn't one of the boys; he went home at night to his wife and children and was back in the morning before anyone else. He did things differently. They didn't understand him, not until he started making money. That's the trading world. You make money for the firm, you're in.

Milken by Milken:

"When I was growing up, I went on field trips with my father, an accountant and a lawyer. I originally went along to carry some of his briefcases and help him with some of his paperwork. And, as I was good with numbers, I not only had the responsibility of sorting checks but eventually I did the bank reconciliations and trial balance sheets. In exchange, I got to ask questions. My father was a captive audience and so were many of his clients. 'Why do you run your business this way?' 'Where do you get the money to build your business?' 'How many employees do you have?' 'What do they do?' 'Who are your suppliers?' 'Who are your customers and why do they do business with you?' This was the beginning of my business education."

According to Chris Andersen, who was an investment banker at Drexel at that time, when Milken began trading high-yield debt at Drexel in the late 1960s and early 1970s there were no analytics. There were no research reports or statistics to which you could go to learn. Chris related to me how Milken developed at this point:

"Michael became the center, and of course, he is a hell of a scholar. So he listened and talked to people and learned everything he could about it. That way he started to build his network of buyers, by understanding how the buyer was looking at something. What the buyer was looking for. He started to develop a knowledge and understanding of the analytical tools and perspective of everybody who was trading in this stuff, and that really was the core base of knowledge. We literally had what, at least for a time, was proprietary knowledge of the structure analytics."

Milken had been attracted to the idea of junk bonds while he was a business student at Wharton. After reading studies by Braddock Hickman done in the 1940s and 1950s, he became intrigued with "fallen angels," or companies that had below-investment-grade bonds with high yields. By 1973 he was trading them for Drexel. The basic premise was that the lower the credit rating of the bond, the higher the return to the investor after defaults. Hickman had found this was true from the turn of the century through World War II. Milken did his work from the postwar period on, and believed that it was even more true for the postwar period. During that time, regulations were put into place that were meant to protect investors from bankruptcy and default.

Andersen filled in the logic:

"The example that is easiest to offer up is Chrysler Corporation trying to go bankrupt. They wouldn't let it. Still, everybody sold Chrysler's paper when it went below investment grade, but they wouldn't let it go bankrupt. Well, what happened? The spread widens, and whoever buys it down there gets the benefit. That basic notion is repeated thousands of times in the economy all the time. The bigger you are, the harder it is for you to go bankrupt."

In 1974 there was a credit crunch, and suddenly the portfolios of some funds were holding bonds that had been downgraded by the bond-rating agencies. First Investors Fund had a large chunk of them in its portfolio, and it wanted to get rid of them before they affected the quality image of the fund. After calling around the Street and being told by everyone that they didn't trade those kind of bonds, but Milken at Drexel did, First Investors called him. Everyone did. The whole Street sent people to Milken because they didn't want to deal with the downgraded bonds.

Milken studied First Investors' portfolio and came back to the fund's managers with an argument that, instead of selling the bonds off, they should specialize in the high-yielding debt. He convinced them that since the fund was marketed for its yield, if it took the highest-yielding securities out of the fund, performance and sales would suffer. They listened. In 1974, 1975, and 1976 First Investors Fund for Income was the top-performing fund in the United States. Its sales grew and Drexel earned a reputation for being part of its success. Of the first seven high-yield bond funds that followed First Investors into the market, Drexel managed five of them.

Milken became the focal point for trading in high-yield bonds, and in the meantime developed an expertise in knowing who was buying them. That enabled him to build up an impressive network of buyers. Andersen said this was when Drexel ran into a problem:

"By the end of the seventies we had become so successful in creating an appetite for this paper that you could no longer rely on natural disasters to create high-yield paper. By the time we had a bunch of high-yield bond funds out there seeking paper, if we didn't have credit crunches and default scares, we didn't have paper to supply them.

"So then the notion hit us that, as opposed to waiting for the deterioration of credit, an investment-grade company downgrade, you could go to smaller-growth companies that were coming up. And if you put debt on their capitalization, they had many of the same credit characteristics, but they were improving, not declining! If you had a company that had a bias that was growing, you had a better-quality piece of paper than trying to catch one that was coming down and trying to turn it around. So we started creating the underwritten market for high-yield bonds."

It was the birth of a market. The Drexel team stirred up the dust, looking either for companies that would not yet have earned investment grade and had been turned down by other securities houses, or for small, risky businesses that didn't realize they could have access to Wall Street's capital to grow.

Other firms had made a stab at underwriting high-yield bonds before Drexel did. One was Lehman Brothers. In 1977 Lehman underwrote high-yield issues for Zapata Oil and PanAm, two of its clients that were having trouble. Andersen remembers being amazed at how the other firms handled the bonds:

"Lehman really should have owned this market. They had everything going for them. They should have been the dominant factor. But Lehman, after they did the Zapata, didn't support it in the after market, because they were afraid to risk their capital. The bonds came off a point or two in the after market, so the partners apparently, from what I heard from the outside, fell upon each other, pointing fingers and yelling about who did this and who created that. They got out of the market. But after Lehman, the next one that should have owned it was Bear Stearns. For years I looked over my back and said, where the hell are they? They should be here. They never came. Lord knows why. But they missed it. We started to create this market . . . "

From the beginning Michael Milken, with his trading and salesmanship, dominated a field on which no one else was playing. The statistics were convincing enough for Drexel to back him with issues. Everyone else was going after the 564 companies that were investment grade, leaving 21,000 publicly traded companies in the category of having revenues over $35 million that had issued stock but were not able to sell bonds. From 1977 to 1987 Milken and Drexel raised $93 billion, their share of the junk bond market that grew to be a $200 billion industry.

How did he create the market out of thin air? Ungraded or downgraded high-yield bonds were thinly traded. It was hard to price them and hard to find them when you wanted to buy or sell one. No one wanted them. Milken found people who did, nontraditional buyers. As he found them and they became clients, Drexel would turn them around into issuers of high-yield bonds themselves. And Milken persuaded high-return mutual funds of the benefits of owning these bonds. Contrary to conventional bond trading, which can have a short-term approach, Milken really knew his companies and touted high-yield bonds as "ownership" in the company. He related his belief that they were more stable in periods of interest rate risk, because they reacted to a company's health or outlook rather than to changes in interest rates. He reasoned that there was less risk in owning high-yield bonds than there was in stocks or bonds in rated companies, especially in a down or volatile market.

Milken saw it as a way for entrepreneurial, even risky, companies that would normally be outsiders on Wall Street to gain access to the capital markets. He is credited with enabling new industries to develop by providing that financing, industries such as cable and the cellular industry. He believed in the promise of people like Craig McCaw, who founded McCaw Cellular, and Ted Turner at CNN. He helped MCI, a company that was started in 1963 with $3,000, which later became the company known for breaking the back of AT&T's hold on the long-distance market. Bill McGowan of MCI once explained:

"MCI challenged what was the largest corporation in the world, a corporation with a government-protected monopoly. But our biggest obstacle was not the opposition of the government or the monopoly position of AT&T. It was the availability of capital. When we started, emerging companies could turn to venture capital firms for early rounds of financing, but they had few places to go when their needs grew larger. The heart of the problem was that banks and institutional investors did not know how to finance growth companies."

Milken raised over $2 billion with junk bonds to make David's dreams of beating Goliath come true. The world's biggest toy maker, Mattel, was saved by Milken's bonds, as were Revlon and TWA. These companies were given a new lease on life, a way to raise money that allowed them to grow and create thousands and thousands of jobs. Of course, he made good money from it. The first question he would ask entrepreneurs was, "What are your hopes and your dreams?"

It sounds wonderful. So how did junk bonds come to be thought of as harmful in the public's mind? Probably because they were used for takeovers starting in the mid-1980s. Nevertheless, Glenn Yago, author of *Junk Bonds*, found that:

"Despite later perceptions and reporting to the contrary, high yield securities were never primarily used for hostile takeovers. For the 1,100 high yield issues occurring between 1980 and 1986, less than 3 percent at most were used for hostile or unsolicited transactions."

How did the firms that issued them use the money? From 1980 through 1986, "a full 73.7 percent of the proceeds were earmarked for corporate growth, and 21.9 percent were used for acquisition financing." They may have not been used very much for hostile takeovers, but when they were, it was for highly publicized transactions by highly publicized corporate raiders. Yago further explained:

"Milken initially opposed the idea of pursuing the takeover market, but was encouraged to do so by his colleagues, who perceived it as a growing source of demand for new high yield issues."

In 1984 the size of takeovers was huge. Merger and acquisition activity was rampant, and Drexel went after the business. It was from Milken's pool of contacts for whom he traded junk bonds, companies like Reliance Insurance and Rapid-American, that Drexel created the junk bond underwriting business.

Drexel underwrote for the casino Golden Nugget in 1984. In 1985 it underwrote T. Boone Pickens's bid for Unocal Corporation. It was on a roll until 1986, when Ivan Boesky pleaded guilty, and plea-bargained by bringing Milken into the story. Then in 1990 Milken plea-bargained to six counts of felony, none of which included insider trading, manipulating stock prices, or bribery, which is what Boesky had plea-bargained for.

Milken had been charged with technical violations for which no one had ever been charged and prosecuted before: concealing stock positions, aiding clients in income tax evasion, and concealed record keeping. For that he paid a $200 million fine, $500 million in civil penalties resulting from lawsuits, and $400 million to the government. He received a ten-year sentence in jail, although he served only two.

In 1989 the *Wall Street Journal* wrote that Milken was "arguably the most important financial thinker of the century." He was picked out as one of the five people who transformed the decade of the 1980s by *Life* magazine. As a trader he had created and dominated the industry.

Milken's next idea? Real estate is one of many. With partners he is investing billions in real estate around the world. He has often talked about real estate that could be packaged and divided up into shares that could be sold to institutional investors, who would then be able to switch their exposure between real estate markets. The securities could be traded easily, and a new liquid market could be developed. He has also shown an agressive interest in education being a commodity available to everyone. One of his companies, Knowledge Universe, is making investments in the future of education. It plans to produce educational books, computer software, and television programs.

Milken on Milken:

"I believe that access to capital is one of the leading components of job creation. I believe when the books are closed on the latter part of the 1980s, we are going to discover that some issues relating to access to capital were misunderstood, thus causing regulation that negatively impacted our economy."

7 CRASHING THE PARTY

YOU HAVE TO BE HEARD, YOU HAVE TO BE AGGRESSIVE. I
THINK A LOT OF WOMEN MAY BE INTIMIDATED BY ALL
THE MEN ON THE FLOOR. I WAS NEVER INTIMIDATED. IN
FACT, I REALLY ENJOY WORKING WITH MEN. I THINK IF
YOU DO YOUR JOB EFFECTIVELY AND YOU ARE SERIOUS
ABOUT WHAT YOU DO, PEOPLE ARE GOING TO TAKE YOU
SERIOUSLY. AND I THINK I HAVE GAINED THEIR RESPECT.

LOUISE JONES

Slowly, and with astounding determination, women have made
inroads into the trading world. The ones who have succeeded are
remarkable. They have had to be not only smarter than scores of
others, but they've had to ask themselves, "Can I take it?" The long
hours, the incredible pressure, the locker room atmosphere of so
many trading floors, putting off plans for marriage or children, the
reality of a lack of balance in their life.

They can take it, and they love it.

WAITING IN A chair outside Muriel Siebert's triangular, monotone
gray office, I spied through the glass door a yellow plastic dog bowl
and some bones placed under the window. I knew then and there

that I would love her. After about ten minutes more I was shown through the door, and I turned to my right. Behind a simple gray desk was a small woman with spectacles and hair slightly electric and wild. With a phone to one ear and her accountant bending down to the other, she beckoned me in.

We later sat down together at a round conference table stacked with her papers and files. At closer range what impressed me about her was that she now looked much younger and that, despite the cool exterior of a tailored linen pantsuit and the now patted-down, coiffed hair, an interior fire came through her eyes, diminished only slightly when Monster Girl, her Chihuahua, came running over to inspect me.

Here in front of me was a woman who had started as a trader on Wall Street at a time when this was unheard of and just unthinkable for a woman. She is sixty-five now, owns one of the largest discount brokerage firms in the world, and exerts tremendous influence. She is fast becoming a household name. Her face is familiar from her television commercials, and her voice from radio ads. She's probably the most famous woman on Wall Street. The First Lady of Finance, if you will—First Lady of Marketing, First Lady of Balls.

Monster was poking through the contents of my purse left on the floor. Muriel, or Mickey, as she prefers to be called, beamed with pride and began excitedly to tell me about the big photo shoot coming up. *Fortune* magazine was doing a pictorial feature on famous people who took their dogs to work. At seven A.M. the following Tuesday her limousine would drop her and Monster Girl off at the hairdressers, then whisk them to a studio where the *Fortune* photographer would take their formal portrait. She couldn't wait.

As I watched her chat on about wanting to take Monster Girl abroad on business trips with her, and the ins and outs of canine air travel, I began to be pulled in. She was human where and when it counted or when she wished to be seen that way and, as others later told me, she was cold and ruthless in business. So what? Someone who once worked for her remarked:

"Muriel Siebert—she's very interesting when you get her up there in front of an audience. Everybody has a great time. She would tell all her old war stories. You have to get her in the mood. She's been through a lot. I mean, you have to understand, she started when there really were no other women."

Muriel looked up from Monster Girl and began to tell me her story:

"I drove from Cleveland to New York in 1954 in a used Studebaker with $500. I was a college dropout and my father had just died of cancer. The first job I got in New York was as a trainee in research at $65 a week. I was given airlines, motion pictures, I wrote some studies, I made money for people. I got my first order from an institution called the Madison Fund and they said, 'We made money from a report you wrote, we owe you an order.' And then I started to make money because I was being given a commission. I went off salary. And I would only recommend stocks I had researched.

"Then I lucked out, because I became partner of Finkle and Company because I knew their son. I learned how to trade and handle orders from Davey Finkle because I found and placed a block that he couldn't once. He said, 'You come here and sit by me.' Well, the first day I was there, this language, I mean I was in shock. And now I use the same language and it doesn't mean anything to me. I try to tell people, if that's the language and you can't accept it, then don't come to the Street. That's just part of it. It doesn't mean anything.

"Of course, mentors didn't exist then for women. I mean, Davey would sit in Switzerland and say, 'Did you call Gerry Tsai today?' And I'd say, 'What am I going to tell him?' And he'd say, 'I don't give a shit, call him. So when he starts buying stocks again he'll think of you.' I mean, he used to pull the phone out of my hand and yell that I didn't know how to close a sale. But then when I learned how to handle orders and how to cross blocks, I mean, if I gave people the research information, I wanted that order. I only handled the things I knew. It's totally different today."

Muriel never married and never had children. She was busy, for one, blazing a path right through the door of one of the most powerful men's clubs in the world at that time, the New York Stock Exchange. Ready to move on and up from Finkle and Company, she began looking into the process of buying a seat on the exchange, something no woman had ever tried to do. Gerry Tsai gave her the idea. This was 1967, and she was turned down by nine out of the first ten men she asked to sponsor her for a seat. She told *Institutional Investor* in an interview in 1987,

"I couldn't get sponsored by anybody who was a member on the floor. Mine were all upstairs people. The people that I had asked, when the time came, they just ran out the door."

Ed Merkle, who ran the Madison Fund, Jim O'Brien, a partner at Salomon Brothers, and Ken Ward, an analyst at Hayden Stone, became her sponsors. Once the letters and forms were completed, she came up against another seemingly insurmountable roadblock.

The stock exchange decided to impose a new rule. She would have to provide them with a letter from her bank guaranteeing her for $300,000 of the $445,000 she needed to buy her seat. But the bank refused to write the letter unless the stock exchange guaranteed that they would admit her. It took her months to cobble together the necessary bank loans and the sponsor letters.

Muriel Siebert & Company became the first woman-owned firm to open on the New York Stock Exchange. That was in 1967, and she was the only woman out of 1,366 members. She readily admits that she was "controversial." When I got my seat the governor of the exchange asked me, 'And how many others are there behind you?'"

It was not until 1970 that the next woman was admitted as a member of the exchange. There wasn't a women's rest room in the New York Stock Exchange Luncheon Club until around 1990.

In the early years it was not easy. She finally joined the all-male Luncheon Club, but only after two years had gone by. She also remembers the humiliation she felt when trying to do business as a woman then. One story relates to a meeting of a financial association of which she was a board member. As she began to walk in the entrance of the club where the meeting was being held, the doorman barred her path and told her she would have to go through the service entrance, through the kitchen and up the back stairs. The great part of the story is that her male colleagues protested by all leaving through the service entrance with her after the meeting.

In 1977 Muriel was appointed by Governor Hugh Carey as the first woman ever to become superintendent of banking for New York State. For five years she made a name for herself holding the highest position in banking regulation ever obtained by a woman, and for exerting an imaginative, forceful, if not controversial, management style.

A devout feminist, she spends a good deal of her time preaching the virtues of women being given a chance:

"American business will find that women executives can be a strong competitive weapon against Japan and Germany and other countries that still limit their executive talent pool to the male 50 percent of their population."

She is founding member and president of the Women's Forum; a member of the Committee of 200, composed of leading women business owners; member of the Financial Women's Association, the Women's Economic Round Table Advisory Council, the Academy of Women Achievers, and on and on, including being the first woman selected as "one who has made a difference" for the Working Women Hall of Fame.

As for women on Wall Street? Muriel says there aren't enough. It is still rough for a lot of them. She admits that there are women traders, but that you find them mostly at the institutions on the buy side. There are a few on the sell side, but not in the key positions in the major firms. And they're not in mergers and acquisitions, but rather in research departments or money management, where they are getting paid well and equally. A lot are coming up in money management, still not many on the trading side.

Now she is at the cutting edge again with online trading facilities on the Internet, through a venture called Siebert OnLine, which offers twenty-four-hour trading and real-time quotes. And she has a municipal bond division, called Siebert, Brandford, Shank & Company, the only woman-owned African American firm in the business. To say Muriel is excited about its prospects is an understatement:

"They are so smart. We were appointed the lead underwriter for the State of California for a $175 million deal, which was a coup. What a story. Susan Shank, who is African American, is a wonder. She graduated from Georgia Tech, practiced engineering for five years, didn't like it—goes to Wharton, gets an MBA. In five years they're all going to say, how did this happen? It's happening right now."

Muriel handed me her background blurb, which had almost three pages listing her awards, board positions, special honors, honorary degrees, and her activities for charity and philanthropy.

I asked this amazing woman what thought she wanted me to leave with, and she said, "Put your head down and charge."

THAT'S JUST WHAT Holly Stark did. She is one of the leading stars among the buy-side traders who work at mutual funds. This, by definition, puts her at the top of the establishment today merely due to the incredible size of the money the buy side has to move in and out of the markets.

From her Midwestern good looks and cascading laugh it was too easy for me to gain the impression that she lacked the intensity or seriousness needed to work on a trading desk. Beneath her breezy exterior I discovered an aggressive woman, a trader at Dalton, Greiner, Hartman, Maher & Company in New York, and vice-chairwoman of a twenty-one-member group representing the largest mutual funds and public and private pension funds in the United States. The group has been influential in discussing various issues about how markets trade and what the big institutions need. Much of what she has lobbied for has appeared in new SEC trading rules:

"We were flabbergasted. It was very satisfying. We have worked very hard and I think we have a decent amount of respect as a group on the Street."

Holly began in the late 1970s, when most investment firms were still hiring women to work as secretaries or assistants:

"I started in this business when I graduated from college in 1978, but I started out doing market administration and economic analysis. When Tim Dalton, who is the chairman of our firm—I worked with him at Oppenheimer Capital Money Management—left to start up something called Dillon Read Capital, he said, 'Gee, Holly, come on along. And you can be the trader too.' It was kind of like the good fairy coming down and saying, 'Bing, and you're a trader!'

"That old saying that ignorance is bliss is really true. Because if I had known what I was getting myself into I would have probably put my tail between my legs and headed for the hills. I was ungodly ignorant. But at the same time, I wasn't shy about saying to people, hello, I don't have a clue as to what I am doing, and please suffer through my very stupid basic questions. The vast majority of people were more than willing to bend over backward to educate you.

"The thing about this business, and perhaps why I love it so much, is that the more you learn, the more you realize you don't know, or that you find that there is to learn. And it is such a dynamic business. The way I trade today is so far removed from the way I traded when I first started, because of the advent of electronic trading. There is always something to learn, and this is what makes it exciting.

"I have been phenomenally lucky. I was given a wonderful

opportunity that not many people are given. Typically one learns to trade by listening in on phone calls and sitting next to senior people. There are very few books you can pick up and say, 'Okay, this is how you trade.'

"There was one guy that I remember telling me to just remember one thing. That your word is everything in this business, and your reputation is everything. And if you think about it, there are billions of dollars changing hands at very, very rapid rates, and it is all done by a phone call. You need to know that the person on the other end of the line is an up-front person."

Situated in a nondescript small room in midtown Manhattan, Holly's trading desk holds four computer screens. There's room for no more than three or four people. Her firm has a strong bias toward buying stocks of small companies, which could mean companies under $500 million. On a good day it might trade 5,000 shares. One of the most difficult aspects for her is to be there when one of her companies' stocks shows up in the market in the size that she needs. Because if she misses the trade, say if 75,000 shares of the stock trades, it could be the largest trade for three months. And if she misses it she's not doing her job. Stocks can trade in so many different places that the buy-side trader constantly has to monitor everything, looking for the most liquidity, worrying that if they miss it in one place, they may miss the opportunity to trade altogether.

"I get up at six A.M. and as I'm coming to consciousness I have CNBC on or CNN to find out what has gone on overseas. I have my *Wall Street Journal* delivered at home so that while I am having my morning tea I am quickly scanning through that. I am in here by quarter of eight, checking up further on the international markets and for news on any of our stocks. I look at Bridge and INSTINET R&A, so you have all this analytical stuff that does all this charting and news recall for you. I start getting my morning calls from about eight-fifteen from brokers to see what they have been saying, and then those calls last until about nine-ten.

"From there on in we are strategizing as to what we are going to be doing with our orders that morning. Then you start getting pre-opening calls at nine-twenty, and then between nine-twenty-eight and nine-thirty-one it is a real crush as you are slamming everything in trying to get stuff into the market.

"Sometimes you don't, you pull back and aggressively watch. That's my favorite phrase. What are you doing? Oh, I'm aggressively watching right now. Sometimes that's what you have to do because you don't want to be in there. Sometimes you just have to sit on the sidelines and wait for an opportunity to present itself.

"I wolf down a sandwich. You don't go out for lunch. You walk out at six or seven. If there is late-breaking news I might keep trading on INSTINET. On the weekends I relax. My husband is in this business as well, so we talk a lot about the market. We escape from the city and go to the country and do nothing. Or I cook and garden."

Although Holly had no problem with being a woman and becoming a trader, she believes that it is tougher in general for women to get their foot in the door, and especially to come on to a trading desk:

"Women typically come on to trading desks by being a sales assistant and handling all the paperwork. It is only in the last few years as they go through the training programs . . . but a lot of times women don't choose to be on a trading desk. It is hard if you are going to have a personal life. The hours aren't very defined. You have to be at your post when the market is open, and you don't take lunches. You are always there. But there is so much going on, you really don't want to step away either. It's very exciting. You turn away, and the whole market in five minutes has changed completely.

"There are some trading desks, no question about it, that are locker rooms where they treat women disgracefully. It tends to be more on the sell side. I enjoy a good joke as much as anyone, but there is appropriate humor and there is appropriate humor. This is not a business for shrinking violets. You can't sit there with your hands folded and be nice. You have to be confident. You have to have the courage of your convictions. Being a trader, you have to make decisions very quickly. Every decision you make is not going to be right, and you have to learn from your mistakes and move on quickly. You can't sit there and agonize over something for two hours. You don't have the luxury of time. For many women that is difficult."

AT SPANISH BAY in Carmel, California, on New Year's Eve Louise Jones had a hole in one: one hundred and thirty-four yards. Then she birdied the eighteenth hole. A par five, over five hundred yards. She was lying three and was eighty yards from the pin. She put it in the cup with the entire clubhouse watching. They continued to watch with interest as the striking blonde with an athletic figure and graceful swing coolly handed her putter to the caddie and began to stroll in.

Single, thirty-three, and co-owner of a firm on the New York Stock Exchange, Louise began life far from the privileged greens of Carmel. "Baby Louise" had been found abandoned at about two days old in a phone booth in New York, a wintry two days before Christmas. Louise surprised me by asking what nationality I thought she was. She still wonders who her mother was, and once found herself walking by that telephone booth hoping for something to happen, someone to walk by that she would recognize.

Incredibly, I detect no bitterness and no pain in her. Her pale blue eyes either crinkle in delight at what you are saying or watch you with warm interest.

"When I was five years old my foster father took me to the local bank, sat me up on the counter, and opened my first account. He taught me what interest was, and I was truly amazed that you could make money with money. From that moment on, my interest in money grew, and I have always been extremely ambitious."

Louise is a floor broker, whose clients expect her to read the crowd on the floor of the exchange, detect the moods, know the players, and trade for them.

"I wake up about six. I'm at the exchange about seven-fifteen. I exercise at night. I'm very into keeping in shape, keeping healthy. I only drink ginger ale. It's so easy to get caught up in habits on Wall Street, drinking after work from stress. I'd rather be working out than sitting at home having a drink.

"So I go up to the Luncheon Club at seven-fifteen and read all the papers, the *Journal, Investors Business Daily*, the *New York Times* business section, *USA Today*. I check all the European markets, see what the currencies are doing, what commodities are doing. I try to find out what the focus of the day is going to be. Then I call and alert my clients what I think is going to happen. It's a great way to start my day. I call each one individually and they put my voice on the squawk box so the whole desk is hearing the call. I do it right from the floor of the exchange. I love being on the floor. Adrenaline. Pure adrenaline. Just a rush. I jumped into it with both feet.

"The whole thing about trading is that you can't put too much emotion into it. You can't get married to positions. You go in it with an idea. I'm going to do this now, if it doesn't work, then I'm out. As long as you take that approach you will be successful. If you get something where you say, oh, I just know I was right and you're very stubborn about it, that's too much emotion. You can't really do that. You really have to be stoic in some respect. You have to do it nine million times a day. As long as you have a plan, then it all makes sense."

Floor traders will often work a series of smaller trades to fill their order, rather than letting everyone know the actual amount of stock they have to move. That would affect the price, so it takes sensitivity and quickness.

Like her beginning in life, obstacles tend to arise for Louise more in a personal sense than in her work. She is addicted to golf, but can't find a club that will allow single women to join. And she is frustrated that in the ones where she can get access, women are limited to playing in the afternoons. She makes tons of money, yet can't always spend it the way she wants to. Her summer house is right on the beach, and playing hours of tennis on weekends is her revenge.

Floating in space above Susan Ollila's head was a luminous square of light, as big as the size of her overly large desk. She radiated beneath it as she looked for a minute out the window, reflecting on how she found her way into this business:

"In the beginning I didn't expect a lot. And that is very odd. I had no idea that I even wanted a career. Like so many of us, I was very curious, willing to work hard. And I was not afraid to say that I didn't understand something, because I didn't have an ego that I was protecting. I didn't press people any harder than they were willing to be pressed. So you don't seem threatening to men. People were very open to me. That was particularly the case at W.R. Grace, where I was for the longest time the only vice-president of that corporation and reported to a group of men who were very senior in the organization. Peter Grace was involved with hiring me. And they were very supportive of my career."

So if she didn't know she wanted a career, how did she get to be the director of fixed income investment at the Ford Foundation in New York, where she oversees a $2 billion portfolio and executes all her own trades?

"I was in a bank training program and was assigned to the trust department. At that time there wasn't much fixed income managed. They were buying municipal bonds for trust accounts because there was no real pension fund business. I taught myself what bonds were all about, and it was a great experience for me.

"I went to work for GE Pension Fund, where I managed a very large fixed income portfolio. And then went to work for W.R. Grace, where I was the fixed income manager as well as the director of all pension fund assets, and then I came here. I am older than most women in the investment business right now. When I started, women were really not seen as people who would be professionals. Women were considered as part of the support staff. I think I was enormously fortunate, thinking back to the bank, that the man I worked for was a wonderful mentor. He encouraged me and let me define my own limits. That was extraordinary. I think my experience was different than most."

Susan Ollila's office looked anything but a place to trade. One computer screen sat to the side, appearing insignificant in the spacious room. Behind her the wall was filled with books, ahead of her there was nothing but a sofa at the far end, and to her right an entire wall of glass that looked out onto a leafy courtyard. It was more of a retreat, an island of peace in which to ponder.

She pushed back her red hair and began to go back over her past again, as if trying to understand it:

"I had never really defined a career path. I never said, I want to go here to here, and at the end of my career I want to be there. Part of it, when I think of myself in 1967, was that I wasn't aware of what the world had to offer. I was very open to what was going to happen to me, so I didn't have my own little agenda. I was willing to walk through a door that was opened for me. I think there are so many opportunities in life if you are just willing to look at them. You don't know where that will take you. And whatever I did, I tried to do it with as much integrity as I could bring to it."

Now she was part of a philanthropic organization that exists to donate grants. There are ten floors in the building; nine of them give away money, hers makes it, enough to support the institution. The majority of the people on the investment floor seem to be women.

"I am investing in bonds around the world. I deal in a variety of time zones. I have to manage currency. I have to understand how to create a hedge and how to put it on and take it off. That is all something that has been a major change in the way we are managing fixed income portfolios. Globalization of the markets has had a real impact.

"The other thing that is a change has been the ability of our country and other countries around the world to control inflation. During the 1970s fixed income markets were depreciating daily because of the ravages that inflation was taking on all markets. And it created an explosion in real estate values because people were looking for hard assets. As the U.S. has understood inflation and has taken steps to control it, the fixed income market has changed.

"Fixed income markets will always be sensitive to interest rate risk, but interest rates will not move like they did during periods of time when inflation was heading toward those double-digit levels. So the taming of inflation has had a major impact on the fixed income market, and on how you would create a fixed income portfolio right now to deliver the kind of risk-reduction return equation that fixed securities are supposed to provide in a balanced portfolio."

I looked back at her small screen and wondered how she traded:

"I am dealing with a broker where they are principals, and I am acting as a principal too, so that I am buying from his position, or selling to his position. For me the execution of a trade is really a reflection of the information that has come to me from a particular dealer, and it has to do oftentimes with his own positioning. And that can work for or against you. But if you have a sense of where the market is, and what you want to do, then it is in your best interest to buy securities from those people who are in a position to actually sell them to you. It would be counterproductive for me, for example, to decide that I wanted to buy some German bunds, and I had developed the idea to buy those securities with an economist at Salomon Brothers, knew that Salomon had a position in bunds—and then turn around and try to buy them from Goldman Sachs, whose traders might be short. The price would be dramatically different."

Down the hall I found Joanne Sage trading equities. She is one of two women traders who work the $3 billion portfolio. She started at the Ford Foundation as a temp in the trading room the year she got out of college, in 1978. Beginning as a staff assistant on the desk and filling in every time someone left, she became a trader:

"I think particularly on the buy side, there are many more opportunities for women. On the sell-side trading desks, we're not there yet. I think there are a handful of sell-side women traders, but it is not as good as it is on the buy side."

In contrast to Susan's, her desk was littered with screens: Bloomberg, Marketrac, INSTINET—although I noticed she did her trading mostly over the phone with her brokers:

"Every morning about eight-fifteen we get a call from all of our brokers with their research, with what their strategists are saying, sort of a recap of what is going on economically, what is going on in the bond market, any economic data coming out. We speak to probably thirty brokers every morning. Sometimes the call is helpful, sometimes not. But that is one of my requisites. I want a call every single morning. Even if they have nothing to say. I want to know if they have nothing to say. That's sometimes saying something also.

"A little after nine I talk with the portfolio manager, go over what they relay to me, and go over our plan for the day of what I am going to be buying and selling. Sometimes I have CNBC on in the background in case there is an important item that might be coming out, or something overnight in one of the foreign markets has gone crazy or something. I'll put on the television just to hear the buzz of what they are saying."

Conservatism in its approach to investing, and taking a long-term outlook, mean that there is a relatively low turnover in the Ford equity portfolio. They are trading every day but not in hundreds of thousands of shares.

For Susan, trading ten or twenty names is a busy day:

"I try to get a good part of the order done immediately if I can, within the framework of the market. Some names are harder than others and you can't sell even 25,000 shares. You've got to wait it out and bide your time and just hope that a buyer or seller shows up so you can get something done. We are fairly price conscious. We don't move big blocks of stock at a time. We'd rather piece it out and see how we do over the longer term.

"I have been in the business long enough to know when somebody knows what they are doing. If it is somebody new, I will be very specific. Sell 5,000 here. Sell another 5,000 there. So they get an idea how I work and how I want our orders handled. Over time you develop relationships. If it is somebody that has been in the business a while, I'll give them more leeway.

"One thing I like about being a trader, as opposed to being an analyst or a portfolio manager, is that the market closes at four, and there is nothing I can do. I could trade in some of the after-hours markets, but after four I've done what I've done. I can't go back. And I can tell whether a trade is a good trade or not, or whether it holds. Now if a trade holds for half an hour you are a genius. I like that aspect of it. It is instant gratification. I go home and I know what I've done and I know how it stacks up by the end of the day."

FREE WEIGHTS AND barbells and exercise mats were scattered all over the floor of the big living room of Carolyn Jackson's penthouse high atop a modern New York skyscraper. Sun was streaming in and New Age music floated across the room.

Everyone in the derivatives industry seems to know Carolyn Jackson, the formerly activist executive director and board member of the International Swaps and Derivatives Association. Now she was somebody else, she had reinvented herself. Dressed in shorts and a tank top, she completely threw me off balance. She looked years younger than her age. She was trim and well toned, with blond hair and myopically large eyes. My mistake was to conclude that she was taking time out away from the industry, away from pressure, to chill out. Behind that beautiful exterior ticked an ambitious mind with a list miles long of goals to achieve. She was just regrouping, redirecting her energy for a while:

"I want to write. I am taking a screenwriting class, also a fiction workshop group where we sit around and trash each other's short stories, which is very supportive. I've really enjoyed that, and I've written more in these past three months than I've ever written in my life, so I'm very happy. I have several chapters of the book I am working on. I have two acts of a screenplay. And three short stories. I never think it is enough."

She wants to write popular novels that use the feel of New York and her experience in the business as a backdrop. She also teaches aerobics classes five times a week, some of them at the Pumping Iron Gym in New York:

"There are three areas that are important to me: writing, derivatives, and fitness. I want to design a life where I can balance being involved in all of them, rather than just being so overinvolved in just the derivatives."

She is a complex person: an A student who has passions in life that take her to the extreme, and she wants to try them all. In my experience, traders are usually single faceted. They are so focused on what they are doing, they don't have much time for anything else. Carolyn was that way while she was a trader. But then all of a sudden she had an epiphany. The only thing that didn't change was the drive.

The speakerphone to her answering machine was constantly chattering away in the background, and it struck me as a metaphor for her life right now. Husky male voices were asking her out, businesslike voices were asking her to speak at functions and lend her support at industry meetings, and to appear as an expert witness in a derivatives case. Others were old friends trying to reach her or people searching for a personal fitness trainer. Does she ever hang out and eat pizza and watch TV? Not likely. She's veered off for a while, but toward other goals:

"The last two years at ISDA, I had to give up three weekends a month to be traveling on the road for them. And so I found that if you drew a pie diagram of one's life, there was basically ISDA and sleep, assuming that I was doing that. And there are so many things that are important to me. Also, I found working in the trade association, that the law was becoming more and more interesting to me. So I have applied to law school. I don't want to lose touch with the derivatives market, but I want to be more a manager of my own time. It is a fantastic industry, and it will always have a huge part of my heart. I was thrilled to have been a part of it and hope in some capacity to always remain a part of it."

Why did she leave it?

"First of all, it is a bit of a misnomer to say that I have left the industry for good. It is very important for me as a personal goal to write a book and finish one. Whether it is a good book or a bad book, the publishing world will determine that. It is something I have wanted to do since I was eight years old. And I have never been able to have the time. It was very very real, turning forty, and thinking of all my personal goals, realizing I was pretty short on the one that had always been my number one priority.

"I have been in this industry for fifteen years, since the beginning, so I almost feel like a grandmother to it. I have a certain pride of ownership and so I would never want to totally just run away. I did find that after fifteen years I had done it all for what I wanted to do in the industry at that time. Which was, be part of the original group at Chase, and that was great. I started as the lowest possible grunt that there could possibly have been, including staying late to make sure that the telex went out.

"I started in 1982, but the group wasn't formed until 1983. I went through the Chase credit development program. I had a rocky beginning in the sense that I was getting my Ph.D. in finance in Rochester at the School of Management, now the William E. Simon School. I was twenty-four at the time. I was doing real well there. I passed all my qualifiers and was a Ph.D. candidate, which means you are working on your dissertation. But it was ludicrous to be a Ph.D. in business and only be twenty-four and never have worked.

"So I approached Cliff Smith, who was my dissertation adviser, and said that I really wanted to work for a bit first. He helped me with an interview at Chase called the Corporate Finance Group. It was made up of people that had either all gone to Chicago or Rochester. It was very much that 'efficient markets' mind-set, so I thought I would fit in real well. Plus, I could work on my dissertation. But unfortunately, the group was disbanded two weeks after I started.

"So, I had just given up my full scholarship and taken an $800-a-month apartment lease. I was a little concerned. Luckily that was the early eighties. I went there and said, 'I would like to go through the credit development program.' And when I came out, this group had just been formed called the Swaps Group, and nobody wanted to go to that area because it was an unknown. They wanted to go to what Chase was known for, like syndication or project finance or a lending area. I said, 'I'll go.' Because I was just happy to have a permanent boss. And then, of course, it became the hot area and Chase was well positioned to be a lead bank in the industry because of their excellent customer base.

"And it was so exciting. It is just so hard to describe those days because everything was new. Every day was totally unpredictable, and you felt like you were at the beginning of something that was really great. I was very aware of it every day, about how fortunate I was. I kept asking myself, if this is so great, how long is it going to last? And that's where I think I was a bit naive. I didn't think it would last as long as it did. I thought something else would be the next wave, and we'd go the way of M&A glory days, or project finance glory days. But the business just kept building, and it added new complexities. So that was fun to be at Chase. And I got to do a lot of things, because the product was evolving. Initially it was very much more corporate finance structure oriented. So you might do a deal once every four months. And there is a lead time, and a lot of money was made on it, but nobody was trading.

"Then you began to do a little bit more trades. And so there was less structuring. My boss left, and a new person came on board. He said we were going to start trading. Because of my quantitative background, he told me I was going to run the trading room. Of course, I had never been a trader in my life. So I had to set up the whole mark to market and the valuation methodology. And at that time I was twenty-eight years old. It was a bit strange to have that much responsibility. But it was great fun and I absolutely loved it because it was new and evolving."

GAIL PANKEY, A floor broker on the New York Stock Exchange, looked as cool and professional as a commentator on the evening news. I was looking forward to seeing at last what a broker trading on the floor did with those telephone trades from across the sea that I would send when I was a fund manager in London. On my side of the pond, when I had wanted to buy or sell a stock, I'd walk an order slip across the floor to my trader. He'd then call a sales trader at a brokerage in London, who would then call his firm's floor broker on the New York Stock Exchange to execute the order. That's where someone like Gail comes in.

People tend to regard brokers on the floor as order handlers rather than traders. But they actively "trade" all day in a fast-paced arena that can be punishing. Their art is knowing exactly when to trade and when to back off and wait. This means they have to be flexible enough to jump into the fray in a split second or to be patient and endure the suspense. The market can change direction within minutes, a stock price within seconds.

I accompanied Gail down a long, nondescript linoleum hall, past a shoeshine stand and through the doors to the main trading floor. We progressed from silence into a sudden surge of loud noise, body heat, and seeming pandemonium.

It felt like déjà vu. Every time a reference is made to the "stock market" on television, they show a picture of this floor with its lofty seven-story trading room. At each reference to how the "Dow" finished at the end of the day, they show the gavel being struck up on the podium and you hear the Pavlovian clanging of the closing bell. Those images and sounds have become the "market" in our heads. You can see and hear it. It is one of the few stock exchanges left in the world where people still physically come together and meet face-to-face to haggle and trade.

A camera crew spotted us and pushed through the crowd to ask Gail if she would do a live report on the market activity. As I stood back to watch, the thought took shape that, surrounded by this mostly male world, she may well be the new face of the exchange. She is a young, self-confident African American woman, a female dynamo who earned her way in. Her rapid-fire analysis for the video camera was honest and hard hitting, with a cutting edge. As they dissolved into the background I noticed that television was a less than subtle presence on the floor. Television booths were up on the balcony and there were screens every few feet all around the room. Traders merely had to glance above their heads to see continuously scrolling stock prices across the bottom of the screens. It almost took away the need to look at the gigantic digital Dow Jones ticker displaying prices across the far wall.

Gail began to tell me about her background:

"I was seventeen coming out of high school and I had to work. I graduated from an all-girl Catholic school on a Friday night, and I was at work on the New York Stock Exchange Monday morning. I kind of walked in blind. You know, these two pigtails . . . 110 pounds soaking wet. And here were all these men, average height five feet ten inches to six feet. Talk about culture shock. Back in 1971 this was a bastion of men.

"So it was very difficult. And it made it maybe even a little more difficult having a tan."

The obstacles to get to this point—being a woman, coming from a different background, having only a high school education—were considerable:

"I was told early on that I was not going to college. Not by any academic superiors, but by my mother. My sister was older and she had gone to college. But I was younger and there was no more money. I had to go to work. She had first dibs on education."

Brokers commuted in on the Erie Lackawanna from suburbs in New Jersey after weekends of golf. Gail took the subway from the inner city.

"This was a higher echelon of people, a more elitist group. So even their vocabulary in a lot of ways escaped me. It meant dealing with different customs. There were different styles of conversations that I was being introduced to for the first time. It was very, very hard.

"So that's how I got here. I had applied to three different places, two of them were insurance companies. Because back then, what did kids do when they came out of high school? They went to banks and insurance companies. I had no concept of what the New York Stock Exchange was, or of stocks, bonds, currencies, or financial risk. They didn't teach it in school."

It's been twenty-six years since Gail started working on the exchange. Now she owns her own seat. As for being a minority female, "It wasn't a glass ceiling, it was a concrete ceiling." She obviously didn't pay attention.

As we talked, the expression on Gail's face changed from confidence to one remembering fear as she recalled what it was like the first time she traded:

"I was scared to death. Scared to death. It's frightening. You are trading millions and millions and millions of dollars. You obviously can't stop to think about that. You have to control your emotions because you are trading someone's money and you don't want to make an error. I remember being so elated and being so afraid at the same time. The emotions were entirely diverse and so intense. But you had to control them. Once you get over that, you love it."

Criss-crossing in a rush around us were rivers of people visibly responding to the ebbs and flows of the market. Motion is good: it means business is being done. Apparent chaos was in reality organized and precise activity. People were on their way to buy or sell their next stock at a trading post located somewhere on the floor. Because there is only one geographic location where you can buy a particular stock, it means navigating your way around to find the appropriate trading point. And if you are in a hurry, it means doing it on the run. Manning the post is the specialist representing four or five stocks, and those are his stocks alone. You can only go to him to buy and sell, for example, IBM.

This was where we were headed. When we got there Gail left me a few steps away while she traded IBM for a client. Her slight frame squeezed into the large group of traders that had formed in front of the specialist for IBM. There must have been news out on the stock—everyone seemed to be clamoring for attention. As the specialist faced them, he acted as an auctioneer for the group. Hundreds of mini-auctions were in progress all over the floor. The action in this one was so fast, it was hard to keep up with what was going on.

Gail, who had minutes ago been charming and laughing, wore a taut expression until she started trading. Then her voice boomed out loudly above the others in sharp calls for prices as she aggressively stood her ground in bidding against the traders around her. It looked like it took the skill of a card player to read the crowd. They all wore poker faces. The more they wanted to prevent the others from knowing what their intentions were, the more inscrutable they were. After years of working on the floor, Gail recognizes the players she is pitted against, and tries to second-guess what their motivations might be, what cards they are really holding in their hands. She pays attention to the conversations going on around her. She watches their eyes. Compared to traders on a commodity exchange who frantically wave their arms in the air as an indication of wanting to buy or sell, here there is less body language to go on, just more eye contact and the nuances of voices.

She's never bored—she's in a constant whirlwind. Weaving in and out of clusters of people, she motioned with her head toward the next huge trading room. On the way, we passed her booth, where her clerks were juggling the phone lines and writing down orders for her to execute. It reminded me of a relay race. Giving them her tickets that were done, taking the orders that she had to do next, and snatching a quick sip of Coke, she walked briskly back out onto the trading floor with me in her wake. They are able to contact her on the floor through the yellow house phones and her beeper. While the clerks' telephone logs accumulate millions of dollars worth of trades throughout the day, Gail's attention is focused on the next trade. Distraction is studiously avoided. Selective focus counts. If she thought about the size of the money she had been negotiating, she would be distracted.

She turned toward me again, spreading her arms to encompass the room:

"I love the energy here. It's addictive. Even when it is quiet, there is always something that is breaking out. There's always news. I love this place because there is no way in hell I could have gotten a college education, in regard to business, that I got on the exchange over the last twenty-five years. It was like a liberal arts and finance course all rolled into one.

"And it makes you very people conscious, because you are working so close together, working elbow to elbow all day long. There's also a lot of discipline involved in trading, you just can't blow up. You have to be professional."

Looking up at computer screens intently while she continued to talk to me, her eyes scanned back and forth over the changing prices of currencies and stocks, hesitating for a minute to watch a CNBC TV screen above her head. By continually monitoring those screens, she absorbs information that the rest of the market is receiving at the same instant. For that moment, she was impervious to everything going on around us. If she could pick up quickly enough on a change in price that might affect one of the stocks she trades for her clients—even twenty seconds before others made the mental connection—she might be able to do a trade at a better price. The more information, the greater the edge:

"I do my homework every morning before I get to work. I get up at five-thirty. I read my *Wall Street Journal*. I flip through channels all morning—CNBC, CNN, Bloomberg—while I am putting on make-up and finding my stockings. If I see there is news out on IBM, I pay attention to what is going on in all the technology stocks. I will watch DEC and Hewlett-Packard as well, because you have to look at the group.

"For me, trading is a mixture of psychological, intellectual, and a gut feeling. You take in the information, think, then trade. So it looks to the layperson as if it is a lot of yelling and screaming. But in reality, there is a thought process going on—thinking, should I do this, should I do that? You have to stay within the parameters of what your client wants you to do at the same time. It's not easy."

By the end of the day I was wiped out. We had been in constant motion. She doesn't go out of the building for lunch, neither do her clerks. It was six hours of muscle-cramping, stomach-knotting intensity. The market had been like a roller coaster, up 80 points in the morning and down 43 by the afternoon. Sometimes it felt like we were just hanging on.

Back at the entrance, she confided:

"My dream was to open my own firm, which is what I did, and it is still embryonic, still a little baby, still has to be nurtured and fed. I am forty-three now. I started my firm five years ago. I took the plunge off the cliff. So far there has been a parachute."

⁸ STATELESS MONEY

WHEN SPECULATORS PROFIT, THE AUTHORITIES HAVE
FAILED IN SOME WAY OR ANOTHER. BUT THEY DON'T
LIKE TO ADMIT FAILURE; THEY WOULD RATHER CALL
FOR SPECULATORS TO BE HUNG FROM LAMPPOSTS THAN
TO ENGAGE IN A LITTLE BIT OF SOUL-SEARCHING TO SEE
WHAT THEY DID WRONG.

GEORGE SOROS, *SOROS ON SOROS*

You have to see a foreign exchange desk work to understand how fast it is and how much personal interplay is part of the process, especially the tension that builds between the traders and the salespeople. While the salespeople are trying to get something for their clients, traders are protecting their bank's capital. A client will ring in and want to sell, say, half a billion dollars worth of yen. The first thing a trader will do is close the trade. He buys it. He is now long (owns) half a billion dollars worth of yen. He then wants to lay that position off—get rid of it, immediately.

He'll stand up and shout, "Yen calls!" And everyone in the dealing room on the foreign exchange floor will hit the phones to get prices on yen. As they get them, they shout those prices back to the trader: "I'm 93 and 1/2!" "Done!" "You're done for 50!" Another guy will say, "I'm 93 for 50!" The trader will respond, "You're done for another 50!" And he lays his position off piece by piece until he has laid off, say, half of it, holding what he is comfortable with.

The art of the trader is protecting his position, not letting the market know the size of the position he is holding. This is one of the most critical pieces of information a currency trader has to protect. The successful ones have honed the skills of manipulating what they have on their books against others in the marketplace.

Michael Paull, who used to manage traders at Union Bank of Switzerland, described what the drill is:

"Traders will deal trader to trader, but most often they deal through brokers. By dealing through a broker, you use the broker to find your counterpart in the marketplace. By dealing via a broker you don't talk to other traders. So you don't give away by your voice, by your hesitation, your inflection—you don't give away that information to a trader on the other side. Additionally, the broker disguises who is doing what in the market. It protects your book position. If you have a big position to move, you don't want the others to know, because they will just mark the prices back against you."

It is widely accepted that only the young can withstand the pressure of trading in the biggest market in the world. Over a trillion dollars trade in a day, and billions can move within seconds from one economy to the next, then into another. Traders plug into their financial world the way we plug into the Internet; one individual connecting to a universal consciousness kept alive by digital blips on a screen in front of them, a universal mind so alive that it surpasses the real world in its reality. Within a nanosecond they can perceive an anomaly and launch a bid for tens of millions of dollars, while at the same time scanning and absorbing tidal waves of information pouring in around them. They thrive not only on information, but in the swirling waters of change and chaos.

Their lot came to the fore after Bretton Woods, the agreement that set fixed exchange rates, broke down in 1973 and exchange rates began to float. The floating dollar caused other currencies to fluctuate, and the volatility brought traders rushing into the market.

They maneuver in a market that follows the sun. Open twenty-four hours a day from Tokyo to London to New York, it allows its participants uninterrupted access to a sea of money. When it is eight A.M. in London, foreign exchange trading is ending in Tokyo and

Hong Kong for the day. When it is one P.M. in London, foreign exchange trading is beginning in New York.

Foreign exchange trading would appear to be borderless, because with the combination of computers and phones you can trade anything from anywhere in the world. But it still is concentrated in many cases in the country of the currency concerned. In Frankfurt, for example, it is almost all deutschmark-related foreign exchange. Sir Paul Newall, who has been the Lord Mayor of London and followed the trends in the financial markets closely, observed:

"London is the only real multicurrency center in Europe. The other centers basically trade their own currencies, whereas in London, only about 10 percent of the foreign exchange traded is sterling related. The triennial BIS Survey last published in autumn 1995 showed that, during the previous three years, London's share of the global forex market had grown from 27 percent to 30 percent, despite the fact that the average daily volume had increased by nearly 50 percent to $1.2 trillion.

"London's share is now as much as that for New York, Tokyo, and Paris put together, and six times the volume of Frankfurt. London is where the liquidity is, and the critical mass."

You would imagine that with world trade expanding and new democracies and emerging countries joining the marketplace, most currency trading would be to facilitate economic concepts like imports and exports. But in fact, of the $300 trillion or more of currency trading transactions done in a year, just over $5 trillion is related to trade in goods and services.

Buying and selling of currencies is based primarily on financial considerations, not commercial ones. It is more a question of where money can find the highest interest rates. Or where money can be earned from the possibility of a currency rising in value due to improving economic conditions in that country. Or where money can find a temporary safe haven during political turmoil. Some of it flows out, fleeing the threat of more regulation, or from a country whose economic condition is deteriorating. Most of the money goes into currency speculation, into making money make money.

FOR MOST PEOPLE the thought that currency trading is mostly done for speculative reasons is disturbing. And there's a commonly expressed fear in establishment circles that currency traders, while speculating, are usurping the power of governments. Governments, in turn, feel it is an infringement of their sovereignty. The currency market is global, public, and free, owned not by governments but by the market participants.

Stanislas Yassukovich ran a bank in London, the European Banking Company, which gained a powerful niche in the foreign exchange market. He found it particularly irksome when government figures attacked foreign exchange traders:

"At the time there were a series of sterling crises, and particularly Labour MPs blamed the traders, most of whom were cockney lads with a trading tradition. Their fathers had so-called barrows in the street markets, where they were active sellers and traders, and these were the kind of people that had a real kind of feel. But they were desperately, almost excessively, pro-British. And if anything, their tendency was to take a bull position on sterling rather than a bear position. You had to contain their desire to be positive.

"So I used to write to these MPs and say, 'You know, I think your accusations are unfounded and you are accusing people who are actually doing a very valuable job. They are making London the biggest foreign exchange center in the world. Why don't you come and actually see them? Come spend the day in the dealing room.' Well, you know, typical MPs—'I haven't got time, I haven't got time.' They exploited the traditional perception of these kind of barrow boys, which made me very upset, because I thought these were basically solid citizens that were doing a valuable job."

Think of currency traders as being the same as reporters on CNN. They observe an event and translate what they think it means in reporting it. The opinion of reporters for CNN, or that of currency traders, demands a speedy response, usually to issues that otherwise might take longer to be resolved. I sometimes think of CNN as a new-age "world government"—in an abstract sense—with correspondent Christiane Amanpour its secretary of state. Not a traditional government, but a more modern concept, where an effective government is one that interacts with its constituency while having an influence on what they think and focus on, and how they behave.

Traditional governments are being made accountable to that overall world government. When CNN turns its camera lights on Bosnia, governments are under pressure to react. When currency traders turn their attention to a sick economy and decide that its currency is overvalued compared to that of a healthy economy, they mark it down as not worthy of that value. This pressures governments to take notice and react. CNN reporters and currency traders have what governments fear—the power to speed the world up and influence foreign affairs.

Should this make us uneasy? There's a free-market process happening here. Thousands of individual currency traders around the world are making individual evaluations of economic conditions, and they are voting with money. They set the fair market price. The prices are found on computer screens on their desks. What currency traders are doing when they cause a currency to drop in value is to point a finger at what prompted their move in the first place.

Stanislas Yassukovich continued with the following thought:

"Governments should be made accountable for their mismanagement. The very same politicians find it perfectly natural that if a company is badly managed, the shareholders sell the shares and the share price collapses, and therefore the company has to either change management or be taken over. They find that perfectly normal.

"But they are absolutely furious when their own mismanagement results in the one barometer, meaning the value of their currency, also being affected. They basically want to avoid being held accountable for financial mismanagement, and the accountability is the foreign exchange market.

"And they talk about the currency traders, well, that's just like shooting the messenger. The currency traders are simply reflecting basic supply and demand. I say, long live currency traders. They may be the last people that keep governments accountable and keep them honest."

But for Muriel Siebert, currency trading for reasons other than facilitating trade has to be questioned:

"It costs a lot of people a lot of money, if you're producing bread or copper or something, to hedge your costs. There are people that are shorting or buying the currencies due to political motivations. They think, this country is weak because . . . then they just go in there and short the currency. The amounts of money are vast.

"I did not realize this until I was in France. I was in Veuve Cliquot, they had named a vine after me a few years ago. The next day I had lunch at Crédit Lyonnais, and that was the day when the franc was under attack by the hedge funds, if you remember. And the

Bank of France called a few times to see what was going on in the markets, and they could not stop the speculators—and here was a major country."

BY DETERMINING THE value of a currency en masse, traders can precipitate a ripple effect. Volatility can destabilize international trade, where one party wins and another loses. It's a matter of whether it would have happened anyway, because it is the shape of the economy itself that determines what currency traders think the prospects for business and consumers there will be.

In stock markets, to draw a comparison, traders sometimes mark down the value of shares of a company after it announces worse than expected earnings. If poor performance continues, the shares will be marked down further. In recent years this has been enough to shake up management into performing better and increasing shareholder value. Sleepy or incompetent managements have to respond and change, or be ousted.

In both cases, whether it is a company or a country, the salient point is inevitability. If markets hadn't become as fast as they have to pass a verdict, the time span for change would be longer. But change would happen at some point. Fast markets, computers, and big money compress the time frame. More important, they bring it to the public's attention as being a situation that has deteriorated to the point of needing to be addressed.

Currency traders can speed up or exacerbate change. Currency volatility is most difficult for companies that do business internationally. It is a major reason that the derivatives market has thrived, to protect against unforeseen changes in currency values.

Large moves obviously affect people's lives. They change the prices of imports and exports, eventually affecting their volume and finally, jobs and personal income. But large moves happened before currency speculators came to the fore. When central banks and governments had control over the value of their currency, there were competitive and sudden devaluations that had perhaps even more disastrous effects.

Economists who study currency speculation argue that inconsistent macroeconomic policies and market expectations can be identified as causing pressures to build toward a currency crisis. Ramon Moreno, senior economist at the Federal Reserve Bank of San Francisco, studying speculation pressures in East Asia from 1980 to 1994, wrote:

"Statistical tests were performed to see whether episodes of speculative pressure appear to be related to unusual behavior in a country's monetary or fiscal policy, or in economic conditions. The statistical analysis reveals that episodes of depreciation in East Asia are associated with large budget deficits and growth in central bank domestic credit more than episodes of appreciation or periods of tranquillity are. This is broadly consistent with speculative pressure arising because macroeconomic policies are not consistent with an exchange rate peg."

Maurice Obstfeld, professor of economics at the University of California at Berkeley, explains that even if macroeconomic policies are consistent with the exchange rate, either adverse economic conditions or market expectations that a government may not be willing to defend the currency can cause pressures to build.

Expectations play a large role in currency speculation, which is why some governments work to develop a reputation for "toughness" in relation to their willingness to keep the currency where they want it. "Talking" a currency up or down is part of the game. Speculators studying the situation may guess that, despite the talk, once a government has defended its currency, it has most probably depleted its reserves and would have trouble defending it against another attack.

HOW IMPORTANT A part do private investment pools of capital play when they speculate in the foreign exchange markets? What Muriel Siebert was referring to in France were funds that were investing for private clients, who, if their traders are well known, are followed by other currency traders in the markets.

In 1992, when the European currencies started their march toward the ERM (European Exchange Rate Mechanism), which is supposed to come together in 1999, currency traders tended to follow the big U.S. private fund traders. What resulted was that the currencies of some countries were devalued while others were pushed out of the existing structure or grid.

This was the time when George Soros and his head trader Stanley Druckenmiller came to the conclusion that the British pound was overvalued and was destined to fall in value. They saw that Germany had initiated a high interest rate policy while the U.K. was in recession, which caused what Soros described as "dynamic disequilibrium in the European Exchange Rate Mechanism." Political wrangling between Germany and the U.K., as well as the signing of the Maastricht Treaty and the realization that the U.K. was probably not going to be a participant, put pressure on sterling. That encouraged people to sell.

By selling the pound, Soros not only reaped an alleged $1 billion in trading profits, but played Pied Piper to other currency traders who follow a big reputation or swim in the wake of the big money. Soros defended their trading by saying that funds will bet against what they perceive to be irrational investment decisions or erratic capital flows, so they actually act to stabilize a market. That 1992 move arguably made Soros and his group one of the world's most famous currency speculators.

But with or without him, it is likely that the moves would have occurred anyway. Large multinational corporations also predicted the weakening of the pound and put through massive sterling sales in anticipation. They traded out. And there's nothing you can do to stop that, other than slapping on currency controls, which as we have seen aren't terribly helpful to an economy. Someone like Soros may spark moves, but currency traders in general look at the same things and move on them at the same time.

Private money can at times take more risks than the public's money. Private investment partnerships made up of wealthy investors, since they expect higher returns than they would get from mutual funds, recognize that they must be prepared to accept higher risk. Risk comes in many forms. In their currency trading, some private funds use options and other derivatives, even bank credit lines, to gear up or leverage their chances of making a greater return. They can control huge amounts during these temporary currency upheavals, and they do magnify the reaction of the currency up or down. However, the market is so big that their impact is just that, either temporary or ineffective.

It wasn't just the hedge funds that precipitated the pound dropping out and the resignation of the U.K. chancellor. It was currency traders and multinational corporations around the world and companies within the U.K. itself that sold the pound.

Currency traders began in 1992 to develop a perception that the deutschmark would be the strong currency. The Spanish peseta dropped 25 percent in value against the deutschmark, and the Italian lira plummeted. The Portuguese and French currencies dropped in value as well. The world's money fled those countries that appeared weak and ready to weaken further if they followed the dictates that would enable them to join the single currency.

France had been under pressure since then as its unemployment continued to rise. Only intervention by the Bundesbank and the Banque de France, and the French government's stern stance, as well as the perception that the governments of France and Germany would do anything to keep their currencies within a narrow range, kept the French franc from drifting lower.

Jacques Chirac once called currency speculation the "AIDS of our economies." He was relentless in talking up the franc and supporting the concept of European Monetary Union. Currency traders took the Paris-Bonn axis seriously for a while. But as unemployment hit 12.9 percent in France, and Chirac was faced with a new socialist counterweight to his policy making, perceptions changed. The currency did not suddenly change value, but for a time was voted down in comparison to the pound and the dollar by traders in the markets. When there is a loss of confidence in an economy and its leaders, or a feeling of uncertainty, traders pull out until they think the situation has passed or will improve.

IN 1994 THERE was a crisis of confidence in Mexico, when the government surprised the markets and devalued the peso, after having said it wouldn't. There was a lack of confidence in the newly elected president. There were predictions of an inflation rate rising to over 20 percent and that the economy would contract by at least 2 percent. There was a large trade deficit and peasant unrest. There were dunes of debt. Does this sound like a good place to put your money? No one wants to board a sinking ship.

Unwilling to forgive weak national finances, traders and investors pulled out of Mexico. As a result, Mexican share prices halved. Shares and other investments were converted to more secure currencies. There was a U.S. bailout to the tune of billions of dollars. Money fled to the perceived stability of the deutschmark.

There were social repercussions, but can it be bad for countries and companies to get their act together and perform in order to attract investor interest and keep it? Can you blame companies and people who are trying to preserve their capital for moving it out quickly? Traders and speculators are part of this process, but it extends far beyond them.

Then look at what was happening in Japan in 1995. Traders were bidding up the yen in a vote of confidence in the economy, considering that consumers would benefit from cheaper imports like food, oil, and paper, and that Japanese companies would cope by cutting costs at home and sending production outside of the country to Malaysia, Thailand, and China, whose currencies are valued at less than the yen. And Japanese export companies seemed to be getting away with raising prices.

Also in 1995, money bled out of Quebec over traders' worries and uncertainty about the province's possible move toward independence. And in the United States in 1996, the fact that progress was made toward a budget agreement was in some part due to fear of what currency traders would do to the U.S. dollar if Congress and the president didn't avoid a government default. The dollar fell sharply prior to each budget deadline. If they had put off an agreement any longer, the dollar would have dropped as traders and investors shifted money into countries where there was a promise of a better economic environment and more government accountability—frankly, where it would be a better investment.

Thailand was subject to a speculative attack on its currency in 1997. The International Monetary Fund (IMF), born out of the now defunct 1944 Bretton Woods agreement, patched together a $17.2 billion bailout loan to support it through the crisis after Thailand's central bank spent billions of its reserves trying to prop up the baht. This was the biggest bailout effort since the Mexican peso crisis in 1994. For more than a year, the IMF had urged Thai politicians and its central bank to allow the currency slowly to move lower. The high value of the baht made Thai exports expensive compared to its competition on the world market, especially in relation to lower-cost China. The country was running an increasingly large trade deficit, had gone through four finance ministers in fourteen months, and had a weak banking system and plunging property prices—not a recipe for success.

The reason given for Thai officials standing firm, despite the damage to the economy, was that its biggest companies that had borrowed abroad would have to earn more to pay off the higher costs of their debt. Despite an economy headed toward disaster, politicians and central bankers alike turned their heads away or declined to take measures that would have not only helped their country, but proved to the international financial community that the economy was in prudent hands and had a chance of improving.

When currency speculation escalates, some of the most harmful effects are within those countries where there is the largest discrepancy between the wealthy and the poor. As we saw with the LDC (lesser developed countries) debt crisis in the 1980s, and are witnessing again in Thailand and other Asian countries, the resulting austerity programs are painful for the poor and underprivileged.

And it is precisely these countries that so desperately need foreign investment, that need foreign money confidently moving into their stock and bond markets. They need to be part of the global economy and international financial community in order to grow and for wealth to be more widely dispersed. The cost of exclusion from the international credit and capital markets is diminished standards of living. The price to pay for inclusion in the global community is good government. Mismanaging a country's economy in a way that discourages capital flows into the country robs the poor and middle class of opportunity. Retaining investor interest is the key to progress. Rational economic and political leadership, lack of political corruption, transparency, and accountability encourage risk capital.

In Thailand's case, pressure from currency speculators forced the government to act. The argument is not that the traders had benevolent intentions or thought that they could help. Rather, it is that in the process of their trading, either for personal profit or to protect their clients' or firm's investments, they were agents of change. Traders provide liquidity and efficiently channel money through the system; without their participation or interest, liquidity dries up. Markets can't function without liquidity, and an economy can't function without markets.

The repercussions felt within the country were painful, but the economy would undoubtedly have worsened without the activity of traders bringing the problems to world attention. Since the Mexican episode in 1994, the IMF had stepped up its endeavors to ward off potential currency crises by monitoring weaker countries and issuing warnings and financial information to investors. There was ample warning in the case of Thailand. Even the Thai central bank made financial data on its situation available on the Internet and thus to the world's press. What was lacking was the will to act on the part of Thai leaders and politicians.

WHAT BEGAN AS distant thunder in Thailand during the summer arrived as a storm by the fall. Following the currency attack, the Thai crisis had spilled over into Indonesia and neighboring countries. Since July 1997 the Malaysian currency had been drifting lower. A surprise announcement that there were to be currency controls and curbs on the trading of shares made the markets even more suspicious when, following that announcement, government officials were unwilling to answer questions from the press. The markets, and especially foreign companies that had invested heavily in Malaysia, perceived all this as threatening at a time when the economy became unstable. Malaysians themselves began dumping their currency in a vote of no confidence.

It was especially difficult to regain investor confidence in the region because financial disclosure in these markets is not very good and they tend to be illiquid. As interest rates were raised to offset the currency crises, stock markets plunged in Malaysia, the Philippines, Thailand, and Hong Kong.

By October Indonesia agreed to an IMF bailout of $23 billion. Its banking system was heavily indebted to foreign banks, there was a threat of debt default, and President Suharto was attacked for running a corrupt government based on cronyism and favoritism.

By that same month Malaysia's ringgit had fallen by 30 percent. Malaysian prime minister, Dr. Mahathir, cemented his reputation for a rigid ideological bias against the West and an inclination toward limiting the freedom of the press. Known for having banned the film *Schindler's List* because he considered it "Jewish propaganda," he became increasingly verbose in ranting against Western liberal values and for Islamic causes. It was understandable that this would accelerate a lack of confidence in the minds of many Western investors.

His attacks in the media against currency traders became more aggressive. In a speech to the World Bank he suggested:

"Currency trading is unnecessary, unproductive, and immoral. It should be stopped. It should be made illegal. We don't need currency trading. We need to buy money only when we want to finance real trade."

As Mahathir jousted in public against the West and especially against George Soros, who he considered the culprit for beginning the attacks on his currency, investors backed away from the region in general. Stock markets in the U.S., England, and Europe began to falter in mid-October as the realization took hold that the situation in Asia appeared out of control, its leaders increasingly incomprehensible, and that the crisis could negatively impact Western economies.

On October 17 the Dow fell 143 points. On October 23 London was down 3 percent and Hong Kong was down 10 percent overnight. On October 27, the Dow plunged 554 points, or 7.18 percent. The next day it was up 337 points. As fund managers agonized over what to do next, traders were just trying to keep their heads in the most volatile trading conditions some of them had ever seen.

With every moon the crisis spread and deepened. By December South Korea joined the list of countries applying for an IMF handout—it asked for $60 billion. Even George Soros, though once called a "moron" by Mahathir, admitted that the Malaysian leader, in his opposition to currency speculation, "has a point":

"Financial markets are inherently unstable, and international financial markets even more so. International capital flows are notorious for their boom-bust pattern. . . . There is no such thing as equilibrium in financial markets. . . . The laissez-faire idea that markets should be left to their own devices remains very influential. I consider it a dangerous idea. The instability of financial markets can cause serious economic and social dislocations."

In December Soros called for the financial community to organize a new global authority to guarantee loans for a fee to international financial institutions.

On January 11 the Dow was down 222 points on Asian worries. The Footsie dropped 98.9 points. There was a risk of an Indonesian debt default. Asian stock markets plunged yet again. People were fighting for food in supermarkets in Indonesia. Critics were attacking the IMF for losing its grip, as one by one the Asian countries delayed IMF reforms. By February workers in Korea were rioting in the streets. Mahathir lashed out again, this time at "foreign Jews" for attacking the Malaysian currency. Singapore's Lee Juan Yew blamed "corrupt foreign lenders" for his country's problems. South Korea stepped up an anti-West, anti-IMF rhetoric as its political leaders sought a scapegoat. Media there labeled the IMF plan a U.S.-Japanese conspiracy.

What was going on?

There was disillusionment on both sides. For foreign investors and banks, things were not as they had seemed. Western banks and investors fell to the same misunderstanding they exhibited in Latin America in the 1980s and in Mexico in 1994. They forgot that local markets are not homogeneous around the world, despite the promise of globalization. International cultural differences make it difficult to assess investing in foreign markets. When it came to light that the much admired Asian tiger economies had a very different set of rules that underlie their economic activity, it was too late. What was normal business practice in Asia was viewed in the West as political corruption, lack of disclosure and transparency, pyramiding of excessive debt, lack of sufficient banking supervision, and more.

For example, Japan suffered a series of financial failures, including the collapse of Yamaichi, one of Japan's largest brokerages, as well as Sanyo Securities and several regional banks. What emerged was the story of a financial system where it was normal to conceal losses in offshore accounts and to pay racketeers protection money.

Western eyes were further opened as Asian leaders displayed reluctance to react to the crisis the way the West thought they should. They were as determined not to give up their sovereignty as European nations were eager to shed it. Sovereignty—the power to govern their country without external control—was a key factor in the countries that had taken an IMF bailout package and not followed IMF dictates, as they were instructed.

By the summer of 1998 the storm had grown to frightening proportions. Rather than heed the pleas of world leaders and his own populace to reform Indonesia's economy, President Suharto had steadfastly refused to meet IMF requirements and after violent student riots was overthrown. Indonesia's currency had lost 70% of its value from March 1997 to March 1998 as the world lost confidence. Mahathir in Malaysia faced rising opposition as anger surged over widespread job losses, high interest rates, and a stock market that had halved from a year and a half earlier.

Japan was in recession, while observers noted with frustration that the Japanese as well appeared to lack the political will to do something about their worsening situation. Losing faith and fearing the worst, currency traders and investors pulled out of the yen. As money fled Asia for safer havens, the yen dropped further and Asian currencies and stock markets tumbled.

Disillusionment in Asia was natural after years of unprecedented high rates of growth. The party was over. Failure of political will had brought them to this point, and an unwillingness to relinquish sovereignty was prolonging their crisis. A reduction in high unemployment and a change in corporate and political culture could take years.

Bailouts take a long time to work. In the interim, social upheaval, political turmoil, and currency and security market volatility may occur or intensify unless the inflexibility on both sides softens and new thinking is employed. Dropping bales of money onto economies that are in crisis, in return for their accepting what they perceive as punishing economic policies dictated by an external body, may be an outmoded prescription. If you believe in fairies, clap your hands. If you don't, hope for new solutions on both sides.

THE DEBATE BETWEEN Stanislas Yassukovich's view that currency traders keep wayward governments in line and Muriel Siebert's view that currency traders who trade for speculative purposes should be restricted by rules boils down to a free-market philosophy versus a belief in government regulation of the markets. Yassukovich worked in the markets, and firmly believes in leaving them free. Siebert was superintendent of banks for New York State and oversaw their international subsidiaries as well. She comes more from a regulatory ideology. It is a private-sector versus public-sector debate. Both schools of thought have their adherents.

Muriel is right in saying that the international currency markets are huge and central banks feel understandably helpless at times. Throwing money into the market to fight off currency speculators, often seriously depleting their reserves, can be futile. Major currency moves seem always to be blamed on currency speculators, who don't have the image of respectability that central banks do. On the other hand, currency traders are free-market players, like bank traders and treasurers of multinational corporations, who can exert a discipline on governments and the bureaucracies running them. Their free-market philosophy naturally extends to how they view the outside world and judge it. The result comes in two forms: countries are either penalized or rewarded.

Are we victims of their maneuverings in the markets for monetary gain? Or are we beneficiaries of their acting as intermediaries in a world that has escalating needs for free capital flows and exertion of disciplinary action on ineffective world leaders? I am of the mind that blaming currency traders and speculators is like treating the symptoms rather than what causes the illness.

Government policy and central bank monetary policy are what initially cause the economic conditions to which traders react when they buy or sell a country's currency, and when companies operating within that country buy or sell the currency. The lack of determination by governments in facing the problems in their economies is under the scrutiny of the financial community every day. Central banks, which formerly managed the monetary policy of a country by artificially controlling it, are not really able to do that anymore.

The free market actually exerts much more control than the central banks do. This seems logical when you think of the tens of thousands of currency traders able to buy and sell a currency versus one central bank trying to control their currency. Power at the central banks has drained away to market participants, similar to the way power is draining away from traditional exchanges to the end users. We're well into another frame of mind.

Officials at the central bank in the United States, the Federal Reserve, are not elected. So there is no public constituency to answer to. Pontification on which direction it thinks the economy is going, and on which direction it thinks it should be going, emanates from its headquarters in Washington. Its intention of guiding the economy and protecting the populace is a benevolent one, but the inevitable connection to politicians' wishes as well as to the banks that own shares in it causes you to pause and think.

The Federal Reserve in effect puts a speed limit on the U.S. economy. Historically, it hasn't always made prudent or popular decisions on that speed limit. And the veil of secrecy under which it operates has the same effect on currency traders as a matador would waving a red cloak in front of the eyes of a bull. Secrecy goes against the philosophical grain of the the trading community. The more secretive the central banks remain, the more traders of corporations and banks will sit as if on beds of nails.

The Bank of England was three centuries old by the time the Federal Reserve came into being in 1913. Like the Federal Reserve, the Bank of England tenders Treasury bills, sets interest rates, and goes into the foreign exchange market to buy and sell currencies to stabilize sterling. The Bank has an unelected committee to decide interest rate policy.

In 1999 the new European Central Bank will take control of monetary policy for all monetary union countries by setting a one-size-fits-all interest rate for them. In influencing economic conditions, central banks enjoy wide room for accountability to the public and to the economy which, after all, are the recipients of their policies. Currency traders are a crude counterweight to their power.

Other than harmful economic policy making, governments can cause problems by "talking up" or "talking down" their currency for political motives. In 1987 U.S. Treasury Secretary James Baker threatened to talk the dollar down again if Germany raised short-term interest rates. Investors dumped stocks after the threat, fearing that further devaluation of the dollar would frighten foreign investors, who would begin pulling their money out of the U.S. markets. A lower dollar would push inflation up and then cause higher interest rates, so this was dangerous talk. This one instance is believed by some to have triggered the 508-point crash in the Dow on October 19, 1987. Stock traders and currency traders reacted in the only way that made sense to protect their investments in the climate of political volleyball that was being played by politicians with their currencies.

The power of the market comes from the sheer weight and speed of the money. The amount of money in the currency markets is mind-boggling. And institutional currency traders tend to move like the wind through a wheat field, en masse and changing direction quickly, taking billions with them when they go. Big international banks and most big multinational corporations are major players.

Either government policy makers or currency traders are going to influence the price of money and the value of a currency. The business community, the layperson, and international investors are left to try to manage their economic lives within that framework. When exchange rates were relatively fixed and stable, it was somewhat easier to plan in the longer term, but there was no stopping bad economic policy, or competitive devaluations, or trade wars. In the end, the self-interest of nations overrode the best intentions to smooth out the workings of the international financial system. Centralized government planning of the value of currencies broke down, and as we may see with the European Monetary Union (EMU), could still having trouble working.

So companies are hedging, trading for profit, locating production facilities in other countries as well as their own, and employing financial engineers to manage interest rate and currency risk. Small companies are learning that to compete in the international marketplace, they have to be savvy about what is happening in the countries with which they do business. It means consulting with their banks and clients about future directions in the economies that affect them. They can then buy or sell currencies and options through foreign exchange brokers or banks.

The first line of defense against speculative currency attacks is to follow what is happening in the economy and the currency markets. Today an astute observer can protect assets and income by watching the markets, listening to commentary, and learning the warning signs. Laypeople and small companies are actually more empowered than ever before in being able to deal with volatility in interest rates and currencies, because information is available from television, newspapers, and the Internet. The information is there, usually well in advance of when it is needed.

Eric Sheinberg traded currencies and found that:

"The people that deal in foreign exchange today are not only the hedge funds, and they make up a huge amount. But you have a huge amount of multinational corporations that have treasury departments that are run as hedge funds. And whether it is Minnesota Mining or Ford Motor, you are talking about billions and billions of dollars that I think most people aren't aware exist.

"All major multinational corporations have treasury departments that are hedging or dealing in foreign exchange. And more so trading than hedging. If you add all these people up together, they are bigger than all the central banks in the world together. Foreign exchange is speculation. Either somebody believes the dollar is going up or the dollar is going down. But it is literally a twenty-four-hour casino, where it used to be an eight-hour casino."

It is a casino where prices of currencies are determined not by one political entity, but by the combined judgment of everybody out there to place a bet. In theory, it should work. In practice, people are finding their own solutions to the endless battle between the self-interest of politicians versus the ideal of international financial cooperation. In the meantime, while we wait for a harmonious world to live in, companies and individuals are dealing with what exists.

9 DERIVATIVES— THE GOOD, THE BAD, AND THE UGLY

Sitting in the darkness of his study, Sol scanned the glowing screen in front of him. He had bought 50 call options—the right to buy stocks at a fixed price—betting that they were headed higher.

Tonight he began to squirm. It was time to get out. He had made some money. Every gyration in the value of the stocks set his nerves on edge. No use pushing his luck. A few keystrokes to enter the sales in his E*Trade account and he was out.

INDIVIDUALS HAVE TAKEN to options, a form of derivative, in a big way. Charles Schwab reported a 55 percent increase in options trading in 1997. The attraction? Leverage. Because of the leverage available, the potential for substantial gain or substantial loss using a small stake of money can be tremendous.

Derivatives take patience to understand. If you are knowledgeable and understand the risk involved, they can enhance the value of your portfolio.

However, they pose an interesting paradox. While bestowing the flexibility of greatly augmenting profits, or protecting assets or income from exposure to interest rate and other financial risk, they can also cause mind-boggling losses in the wrong hands.

The surprising fact has come to light that there are corporate treasurers, pension fund managers, and managements of banks who really don't understand derivatives. Yet they have used them; or allowed, indeed encouraged, people within their organizations to use them. The ones who do understand them utilize them for two purposes: as insurance against uncertainty, or for speculation. In either case, they involve speculation. And if you've speculated badly, you're in trouble to the degree that you have loaded on leverage over the amount that is acceptable if you are on the losing side of the bet.

As ABSTRACTIONS, PROXIES, or substitutes, derivatives offer a multitude of benefits to people managing money.

They are, in the simplest of terms, financial products that *derive* their value from the price of an underlying security such as a bond, stock, commodity, or currency. When you buy a stock, you are buying a part of a company. When you buy a derivative, you are buying a contract whose value is related to the underlying asset. You don't own anything tangible, just a product that has an expiration date. For example, a stock option is a derivative that has value depending on the changing value of the underlying stock, giving you the right either to buy or to sell the stock when it reaches a certain price. *Futures* are derivatives. *Currency options* are derivatives. *Stock index futures* are derivatives. *Swaps* are derivatives. So are *floors, collars, swaptions, caps,* and *straddles.*

There are good and sensible reasons for using derivatives. Companies utilize them as insurance to protect themselves from risk and uncertainty. It may be to protect against the unpredictable: a rise in interest rates, a change in currency values, or a variety of other reasons. A change in exchange rates, for example, could affect General Motors, which is exporting cars and is in competition with car manufacturers around the world. GM could be forced to bring its price down to meet that of a car in another country.

General Motors may decide to enter into a foreign exchange contract to protect against the chance of a loss in earnings due to an unforeseen change in the exchange rate.

Or a change in interest rates could push General Motors' costs up because borrowing becomes more expensive. So it may use a derivative to lock in its interest rate expense on its borrowings so that it can properly budget and count on what its costs will be.

What General Motors is doing in these instances is risk management: it is studying the risks involved and how much of those risks it wants to accept or protect against. The key, when its treasurer is using derivatives, is whether he is making the right judgment about the size of the risk involved, since he could actually hurt the company if he made the wrong bet.

Multinational corporations, banks, and fund managers also actively speculate with derivatives. They make money by betting on the direction of a market, interest rates, currency, or a security. They're trading for profit. If they're good at it, they make a lot of money for their companies or funds. Again, it depends on judgment and acceptance of reasonable risk. When leverage of unreasonable proportion is used and the bet goes wrong, spectacular losses can result. Risky bets and wild, off-the-wall speculation with your own money are fine if you can accept the risk and afford the loss. When they concern other people's money—whether shareholders or clients or retirees—they are not.

FROM A HISTORICAL perspective, the impetus toward derivatives began with the genesis of financial futures and advances in technology. Fischer Black, a consultant at Arthur D. Little, and Myron Scholes, a young professor of finance at MIT's Sloan School of Management, published a paper in 1973 that proposed a way for people to value options with a mathematical equation. The model gave birth to a whole industry of products that people were able to value according to the risk involved.

The technological revolution was a springboard for the derivatives markets. Traders using computers could do intricate calculations, analyze financial risk, and dream up new complex products. Heather Pilley, a lawyer in London who works on derivatives, has seen through her experience that "derivatives provide a highly flexible tool for structuring financial products."

The impetus also came from economic need. Once upon a time there was less volatility. Then things changed. In the United States in 1972 the prime lending rate that banks charged companies was 5 percent; by the end of 1973 it had doubled to 10 percent. In 1974, after the lifting of wage and price controls and the oil crisis, prices surged. Interest rates rose again to fight inflation, and the 1974 credit crunch was upon us. Then from 1977 through 1981, companies were hit with long-term interest rates that doubled and a prime lending rate that tripled. The surge in prices sent the price of commodities up. Oil was the first. Layer on to that scenario the fact that when the Bretton Woods agreement that set fixed exchange rates broke down in 1973, companies were broadsided by volatile exchange rates. The unstable environment stimulated the need for companies to find a way to deal with the escalating risk to their earnings.

The other historical incentive came from world events. Leo Melamed offers this as one of the prime reasons that the use of derivatives became more and more important to businesses:

"Globalization had come upon us in the eighties. We were competing internationally, so everyone was looking for a financial advantage to protect their stake, protect their positions, hedge their exposures; and that was going to be true whether there were financial upheavals or not.

"Then you had the collapse of the Communist empire. You had three billion more people coming into the marketplace, 70 percent of the world, whereas it used to be 25 percent of the world. So suddenly competition got more competitive and the world really became much more globalized than in the eighties. Suddenly now, everywhere you looked almost, we were a free-market economy—competing for the capital, competing to build financial markets, competing for profits. Risk management became much more intense and much more competitive in the nineties than it was in the eighties as a result of this. And at the same time, capital flows were moving so easily that there were no limitations to it around the world."

The first successful derivatives market in currencies appeared in 1972 when the International Monetary Market in Chicago introduced futures contracts on the pound, Canadian dollar, deutschmark, yen, and Swiss franc. With currency futures you could agree to buy or sell currency at a fixed price at a future date. So a company could plan on being able to exchange a currency at a future date at a certain price, perhaps when the company received payment from abroad and wanted to change it into dollars.

Financial futures can be used to offset, or *hedge*, risk. They transfer risk from one company or person to another, from one who does not want it, to one who is willing to take it on in the hope of making a profit from it, or who has the opposite risk. Futures therefore reduce or eliminate risk for the risk averse. When a company or person is fully hedged, they won't profit, but neither will they lose anything. The companies or people who are willing to take the risk that they can make a profit are speculating, while the risk averse are managing risk or fully hedging. It's similar to the way insurance works. Lloyd's of London will insure a cargo ship on the chance that it will make it safely back into harbor. It is speculating that it will profit. The owner of the ship, who is risk averse, has insured, or fully hedged, himself against calamity.

Following the introduction of futures were currency swaps, which allowed a company that was holding, say, deutschmarks to swap them with a company that was holding dollars. Both desired the other's currency. Options on currencies were introduced so that you could, if you thought a particular currency was going to change in value, have the option of buying or selling it at a certain price. The Philadelphia Exchange began offering these in 1982, and commercial banks followed their lead.

Interest rate management derivatives came to life in the early 1980s. IBM and the World Bank were reputedly the first to negotiate an interest rate swap in 1981. Interest rate swaps allow two parties to exchange cash flows over a period of time. Motivation might arise from wanting to pay a fixed rate of interest rather than a floating rate. So you swap your floating rate amounts with someone who has fixed rate amounts. Your counter-party obviously prefers paying a floating rate. You pay amounts relating to each other's interest obligations, no payments relating to the principal. Banks such as J.P. Morgan, Merrill Lynch, Morgan Stanley, Swiss Bank, and Goldman now typically take the other side on their own books.

Carolyn Jackson, a member of the original swaps team at Chase, was in on the birth of the swaps market:

"Initially the market started in 1983, primarily focused on large currency swaps. The reason people were doing those was for market arbitrage purposes. Until the swap product came along, if you were a

U.S. company, you tended to borrow in the U.S. because you didn't want to go borrow in Switzerland and then have exposure to the Swiss franc.

"And that was the way the world worked. So if you were a Swiss company, you borrowed in Swiss francs in Switzerland. With swaps, what was interesting was, a U.S. company could borrow in Swiss francs and do a swap and change it back into dollars for the whole life of the transaction. And similarly, the Swiss company could borrow in the U.S. and change it back into Swiss francs. And because Swiss investors had never been able to hold U.S. company paper, they were able to get a much, much lower rate, by the time you borrowed in Swiss, and switched it back into the equivalent dollar rate. That was really making the markets twenty-four hours, truly global. But like with any arbitrage, that goes away over time. There are still those types of transactions done, but they are like a window of opportunity."

By the late 1980s banks started to step up their derivatives operations to supplement the income they were losing from regular banking business that nonbank institutions were luring away. Corporate clients bought the banks' derivatives to hedge currency and interest rate risk. They were turning out to be increasingly popular and profitable products. Right up until 1994, big banks like Citibank and Bankers Trust did a booming business, with Bankers Trust earning almost a third of its net income in 1993 from its lucrative derivatives operations. After the 1994-95 derivatives-related blowups that grabbed the world's headlines, the public suddenly became aware of derivatives.

NINETEEN NINETY-FOUR was a watershed year. U.S. interest rates suddenly swerved up. There were seven interest rate hikes in a twelve-month period. Derivatives-related disasters ensued at Metallgesellschaft, Askin, Procter & Gamble, Gibson Greetings, Harris Trust, Barings, and Glaxo Holdings, among others. The resulting debate was over whether derivatives were valuable tools or highly leveraged time bombs. Investors pulled away from using them in such numbers that some banks suffered big losses. J.P. Morgan's revenue from derivatives trading slumped 17 percent in 1994, Chase Manhattan's was down significantly, and Citibank's derivatives revenue dropped by 50 percent in the first nine months of the year. Bankers Trust, which had been one of the biggest players in the business, was hit with lawsuits and customer complaints, resulting in a big loss in market share. Wary customers eventually came back, but were buying more conservative variations than previously.

The immense leverage that can be available in the derivatives markets is problematic for market observers. When interest rates were low, leverage could be embedded into a derivative that could give you, through complex mathematical structures, a significantly greater return than was available from other instruments. The problems arise when people forget that interest rates can suddenly move up, and stay up.

Almost any bank or institution now has guidelines and internal restrictions that require their salespeople to make customers very aware of the leverage they are buying. Derivatives are available for those who want it, but they aren't the right product for everybody. Some derivatives have high leverage, some have medium leverage, some have very low leverage. Caveat emptor. It's imperative that customers make a knowledgeable and reasonable assessment of which notch up on the leverage pole they take. The sad fact is that even if customers are knowledgeable, they are not always reasonable. As Heather Pilley pointed out, "Even though derivatives have many beneficial uses, they, like other financial instruments, are capable of misuse."

In 1994 the $7.4 billion portfolio of Orange County, California, sustained losses of $1.7 billion, which caused the county to declare bankruptcy. It was a case of a money manager using bad judgment. Treasurer Robert Citron had leveraged the county's investment portfolio up to $20 billion on the bet that interest rates would not rise. They did. When the county recognized the tremendous losses Citron had tallied up, it fired him. Citron was sentenced to one year in jail and fined $100,000. He was also given five years' probation and ordered to serve 1,000 hours of community service.

In the ensuing melee, Citron blamed Merrill Lynch for selling him highly risky investments, and the county sued for $3 billion. Merrill Lynch claimed that it was being used as a scapegoat and that it had for years warned Citron he was taking on inordinate risk. Citron, called "imperialistic and dictatorial" by a former member of the county's retirement board, apparently had a reputation for thinking he knew better than the investment professionals he was using. He had bought securities with options and other derivatives attached that were related to different interest rates. He had taken on debt to leverage the portfolio.

Listen to one trader's explanation of what was in Citron's portfolio: "It includes inverse floaters with complex index amortizing structures as well as notes where coupon resets are inversely leveraged."

Up to 80 percent of the portfolio was inverse floaters, which reward you if interest rates drop and penalize you if interest rates rise. As early as 1994 the portfolio was 300 percent leveraged. Using inverse floaters to that degree to make a bet on interest rates, then leveraging that bet threefold, is insane.

In more cases than not, the fault lies with managers of funds, or corporate treasurers who either don't know what they are doing, or worse yet, are irresponsible with someone else's money. Carolyn Jackson analyzed the situation at Orange Country as follows:

"Citron understood what he was doing. I think he definitely understood. He was one of those people that, as long as interest rates remained at 3 percent, he was getting an 18 percent yield in a 3 percent environment. The most complex math you'd have to do is take 3 to the second power—you could figure out in an interest rate scenario how much money you would lose. It doesn't take a mathematical genius to do that.

"He wasn't supervised, and I am sure he never bothered to explain the leverage he was taking implicitly in his portfolio. Like with Nick Leeson, as long as they are making money, people don't question. When he was making tons of money when interest rates were low, people thought he was a genius. Unfortunately, coming from my background, when you see somebody getting a lot ahead, it's from a coin toss and you should get suspicious."

Leo Melamed's view on the so-called derivatives blowups is that regulation wouldn't have prevented them from happening:

"Those things were just bad speculation. And you don't regulate bad speculation. Someone who makes an error makes an error. Orange County was an error of judgment; so was Metallgesellschaft."

The problem with Metallgesellschaft in Germany was that it had offered its clients long-term fixed-price oil-supply contracts that it could not meet because it did not have enough oil. So it used leverage to hedge itself by buying short-term oil derivatives, thinking that oil prices were going to rise. Its expected profits from the derivatives would then offset losses from having to buy oil at higher prices to meet its undersupply need. Instead, its derivatives produced a loss when short-term prices fell. Metallgesellschaft lost $1.3 billion by making the wrong bet on the price of oil.

Gibson Greeting lost $20 million. In that case, the SEC ruled that Bankers Trust misled it about the value of the derivatives Gibson had bought. Bankers Trust discovered from listening to internal tapes that one of its derivatives salesmen had lied about the size of Gibson's losses. The bank hid those losses for two years, which resulted in Gibson's losing $20 million. Bankers Trust did not admit guilt, but ended up paying damages of $14 million to Gibson as well as $10 million to the government.

This had nothing to do with trading, but rather was due to a salesman who repeatedly lied. Another Bankers Trust salesman was quoted as saying that he "lured people into that total calm and then totally fucked them." The implications of employing salespeople like these? Humiliation, staff defections, client lawsuits. Bankers Trust hired a new chief financial officer. It stepped up training programs. Salespeople were indoctrinated to go out of their way in their explanations to clients. And Bankers Trust set aside $423 million for potential derivatives losses.

Procter & Gamble lost $157 million. One of the derivatives it used was a diff (differential) swap. Tailored over a five-year span, it would pay off depending on the difference between three-year German and U.S. interest rates. It thought that German interest rates would fall less and U.S. interest rates rise less than the yield curve for forward interest rates inferred. It was wrong. Not only did this reflect bad judgment, but it was later reported that Procter & Gamble's treasurer signed the swap contract without reading it, then didn't tell his boss when he discovered he was in trouble.

In the majority of the derivatives-related scandals, it was money managers, corporate treasurers, and bank managers who initiated the use of derivatives. And although traders were responsible for only a couple of the problems, as a result of the fallout from the 1994 debacles, derivatives traders in general suffered. Salaries and bonuses were cut, and jobs lost. Traders who had earned $1 million to $1.5 million in 1993 were earning $500,000 to $700,000 in 1995. After the slew of articles in the press, they found themselves the topic of unwanted attention. Jeffrey Larsen at Chemical Bank complained:

"I used to say, 'I'm in trading.' Now if I say derivatives and people give me a funny look, I tell them, 'By the way, if you have a home mortgage with a prepayment option, how do you think the bank deals with that uncertainty—derivatives!'"

Bad publicity caused trading volume to shrink on the exchanges as well as over the counter.

The positive legacy of the derivatives scandals was that they caused everyone to take a second look at their risk management and actually do something about it. Following the string of problems that arose, more attention was paid by the firms that sell them to control their operations and salespeople. And more attention was paid by the regulatory authorities, which worked together with the banks and securities firms to tighten up their sales and trading practices. A new mechanism for senior management was developed to monitor and control derivatives risk, called value-at-risk (VAR). Financial firms and banks are using this method to determine at the end of the day how much of the firm's money is at risk from derivatives. What it does in effect is tell you how much you could lose, by using averages of volatility attached to your currency, interest rate, and commodity exposures.

New SEC rules in the United States require companies in their financial statements and annual reports to disclose their derivatives exposure, which can be determined using value-at-risk calculations. Derivatives would be listed with their maturity dates and then the corresponding value depending on an increase or decrease in interest rates. And individual investors learned from reading the papers that, if they were concerned about their pension fund or mutual fund using derivatives, they could call or write and ask whether the fund uses derivatives and if it uses leverage. If it does and they are risk averse, they can switch to another fund.

So far, and for good reason, supervisory bodies have issued studies but have not called for regulation of the derivatives market. The Futures and Options Association in the U.K. issued a guide for companies and investors on the procedures to be followed and the questions that should be asked when using derivatives. Futures regulators from sixteen countries agreed in 1995 to cooperate and work on reforms in crisis management, supervision, and the exchange of information relating to derivatives. A report was also issued by the Group of 30, a think tank of bankers and public officials. And the general manager for the Bank for International Settlements, Andrew Crockett, weighed in against regulating the derivatives market itself, saying this was not needed, but claimed rather that firms should exercise internal supervision and controls. Consulting firms and software boutiques are making fortunes from crafting risk-management tools for financial firms selling derivatives. For the companies using them, this is a clear indication that no one wants to be caught in a financially difficult situation or a public relations mess again.

Furthermore, the transaction sizes have gotten smaller. Carolyn Jackson witnessed it happening in the swaps market:

"When companies were first doing the large currency swaps, if you are issuing debt in the market, you very rarely did something for less than $100 million, so that was an average size. Maybe $50 million. Whereas now I think the average transaction size is $22.5 million. People are doing transactions more at the margin. The volume of transactions is huge, but the size of the transaction has gotten smaller."

One of the founders of the derivatives markets sees the answer in using sound risk-management practices of the type issued by the G-30 Report and the Federal Reserve. Leo Melamed pointed out in 1994 that options in particular need thorough understanding, internal controls, and surveillance:

"There are yet unknown dangers created by a wide assortment of OTC financial options, and to an extent, even exchange-traded options. These range from simple standard options to a complex species of hybrid instruments that combine futures, swaps, and options.

"There is also an emerging genre of contingent options where payment is a function of multiple possibilities. Since these contingent options create risks that cannot be perfectly hedged, the resulting risks normally need to be managed through a process of dynamic hedging—an inexact science that can heighten price movements and produce unknown consequences."

That's for the users of derivatives. For the firms that market them or provide a counter-party service, greater internal control and education of derivatives salespeople are being called for. Officials from the Government Finance Officers Association, a group that petitioned for rules to be implemented to rein in sales practices, testified to the U.S. Congress that "many cautious finance officers believe they have been misled" by salespeople at the banks. They said that "derivatives are being aggressively marketed to governments, which are assured in many cases by the sales force that the products are safe, government-guaranteed, and will protect principal."

David Shaw observed:

"I don't think derivatives are bad, and I think that many of the efforts to stamp them out or restrict them in a very heavy-handed way is misguided. At the same time, I think it is important that people not take advantage of institutions that don't understand what is going on. The gray area perhaps is selling products that you know aren't really a good deal."

Salespeople are under pressure to get clients to ask for trades. If they don't, they lose their job. That means room must be made for educating salespeople about the additional requirement that they don't lie to clients, that they thoroughly understand the products they are selling, and that they inform the client of the risks.

BANKS AND BROKER/DEALERS sell the vast majority of derivatives in the over-the-counter market (OTC), a private marketplace that dwarfs the trading volume provided by commodities exchanges. The OTC market is absolutely huge. The International Swaps and Derivatives Association (ISDA) reported that as of June 30, 1997, outstanding contracts in over-the-counter derivatives stood at $28.7 trillion. In the first half of 1997, OTC derivative transactions grew by 46 percent from the previous six months.

There are marked differences between the two marketplaces—over-the-counter versus commodities exchanges—and distinct reasons for people choosing one or the other. The OTC market has no physicality. It is very comfortable with a computer screen and a telephone. Multimillion-dollar deals can be done in seconds. In the exchange marketplace, derivatives trading is done on the floor of the exchange, face-to-face in the commodity pits, and in smaller amounts. You can't even attempt to compare the over-the-counter market in terms of size or temperament to the market for derivatives on the commodities exchanges. They are two different animals, one free, the other caged.

Over the counter means private. It is a cash network that operates over the phone or on a screen rather than publicly and in the open on an exchange. Basically, you phone certain dealers and they take the other side for you. Over-the-counter derivatives are custom-tailored, nonstandard instruments used for risk management in relation to interest rates, currencies, commodities, and equities. They are not traded on exchanges. In the United States, the over-the-counter derivatives market is unregulated. In the U.K., they usually operate under a "code of conduct" enforced by the central bank. In the United States the regulated exchanges are visibly chafing under the restrictions they have as business drains away like a river to the sea.

The regulated market feels it cannot compete. OTC market players can come up with an idea for a product and offer a contract specifically crafted to meet a company's needs. If the exchanges come up with the same idea, they have to take the time to satisfy regulatory requirements and paperwork before they can offer the contract, so from their point of view, they are at a regulatory disadvantage. The struggle between the two markets for business has heated up, and both sides can become defensive when referring to the other.

When I discussed this with Carolyn Jackson, she agreed that it is harder for the exchanges to introduce a new product, but pointed out that the high volume is not in new products, but in plain and simple transactions. She also pointed out that the OTC market brings business to the exchanges:

"The Eurodollar part of the IMM ought to thank its lucky stars that swaps were developed. Because otherwise it would probably still just have those four little dinky contracts that nobody used. As swaps progressed, the Eurodollar volume picked up and new products had been introduced to provide hedges to the swappers.

"And it is not like, gee, if swaps never got invented, the Eurodollar business would have all this volume itself, because it has been my experience dealing with corporations that they don't want to deal with the mess, if you will, of Eurodollars, which are contracts that are daily, market to market; and they can't exactly tailor the cash flows."

There is a multitude of reasons for the over-the-counter market to be gaining ground. One, as discussed, there is no regulation. Securities firms in New York have stepped up internal controls and report voluntarily to the SEC, but there are fewer legal restrictions. Two, exchange derivatives are standard. They have a specific size and price and specific date in the future. Over the counter can custom tailor a derivative exactly to your needs. In at least one area, exchanges are fighting back, with flex options that allow for custom-tailored options on some big stocks.

The third reason is size. The over-the-counter market, for instance in currencies, can offer multimillion-dollar contracts. The Chicago Mercantile Exchange's average currency contract is $200,000. Four, for short-term trading, listed derivatives on exchanges are efficient, but for longer-term contracts that can be tailored out a significant time in the future, over the counter is more practical. Five, the exchanges have margin requirements. You have to put down money on the positions that you put out. (However, the London Metals Exchange does not require cash margins.) In OTC they don't necessarily do that. The banks and big brokerages will issue a line of credit, so there isn't an initial margin to put up. Instead there will be payment periods that are time related and product related.

Six, institutions with large transactions may for a variety of reasons want the anonymity that private over-the-counter dealing offers them, for example to avoid price impact on their transaction. If it was surmised by the traders on the public exchanges that a big order was going through or was about to happen, the price of the derivative would be bid up or bid down in anticipation of that, and the price on that big order would suffer.

Gary Lapayover explains the concerns the exchanges have:

"The OTC market has made major incursions into the futures industry and in fact has taken away a lot of the play of the financial futures markets out in Chicago. That's why their volume has dropped precipitously in the financial futures area, because OTC competition offers cheaper pricing, and no government reporting requirements. And that's why a lot of fellows on the exchange are getting really upset. A lot of our options traders are upset about the fact that we don't have enough strikes in our system, our margins are high, and our fee structure is high. They are losing a lot of their business that came into our options on energy.

"Also, the OTC is doing big blocks, so you don't have the price movement volatility that you do in futures. They'll give you just a monstrous size. They'll offer huge blocks with one price. Which appeals to managed money at pension funds and mutual funds, because it means it is much easier to distribute amongst a large number of investors that are in a fund. You have to offer equal apportionment of whatever price it is to all the customers within a fund."

Because derivatives can be custom tailored, they can be highly technical instruments to understand, value, and trade. Their value is extremely volatile. Mathematically adept traders have to have the analytical skills to grasp quickly the relationship of what they have and how it will act to the direction of the underlying asset. Valuing derivatives, which are constantly changing, is done by using models that are either bought as software packages or are ones traders develop themselves. Sun workstations make it possible for them to calculate at lightening speed.

Goldman Sachs has a team of quants working under Emanual Derman, a particle physicist and former research scientist at Bell Labs. Derman developed a model in 1990 called the Black-Derman-Toy that has become the standard for valuing interest rate options. To use the model as a tool, traders have to be quants themselves. They have to be able to judge how other variables in the marketplace will affect the value the model has produced. And they're not always trading or studying one at a time. Some derivatives traders have to manage an entire portfolio of them, in securities in different currencies.

The original architects of derivatives are still active in the business, people like Leo Melamed, who developed the currency futures contract on the Chicago Mercantile Exchange; Myron Scholes, who with Fischer Black developed the first options pricing model (Black-Scholes) and in 1997 shared the Nobel prize for economics for helping develop a way to value derivatives; and Alan Wheat, who constructed some of the first interest rate swaps. But the vast majority of traders in the markets are, on average, thirty years old. For them the business is more often than not referred to as risk management, and they as financial engineers. They can make millions if they are successful. In 1992, for example, it was estimated that almost 40 percent of Goldman Sachs's trading profits were related to the use of derivatives. Traders who can generate that kind of profit for a firm are rewarded well, and they are gaining ascendancy in trading rooms.

For a trader, predicting how volatile something will be is critical to making money. Their normal approach has long been to consider historical volatility. But the quants are now looking increasingly at recent volatility in relation to an underlying asset to predict the future. Perhaps that is reflective of the speed with which market cycles and market instruments are writing their own history. Cycles are being compressed from what had previously taken years, down to months, weeks, even days. Building recent volatility into their mathematical models may also allow them to recognize danger signals more quickly. Some quants are inputting volatility variables into neural networks—computer programs that can learn to predict volatility on their own from the original input.

Risk and the management of risk are at the heart of derivatives trading. The ability to take it on and slough it off between two parties is facilitated by the derivatives trader who enables the transaction to take place. A respect for risk and an understanding of it is part of any trader's job, but this is especially so for a derivatives trader. Risk escalates as money moves faster than ever before, and as the amount of leverage used becomes outsized in proportion to what you are willing to lose. Despite thorough analysis of all the factors determining risk, it doesn't change the fact that risk remains. You can diminish it or you can pyramid it. The only way to control it is to decide how much of it you can take: what is the predetermined monetary amount that is acceptable for you to lose or gain?

10 THE RISE OF THE BUY SIDE

Matt Newton took off his jacket, leaned forward, and began to work the phones with a professional air. He was receiving "first calls," which go to traders and fund managers to alert them ahead of the market opening what the brokerage will be recommending. Or if they will be changing a rating on a company their analysts cover. Calls also come in directly from the floor of the exchange to give an indication about the feel of the marketplace just minutes prior to the opening bell. He looked forward to these calls, because if a trader perceives something before the rest of the Street, he has an advantage.

He used them to absorb the information he would need. Already this morning he had programmed a $400 million portfolio into one of the computers that would automatically sell off pieces of it without his intervention throughout the day. He would still monitor it, and he could change parameters if he wanted. But it was relatively effortless.

He had been training on the desk under the head trader, answering the phones, running for coffee, watching every piece of information flowing in green lines in front of him on the bank of computer screens that sat two high and eight across on his desk. If he were asked almost anything, he would know the answer. If he didn't, he wouldn't last long. There were others in line. He was working at Scudder, Stevens & Clark, a mutual fund with over $100 billion under management. And he was in New York, the most competitive place in the world to work. And he knew he always, always had to be the best.

THIS IS PERHAPS one of the biggest, and historically most significant, stories of the 1990s—the rise of the buy-side trader and his use of leading-edge technology. The trading world is in the midst of a major transition. As this new group has ascended, they have promoted change and are directing the future of the markets.

Look at why. The growth in retirement funds and mutual funds in the United States has been astonishing. They began to grow in the 1940s and 1950s, but really got a boost when ERISA was passed in 1974, allowing people to open their own Individual Retirement Accounts (IRAs). Another jump came in 1978 when 401(k) employee retirement (company) plans were created. Since then mutual funds and pension funds have grown in popularity with the public. As of February 1998 the combined assets of the nation's mutual funds were $4.8 trillion. By comparison, in the U.K., unit trusts plus investment trusts totaled $380 billion.

Muriel Siebert explained why mutual funds have become the predominant investment vehicle for individuals:

"The public now realizes that Social Security is not a permanent retirement fund. It was for their grandparents and parents. The average family would have a paid-up house, and if they sold it they could buy a condominium in Florida or Arizona or California, in a warmer climate where expenses are much lower. And they probably had $50,000 or $60,000 left over from selling their house. They had Social Security, they probably had a small pension, and they lived well.

"For baby boomers today, Social Security is not going to pay for them. In the 1980s people were buying homes and upgrading them because they were going up at the rate of inflation. If the house went up 30 percent in two years, they would sell and take that equity. That's not happening today because real estate in some cases went down. The rate of inflation stopped. You have a different situation now. So they are putting the money right into mutual funds, and for many that is their first investment."

As we move further away from memories of the Depression, and then further away from memories of the 1987 crash, behavior has become more aggressive, short term, and more willing to take on risk. There has been a shift in attitude and preferences. There's no personal memory of financial loss and what it feels like. The present generation seems to have less fear than its predecessors, who exhibited conservatism and caution concerning their personal finances. Baby boomers and those younger prefer to take on credit card debt, buy on margin, and put money into the markets rather than into an insured savings account, which is risk free. Their willingness to incorporate *risk* into the word *saving* has driven the market for mutual funds.

Like the generation that saw technological breakthroughs with the advent of the jet and color TV, for baby boomers technology has caused perceptions and behavior to change dramatically as well. The short term has become the reality. The long term has been redefined as the short term. The change in the perception of time—its compression—permits them easily to accept great speed, volatility, and change as normal rather than as something to fear. The irony is that this generation is massively investing in mutual funds for their retirement, which implies that these are regarded as safe vehicles, while accepting at the same time the reality that the markets are ever more volatile and risky—indeed wild at times.

Industry experts from an older generation find this trend worrisome, and have expressed concern that so many of the people participating in the markets today are young enough that they have not seen a bad market, and their judgment, from a historical perspective, is frighteningly naive. They don't understand that they can lose a great deal. But I'm from that generation that shrugs its shoulders and accepts risk. Knowledge tells me that, while in the 1970s it took almost ten years for financial investments to regain their value, after the 1987 crash it took less. I can wait. I'm young enough. What is more to the point is that while accepting risk with equanimity, I also fully understand what I can afford to lose.

To give an idea of the acceleration of money into these investment vehicles, in 1940 there were fewer than eighty funds in the United States, with assets totaling $500 million. In 1960 assets totaled $17 billion. In 1980 they grew to $135 billion. As of February 1998 assets had grown to $4.8 trillion.

And think of the trading volume this is generating. Buy-side institutions account for the lion's share of trading volume. Fund managers are rotating in and out of stocks and bonds—not necessarily sitting on them.

With the power that the size of the money bestows on them comes rivalry. The number of funds operating in the United States is as dramatic as the amount of money they have under management. In 1987 there were just over 2,000 mutual funds for investors to choose from. Today there are over 7,500 mutual funds. That means the managed money fund environment is intensely competitive. It is heating up, inciting participants to advertise with glitzy television commercials and slick one-page ads in newspapers. An individual working for INSTINET in New York told me:

"The difference between the number one and the number two fund manager over a five-year performance period may be 30 basis points. It is sort of like Olympic swimmers. They shave their heads and bodies to get that extra hundredth of a second advantage over their competitor. It is the same thing in money management today."

Performance is measured on a monthly basis, or even more frequently, and that puts tremendous pressure on mutual fund managers to achieve better ratings than their competition over the very short term. How good their ratings are determines how much money they attract to their fund. As fund managers look under the rocks for ways to "shave their head," their focus has turned to more than just picking stocks better than the next fund. It has zeroed in on the trading function itself as a place where they can squeeze out extra performance points. It is up to the buy-side trader, therefore, not only to have a shorter time horizon because his manager does, but also to add value and contribute by controlling or cutting transaction costs.

He is the person responsible for shepherding these huge flows into the markets. The mutual or pension fund manager will decide what to buy; the trader will decide where, how, and to whom that money is directed.

HISTORICALLY, THERE HAVE been marked differences between the type of trader found on the buy side and those found on the sell side. The buy side gives orders to the sell side as members of an exchange, to transact for them. Because of the function of their end intentions, the two institutions attracted and needed two very different kinds of people for their trading desks.

Sell-side traders have been the ones we most like to imagine as the Masters of the Universe. Their job takes nerves and persistence and aggression. There's pressure to perform, which puts an edge on what they do. These traders have been considered the stars because they have been the ones who took on risk, at times staking their firm's money to take on board the buy side's huge blocks of stock. And they had to be very smart—especially the proprietary trader, who traded the firm's money rather than the clients', and who made the actual decisions himself on what and where to buy.

For the average sell-side trader who puts through the buy side's trades, below the typical surface bravado there is a complex blend of skills needed to do the job well. They walk a tightrope between their firm and their clients. They want to do the best for both; yet both have opposing goals which the trader has to meet. It requires toughness to negotiate and win a point; diplomacy and the ability to gather the support and respect of others in the firm.

The contributions of a lot of other people go into making a good sell-side trader. The traders rely on research analysts to feed them the best information, block desk traders to work with them, people to bounce ideas off of, and good contacts at the exchanges. The sell-side "proprietary" trader is the risk taker, the one who increasingly is under pressure to produce profits for the firm by trading the firm's own money. Sell-side traders as a whole are still the big earners. Their bonuses are for the most part tied to trading profits they generate, and if they are good, they can take home millions every year. So the image lingers of its being the sexy side of the business.

But buy-side traders are catching up. Their attitude and aptitude are completely different from those on the sell side. There isn't that constant striving that you have on the sell side. They are in control and are the key intermediaries in investment flows. As the growth in mutual funds and pension funds exploded to gargantuan proportions, buy-side traders began to gain an inordinate amount of power that previously had belonged to the sell side.

The only aspect that still does not reflect the power they have attained compared to the sell side is compensation. Although it is steadily increasing, for the majority it is well behind the sell side's.

The buy side represents individual retail investors around the world who have been putting into mutual funds the money they would normally put into savings. Traders have a fiduciary obligation to get the best execution and price for investors. For the firm they can add value if they are good at negotiating commissions, good at getting the first call from the sell side before the market opens, and before other traders get it. They have a direct tap into the stream of information in the markets, which can be fed back into the firm and used to change or create strategy. They are good if they can find the truth in the market chatter. The best utilize the latest technology to gain an edge.

Matt Newton's boss, Peter Jenkins, is managing director, head of global equity trading at Scudder, Stevens & Clark, as well as having another role in the industry as chairman of the Security Traders Association's Institutional Committee. Peter and Holly Stark, senior vice-president and buy-side trader at Dalton, Greiner, Hartman, Maher & Company, are leading the charge toward making the financial community sit up and take notice that the power has shifted to their side because of the explosive growth in investment funds. And they are leading the charge toward changing the rules that govern the industry. Both are politically involved and influential. They, along with Harold Bradley at Investors Research Corporation, regularly lobby the SEC, write position papers, and give speeches at conferences to raise consciousness of their side of the market and their needs. All this to change rules that have dominated an industry they think has been historically biased toward the sell side.

Buy-side traders today have so much money to put in and take out of the markets that they need deep pools to trade in. Whereas a decade ago their positions may have been in hundreds of thousands of shares, now they are in many millions of shares of one security. And this poses a problem in finding liquidity. There is lots of money, but not always enough liquidity. Does that make sense? It's because big institutions tend to make their decisions in the same direction. They all seem to want to buy IBM at the same time, but there aren't always enough sellers to accommodate them.

So every morning the buy-side trader sits down and tries to put together the puzzle. They have to decide where they are going to buy and sell their securities. Once long ago they only had a central marketplace like the New York Stock Exchange to go to. Then NASDAQ came along as a marketplace for smaller companies, so there were two marketplaces to go to. And then there were three, when firms that were not members of the stock exchange began buying and selling securities. So the trader could go to this "third market" to trade.

The big brokerage houses provide an "upstairs" function, where they put through huge block trades for the buy side. Goldman Sachs, Morgan Stanley, Salomon Brothers—they all began to put up their own capital to provide immediate buys or sells for the buy side and liquidity for the market.

Buy-side traders will go anywhere there is a deep enough market and good price at the time they want to trade. They want liquidity above all. They want to access it quickly and to be able to transact with it quickly. If the liquidity is in INSTINET, they will trade there. If it is in POSIT, they will put their orders through POSIT. If the liquidity is on the floor of the exchange, they will use that. If they need the help of a broker to place a block of stock, they will do that. And the choices are growing.

In one way this is a good thing, but in another way it makes their job harder—they have to decide which avenue to take, and must continually monitor them all. Market fragmentation can complicate things. When trading systems like POSIT and INSTINET and Bloomberg came along, they were accessible and viewable on a trader's computer. He could be trading through a broker on the New York Stock Exchange and notice that INSTINET or the third market was offering a better price. He could cancel his order to the broker transacting on the exchange and switch it over to the third market. The telephone is very important. Traders have banks of them, and each line is another possible source of liquidity. So not only are their choices growing, but the markets are speeding up and becoming more changeable from minute to minute, forcing traders constantly to scan and be ready to hit the bid or offer when they see an opportunity.

There are different ways to go about it, depending on what trading strategy you use. Your way of trading may be very different from mine. If I wanted to use technology, I could go to ITG in New York and have their quants help me work up a program and system to trade automatically according to the parameters I give them for a portfolio. In the simplest of terms, the program would have to know if it is a buy or a sell, how and when I want to trade. It can be programmed to know when I want to back off a bit, and will do it automatically for me. The program will do this for 100 stocks or 1,500 stocks at the same time, on Unix workstations that are very fast and do all the calculations, take in all the information, assimilate it, get it into order form, compile the orders, and send them to the floor. The program can be set up so that it won't buy, for instance, if there is too much stock on offer for sale, and will back off an eighth. It will know that if supply dries up, it has to get aggressive.

If you are trading manually, on the other hand, and want to buy 300,000 shares, you can call up a good broker who knows how to handle the crowd on the floor. If the broker sees a lot of sellers coming into the crowd, he will back away and let the stock fade or drop in price before he steps in to buy.

If you are a big fund trader with a hundred-million-dollar list of securities to buy and a hundred-million-dollar list of securities to sell at the same time, you are almost forced to use electronic systems. It's not humanly possible to watch every single stock. You can opt to send orders electronically to the New York Stock Exchange through the SuperDot system of the exchange, or use other electronic systems.

With the avalanche of money falling onto their desks, buy-side traders have been pushed to find innovative ways to maneuver. Some have moved toward "basket trading," a kind of program trading. This means that they will have a long list of stocks to buy and a long list of stocks to sell, and they will do both simultaneously. Each side of the trade could be worth hundreds of millions of dollars. The reason they use this technique could be that portfolios have to be sold quickly to raise cash to pay for redemptions, or new money has come in that has to be put to work, or they are just rebalancing a portfolio. In the interest of speed, they get the money in the market faster to make it work for them, or they get it out faster because clients want to have the cash. Without technology to help traders analyze the risk, liquidity, and volatility characteristics of the stocks in the basket, basket trading wouldn't have evolved.

Peter and Holly and Harold are strong adherents of electronic trading systems where two institutions can trade with each other directly and pay a commission for the service, because this shields their identity. They buy or sell sizable blocks of stock, and if a broker knows it is their firm doing the transaction, the broker may buy ahead of them because he knows a big order will drive the price up. That hurts not only the traders' performances, but ultimately the retail investors who have invested his money with them. Information leaked or surmised by brokers is a worry. Without anonymity for these huge trades, they feel that they lose the chance for the best price they can get. In a survey by the Institutional Committee of the Security Traders' Association in 1996, 78 percent of the buy-side traders polled responded that they use electronic networks such as INSTINET and Posit regularly. Peter explained to me:

"Technology has given the buy side the ability to get closer to the point of sale. Through my INSTINET computer screen, and with Bloomberg creating their own system, I'm able to go in and put a bid or offer in, and that can be exposed to hundreds of players, or thousands of players, that have the INSTINET screen sitting on their desk. I have immediate access and can go right to the point of sale. It is a very powerful tool for the buy-side trader. My broker would be INSTINET, which is a computer, but I use my own strategy and I don't have some broker telling me what to do. Also, the New York Stock Exchange has made it easy to enter orders electronically to the specialist booth. So the floor of the exchange has come a long way toward making it easier to route orders to them. And that has helped the buy side."

Because huge waves of money from the buy side flood in and out, the markets can move up or down quickly. It's one more ever-changing variable that traders keep a close eye on and have to factor in to their trading strategy. As an indication, in January 1997 small investors put $24 billion into mutual funds during the month, double the figure for December 1996. All boats rise with the tide. At high tide not only will prices move up from that increased buy-side inflow, but actual trading activity can be anticipated to grow in volume.

Traders also track the movements of well-known players in the market. They can pick up unusual volume or trading behavior from watching their computer screens. If one institution picks up a pattern of another institution buying or selling a block of stock, it follows—or in some cases stands back. For example, in a market where "momentum" investors or traders are prominently moving certain stocks and creating unusual volatility, a trader can go to his computer to investigate. Not only can he access volume, price, and historical data instantaneously on the stock in question, but he can then immediately pull up the most recent SEC filings on the ownership of that stock.

By scanning down the list of owners, he can quickly deduce if they are the momentum players, which tells him that he should watch the stock carefully. He's almost forced at this point to "go with the flow"—follow what they are doing—or to go to the other extreme and sit and wait until they have taken the stock all the way in one direction or the other. This can be disastrous for him if he owns the stock and the direction is down.

Once momentum players hit a stock and decide it is time to sell it, they all pile out at once. A $50 dollar stock can drop to $7 in a day. Does the mutual fund trader buy it then because it looks cheap? Maybe not. That stock could drop to $3 the following day and halve the value of his position. When momentum players are in the market and feeding on a particular stock, nonmomentum institutions can behave like a rabbit caught in the headlights, holding back for fear of what might happen. On the other hand, if they study the patterns of how these people tend to move, and try to second-guess their trading behavior, they can decide to ride in their tailwind rather than get run over by them.

Because technology and the size of the money tipped the balance of power to the buy side, it doesn't always call for using the sell-side trader anymore. Holly told me that she only uses the sell side if she has to:

"We don't need them as much as they like to think we do. The sell side has made the argument that they are there to provide principal, to facilitate trades by using their capital. Given the size of institutional positions today, a broker is not going to have enough capital to be the other side of your trade.

"So you want the broker to act as your agent and find the natural other side. They are not necessarily good at that because sometimes it takes more work than they want to do. And sometimes the information about your trade is given to the wrong people and the price is negatively impacted. So if you can go out and find the other side of the trade yourself, that's the ideal trade. You're trying to do that anonymously, be it through INSTINET or whatever."

Is it true that the sell-side trader's star is fading? Bob Schwartz, professor of finance at NYU, thinks so:

"The buy side is the big winner. The sell side, and the extent that the sell side doesn't win, that's what happens with technology. You can't feel sorry for the guys who produced buggy whips and horse carts and the like and say, well, how do you make them happy in an era where we are all moving toward automobiles?"

The problem is that, as the mutual funds have grown and the blocks of stocks have grown, the money needed by the brokerages to temporarily buy those blocks has become huge. The Gus Levys and Jay Perrys of the past would probably be shocked at the size of the positions their firms are carrying in the market today. Peter Jenkins commented:

"The flow of merchandise has gone from the sell side, who dominated that because of their capital. You know, they used their capital to facilitate trades for the buy side. Now if I have 3.5 million shares to buy or sell, I am going to make the call where that stock is going to trade, and who I am going to trade with. So that is now the power we have. Brokers don't have the huge capital to put up to get big trades done now."

And when they do buy a block, it can be a large position and risk to have on their books.

But something else gave the buy side muscle. May Day 1975 was a red circle day for buy-side equity traders. The rules changed, and fixed commissions were abolished, drifting down from 40 cents a share to 15 cents. Today they are around 5 cents a share. From May Day on, the buy side used its power to squeeze the rates it was charged, bringing the sell side's margins and revenues crashing down. The buy-side focus on reducing trading costs was one way to have better performance in a world where information had become instantly available to everyone. Transparency—no shadows, no secret information—meant that any information advantage that one trader previously had over the other had dissipated. So they had to look elsewhere to improve performance.

For the sell side it was a body blow. With guaranteed commissions gone, trading took on new meaning and was actively accelerated to make up for lost revenues. Chris Andersen pointed out that, where there were twenty-three sub-major investment banks in 1972, over the following four years, twenty of them ceased to exist.

"It was as if somebody threw a grenade in a box. A lot of those were partnerships. It all happened like that, in three years. What happened was that those people had been protected from economics by the fixed rate commission, and they had forgotten what their value added was."

Although their role has changed, the sell side still thinks the buy side needs them. Eric Sheinberg responded to Holly's comments:

"The reason they need the sell side is because all of a sudden, if Goldman Sachs files a deal for Ralph Lauren, a portfolio manager will walk in to his trader and say, I want that stock and I want 200,000 shares. That's why they need us, because where are they going to get it? And that's why the new issue area is so important, such an integral part of the business.

"And as far as using INSTINET, it doesn't work all the time. INSTINET only works if there is somebody on the other side. If there is no one on the other side, forget it, you could wait forever. You can't make somebody in INSTINET do something they don't want to do."

Because you can't always find a match in buyers and sellers, you need somebody to take the position in the middle, which is the sell side. Linda Strumpf, chief investment officer at the Ford Foundation, weighed in with her vote for the sell side:

"In our case, I am sure we get excellent execution from them. But we also want to hav e a relationship with the Street so we have access to the analysts. We are not that big in the scheme of things, so in order to get the attention, we have to treat them well, so they treat us well."

IN LONDON, BUY-SIDE traders are becoming more aggressive and are taking on a noticeably higher profile. There are major differences between the United States and London, in large part due to the fact that London is a small place and New York is a big place with thousands and thousands of funds, extreme competition, and oceans of money. To put size in perspective, take the example of just one U.S. firm: Merrill Lynch. It employs 38,000 people in the private client area alone, including salespeople and all the support staff. That's more than the whole industry in London. The private client side of Merrill has over $750 billion in assets under management. That's about double the reserves of the Bank of England.

Despite the difference in magnitude and money under management, the buy side in London is undergoing a mirror image of the changes the buy side in the United States went through. Alan Line, head of dealing at Foreign and Colonial in London, was previously a sell-side trader who switched to the buy side:

"I worked for a broker for six years where you were paid for results. At the time I switched to the buy side, many of the dealers were to a large extent just order clerks. That has changed a lot, and the cachet of the buy-side trader is getting higher and higher. Salaries are improving and our status within our own organizations is improving, as evidenced by many of us being directors of our companies."

Alan thinks that the evolution of the buy-side trader in London was generated from the U.S. way of dealing, which he thinks is driven by consultants convincing firms that trading evaluation systems should be put in place to analyze their traders' performance. That way firms can compare how they are doing against their peer group. And that naturally adds pressure, which has caused the change from a functional role to an added-value role.

Alan has worked to add value to the industry as well. In March 1994 he formed the Institutional Dealers Group, which held discussions with regulators and the exchanges in an effort to make their views heard when there were changes that were going to be brought about in the London market. He is also chairman of the International FIX (Financial Information Exchange) committee in London, which concerns an information protocol, and is involved in speaking at industry forums to discuss electronic and computerized trading.

He believes, like his U.S. counterparts, that electronic technology is going to drive the industry in London:

"We are having a change in our system on the equity side, bringing in the Stock Exchange Electronic Trading Service (SETS), which is the order-driven system. This Big Bang is going to have a much more fundamental change to the way the market operates than the previous Big Bang in 1986. The more people that are involved in a trade, the more expensive it is. As an end user, you need to get to another end user as quickly as possible, thus making the trade as cheap as possible. Electronic trading can provide this disintermediation by allowing you to enter bids and offers, normally within the quote, to seek out natural liquidity. This also allows you to trade without market impact. Whilst it will not always be the answer, I am sure it will become an ever-increasing part of what we do.

"There will be brighter people in the business, that are much more computer literate, that are much more able to assess risk in a structured and quantitative way. People have to understand the mentality change of the buy-side traders in London, the way they are going to change their trading. Because if they are basing the way the market is going to be on the way that things happen now, they are completely wrong."

11 BLACK SHEEP

What happens when a trader blows up?

In February 1995 the directors of the Bank of England were presented with a situation they had dared hope would never happen, the imminent likelihood of Baring Brothers going under.

Governor Eddie George, head of the Bank of England as well as a friend of Barings' chairman Peter Baring, was concerned about "moral hazard." He knew that if he lost sight of the cold facts and supported Barings, he would be signaling to the City banks that they could behave as they wished and the Bank would clean up the mess for them. It would be like pumping water out of the boat as fast as it was sinking. On the other hand, he worried that if he did not succeed in raising the money needed to bail out Barings, there was a chance of systemic damage to the international financial markets.

It was hard for George to face the prospect that such a prestigious institution could go under. Barings, the oldest merchant bank in London, had survived longer than many of the companies and governments to which it had lent. It had survived world wars, the Blitz, and numerous financial crises.

Now its light could be extinguished by the actions of one trader. Letting Barings fail without attempting to provide a safety net was similar to tearing down a historic castle to make way for a modern skyscraper; just as modernity defines us, so by definition does history. The unique place that Barings held in the history of the City of London deserved thoughtful consideration.

Its illustrious past was filled with intrigue and power broking. Along the way the Baring family earned itself five separate aristocratic peerages. In the past one hundred years, various family members had served as the governor of the Bank of England and several had been on its board of directors. Diana, Princess of Wales, had a Baring in her bloodline.

Barings had bankrolled President Jefferson's Louisiana Purchase from France in 1803, which effectively doubled the size of the United States; ironically, the $15 million that France made in the deal would finance Napoleon in his war against England. Barings had financed trade around the world, running its own ships in the China tea trade, lending money to Portugal, France, Russia, India, Iraq, Egypt, Belgium, and other countries. Not only was it a king-maker, it had more resources at times than kings or the Bank of England itself.

Newspaper headlines told the story:

"Busted! A 28-year-old loses a billion dollars and takes down the investment firm that financed the Louisiana Purchase."

"£400 million crash hits Barings. Bank of England called in to avert world market panic."

"Barings bank goes bust. Mayhem feared in markets."

"£500 million cheat busts Queen's bank."

The Bank of England held emergency meetings over the weekend after it learned of Neeson's activities, as well as a final meeting in Peter Baring's office that Sunday night, all of which failed to find an individual, bank, or group of investors to put up the money needed to save Barings from bankruptcy. The news wires were rapidly transmitting in neon dot-words from left to right across digital screens that a 28-year-old "rogue" trader in Singapore had placed a spectacular bet and lost, wiping out more than the entire capital of the bank. Vultures were already circling over the oldest merchant bank in England. The news was like a bolt from the blue not only for the four thousand employees of Barings all over the world, not only for Queen Elizabeth, Prince Charles, sultans, and other royal clients, but also for the Baring family, whose identities were so entwined with that of the bank. For the employees of the bank, there was nothing but shock: heads were bowed, hands shielded eyes. Some just sank to the floor and sat staring, unbelieving.

Originally Nick Leeson's job had simply been that of an order taker. He would take calls on the floor of the Singapore International Monetary Exchange (SIMEX) and make sure the Barings' trader got the information on the orders to buy and sell futures and options for Barings' clients.

But then he started to trade. Normally, Barings Futures Singapore was meant to arbitrage between two markets—the one in Osaka, Japan, and the one in Singapore—and find small price discrepancies between the two for a profit. The group would make money from the commissions on those transactions. Evolving from what Barings allegedly thought was a relatively risk-free platform, Leeson began to take bullish positions on the future direction of the Japanese market. Through this unauthorized trading he accumulated a long position in futures on the Nikkei 225 Index without hedging to protect his position. While seemingly generating profits, in reality he was concealing losses in an error account. He was able to get away with this because he was responsible for the back office accounting of trades as well as the trading floor operation. This is not normal practice in the industry.

His trading losses mounted. By the end of 1993 the error account had a loss of £23 million, by the end of 1994 a loss of £208 million, and by the end of February 1995 a loss of £827 million. He sold options and credited the money to the account to offset the losses, in effect balancing the account. But Barings was now exposed to even greater risk, because of the options, which, along with the futures, were dependent on the Nikkei not dropping below the 18,500 level.

On January 17, 1995 there was an earthquake in Kobe, Japan. In response to the devastation and economic uncertainty, the markets became volatile. Guessing that they would bounce back, Leeson bought more futures contracts. On January 23 the Nikkei fell 1,000 points to the 17,800 level. Instead of pulling out then and taking his losses, Leeson doubled his bets. He bid desperately against the market, believing he could hold it up. By February 23 he held over 60,000 futures contracts. In his book, *Rogue Trader*, he recounts that on that day, "I'd bought everything the market had to offer." By the end of the day, he had almost 50 percent of the open interest on one futures contract and 24 percent of another. That night he left the trading floor, never to return. His losses were so great that they brought the bank down: by February 26 Barings was officially bankrupt with total losses of £927 million.

Where were the auditors, both internal and external? And how good were they anyway? When they had questioned him in January 1995 he had whipped up a fake letter from a supposed client to justify a deficit in his account. In February he had forged other letters and signatures, and the auditors accepted them as proof, despite the fact that they had a "From Nick and Lisa" fax identification at the top.

For Leeson, his adventure in Singapore at first had been a dream. A poor boy with the wrong accent and few credentials, he had made the most of his life, and at twenty-eight was reaping an abundant financial harvest for himself and Barings, far away from Watford where he grew up.

Barings hired Leeson in 1989 as a back-office clerk for settlements. By 1992 he had been transferred to Singapore. In 1993 his group accounted for 20 percent of the firm's overall profits, and Leeson earned a $200,000 bonus. And in 1994 he made a reported $30 million in profit for Barings and was supposed to receive a bonus of $720,000. The frontier mentality of the SIMEX provided a unique environment for Leeson to grow in, allowing for his spectacular rise. Cowboys roam territory ordinary people would find overwhelming.

In a euphoric market atmosphere where trading volume on the SIMEX was booming, local traders watched Leeson because they saw he could move markets. Someone at Barings should have had bells ringing in their ears, especially since management kept sending him money to meet his mounting margin calls. As Leeson quickly amassed his futures contracts, other banks in the Asian markets began to pay attention, and the rumor mill began. On February 17 Morgan Stanley and Goldman Sachs warned in their morning wires that there was possible counter-party risk in using Barings. The rumors in Asia were finally out in the open.

At his trial, Leeson pleaded guilty to two offenses of deceiving the auditors at Barings and to cheating the SIMEX. He was given a six-and-a-half-year prison sentence, which he is serving in Singapore.

In Leeson's autobiography, he casts about endlessly for someone to blame other than himself, although he admits, "I was a fraud and a cheat." He was street smart, there's no doubt about that. He was thrown into a situation ripe with opportunity and he made it for himself. The problem was the way he made it happen. He worked hard. Leeson started on the trading floor at six A.M. and left at seven P.M. It's simply that his values were not those of the rest of the trading world.

He was doing unauthorized proprietary trading, allegedly without using pricing models or hedging, incurring big losses, and concealing them in an error account. The losses he racked up were big enough to cause Barings' collapse.

Once the horrific news was out, international magazines and newspapers fastened on the fact of his young age and of his making a lot of money—their conclusion being that greed was a crucial element. All of this misses the point. Twenty-eight isn't young in the trading world, and a lot of people make a lot of money trading in the markets without resorting to illegal activity. The point is that Leeson saw nothing wrong in making up his own rules as he went along. If they were illegal, he found ways to justify his actions in his own mind. He wrote:

"Lies and lies: I was building up a towering pile of lies and if one of them was found out, they'd tumble all over me."

And this was in an industry that is strangely vulnerable to people like him because it has always been conducted on the basis of trust. It was this bond of trust that built financial empires and reputations, and it was the betrayal of that trust that brought them down.

All the warning signs had apparently been ignored by management. Leeson's daily requests to London for money for the collateral that SIMEX demanded at the end of each trading day were large and were adding up. It was known in London that Leeson had made at least one trade four times over his authorized limit. He had a trading limit of 200 Nikkei futures, but he went way over that. The fact that he did it once should have told his bosses that he'd do it again.

Anytime a trader repeatedly reports extraordinarily large profits, a red flag should go up. Someone should be watching him, because those kinds of profits mean those kinds of risks. Leeson was treated as an expert by staff at Barings. There are many calls on record where his supervisors accepted his explanations of the markets and why he was putting off cutting his positions, and they trusted him.

It was a peculiar breakdown of management control. His position should never have been allowed to grow to that size. If someone had closed him down at a £40 or £50 million loss, it would have been easily absorbed by Barings. Betting the bank against the market was an act of insanity. And the whole marketplace knew what his position was, so as soon as Leeson sent his traders back into the pit, everyone else in the pit knew that they were buying, and they'd mark their prices accordingly. Once the market knows your position and what you want to do, it becomes very expensive to trade.

Another disturbing aspect is the possibility that Leeson wasn't properly supervised because people working at Barings in London received bonuses dependent on the earnings of his unit, and as long as he was turning in supposed profits they left him alone. When managers have a piece of the trader's action, their willingness to sit on that trader is often compromised.

Stanislas Yassukovich has a philosophy about traders who are too successful:

"I remember an old partner of mine from White Weld, called Harold Mendelson, who had told me very early on, the secret to managing traders is basically very simple. The more successful a trader is, the more you watch him. When he's really successful you fire him. And I always remembered that. In fact, what people have done is exactly the opposite. When traders have been apparently successful, the less watched they are. The more a trader has been able to say to his manager, leave me alone, if you interfere with what I am doing, you will actually reduce my profitability, the more trouble you get in.

"And the Barings thing . . . the fault was entirely with management. To send that young man, particularly because he already had a question mark against his name—his SFA application had been turned down—to send him to Singapore, he had never been abroad before. He was a complete innocent. To send him out to a distant marketplace, without any look or mentoring or supervision, was a piece of criminal mismanagement of people. I mean, it was a fundamental management error."

Leo Melamed has thought about the situation as well, and offered his opinion:

"Barings is the best example I know of lack of internal controls, that begot what it begot. You can't have managers so incognizant of today's dangers that they cannot guard themselves from their traders, and they must be conscious of it. Both Barings as well as Sumitomo and Daiwa proved to the greater part of the financial community that you must have internal controls sufficient to protect the management and the company from any given trader's wiles."

Eric Sheinberg had another take on Leeson:

"In the United States, it would be very hard to have a Leeson take a firm down. Not to say that we haven't had our problems going back, where you had Jett at Kidder Peabody, but $300 million wasn't going to take a firm down. I think the real problem is that the business changed so much. What Leeson was doing, probably most of the people at Barings didn't have a clue what a 'future' was. As long as his numbers looked all right, nobody asked questions. Why it took them so long to ask questions, I don't know."

Carolyn Jackson said that the Leeson incident was one of the main reasons she felt an urgency to leave the derivatives industry and work at the International Swaps and Derivatives Association:

"I had been in the market for thirteen years and all the press had come out following Nick Leeson. First of all, it was just one market, but the press wanted to sweep everything in. I really thought it was time to give back to the industry so much of what it had given me. I wanted to work on the campaign to try to keep the regulators understanding how valuable the markets are, what a good function they serve, and that increased regulation would not benefit anyone."

As NICK LEESON'S face stared out eerily from the cover of *Time* magazine, the public read about two other traders as well: Toshihide Iguchi and Yasuo Hamanaka. We heard about their backgrounds and their lifestyles and how they hid their trades from management.

Yasuo Hamanaka, "Mr. Five Percent," allegedly engaged in unauthorized trading in the copper market, which produced over $2.6 billion of losses for his firm, Sumitomo Corporation. Hedge funds in the United States had studied the market and determined that Hamanaka would be vulnerable to what they perceived as an oversupply of copper in the world. So they began selling heavily, effectively flushing out Hamanaka, causing losses on his positions. His losses were probably the biggest ever attributed to one trader.

Hamanaka was one of the world's largest and most powerful

copper traders. Being big gave him credibility. His huge trades were no secret. That's how he acquired his nickname, which he'd had for years, because it was calculated that he had 5 percent of the global copper market. And it was later reported that Sumitomo owned or had control of almost 70 percent of the copper stored in a warehouse in California owned by the London Metals Exchange (LME). With that amount of copper Hamanaka was apparently able to influence copper trading prices to artificially high levels.

The president of Sumitomo revealed that, although the company's reported copper trading for 1995 was $9.4 billion, in fact a separate and secret set of books was kept by Hamanaka showing a tally of $20 billion in copper trading annually. It was alleged that for ten years he had maintained a separate trading operation, having correspondence related to his unauthorized trading delivered to him rather than to the company's accounting department; and that he had also maintained secret bank accounts.

His logic apparently included selling copper below his cost to facilitate customers and secure their business in the future. He'd trade derivatives to try to make up the money he lost, keeping track of the losses in separate books. A hint of something odd had previously come from a trader in Vermont. David Threlkeld emerged on the scene as early as 1991 with a letter addressed to him from Hamanaka asking him to write confirming $500 million of false trades. He claims he alerted the LME to the letter, but no action was taken.

The U.S. regulatory arm, the Commodity Futures Trading Commission (CFTC), had reason for suspecting that Hamanaka had something to do with market abnormalities, and it put pressure on British regulators. Together they persuaded Sumitomo officials to look into Hamanaka's dealings. When Hamanaka learned that Sumitomo's examination of a bank statement was going to lead to its questioning him, he went to his superiors and confessed. The effect of the blowup was that the day after Hamanaka admitted to his superiors that he had massive losses, copper prices fell 10 percent. In March 1998 Hamanaka was sentenced in Tokyo District Court to eight years in prison for forgery and fraud.

Did Sumitomo know about Hamanaka's activities and just brush them under the rug, hoping things would all turn out? Or did it simply exercise lax supervision and an unbelievable lack of controls?

Hamanaka's downfall raised questions as to whether he was acting alone, whether there was a web of conspiracy, or whether his working environment in Tokyo was to blame.

The London Metals Exchange, auction arena for trading in copper and five other base metals, has annual metals trading volume of almost $2.5 trillion a year. About 90 percent of all copper trading is done on the LME. For years it had been the subject of press comments about lax regulations. Just the year before, the LME had come under fire because another trader named Juan Pablo Davila lost over $200 million for Codelco, the state-owned copper company of Chile. During the Hamanaka scandal, the exchange suffered another blow to its image.

An informed source in London provided me with an entirely different insight:

"When the news broke about the Sumitomo trader who was operating from Japan but trading on the LME in London, the price of copper plunged. And the LME managed to maintain an orderly market, which is quite amazing. And not one single newspaper [reported that fact] . . . we heard their moans about how we should regulate the metal exchanges, not a bit of it. London got the business, thank you very much. And the LME's global market share was up again because people saw that it worked. It was a great big feather in its cap.

"But the media would not see it that way. It was all gloom and, oh, isn't it terrible. That was the lesson of that. If you are going to deal in size you are going to have to do it in London. The LME has its own rules, but anybody in the world can ring up and deal with an LME firm and place an order. He was a client, that is all. The point was—the main purpose of the market is to fulfill the clients' requirements, to provide liquidity, and to maintain an orderly market. And the LME fulfilled that requirement very well."

Sumitomo was not a member of the London Metal Exchange, only a client, so was not subject to its rules of jurisdiction. It was U.S. commodities regulators that stepped up the pressure to investigate what they perceived might be market manipulation.

Post-Hamanaka, many observers were convinced that Sumitomo may have been partly to blame by giving him free rein. After the affair, Sumitomo devised a new rotation system so that the head traders on its foreign exchange and commodities desks would not be allowed to stay in a position for longer than four years, and those under them for three years. It felt this would reduce the possibility of a trader racking up hidden losses over long years, as Hamanaka had done. On a larger scale, the Ministry of Finance in Japan issued a guide to financial institutions recommending that they set limits on trading volume and establish a structure of rules that must be followed.

Toshihide Iguchi was another supposed magician. For an incredible eleven years, he concocted false trades and hid 30,000 unauthorized trades as the senior bond trader in New York for the Daiwa Bank, the fifth-largest bank in Japan. Initially Iguchi had a $200,000 trading loss that he wanted to hide. It snowballed from there.

The accumulated losses forced Daiwa not only to pay $340 million in fines to U.S. regulators and take a $1.1 billion charge against earnings, but also to close its U.S. operations. Iguchi was sentenced by a U.S. judge to four years in prison and fines of nearly $2.6 million on charges of embezzlement, financial fraud, and conspiracy. It sent shock waves through the financial markets that yet another trader had the apparent power to cause anxiety in the markets. Not only that, but it was unsettling that for two months, officials at his bank hid the truth about his trades from U.S. authorities. Daiwa employees testified that management had conspired with Iguchi to cover up the losses after his confession to them, and that they told him to keep quiet about it for a few months while they thought about what to do.

Then there was Joseph Jett, the African American educated at MIT and Harvard, a rising star at Kidder Peabody. He allegedly created $348 million in false profits and hid $83 million in losses over a two-and-a-half year period as head of the government bond trading desk. At some points he represented 50 to 60 percent of the market. Similar to those at Barings, his immediate supervisors enjoyed increasing bonuses due in part to Jett's input on the trading desk.

An SEC filing alleged that his supervisor only looked at the net day inventory and not at Jett's order tickets, settlements, or counterparties. And he apparently didn't look into the reasons for Jett's making big profits. The filing noted that Jett's profits in 1992 were "100 percent greater than Kidder's best ever profits from trading Strips."

Jett had been trading U.S. Treasury bonds, and the zero coupon components of those bonds, in transactions called strips and reconstitution. He allegedly used an anomaly in the accounting system that resulted in the transactions showing up as profits, and supposedly entered trades in strips and reconstitutions into the company's computer system with instructions to settle more than one day forward. The system translated his instructions to mean that they were actual trades, would produce order tickets, and the accounting information would be recorded on the company's books. The system recorded them as profitable when actually they were bought and sold with no monetary gain or profit. Jett's ascendancy within two years from being a junior trader to being managing director and head of all government bond trading, with fifteen people under him, was swift by normal standards. He had received a bonus in 1993 of $9 million, and Kidder had bestowed on him the Chairman's Award for being a top moneymaker at the firm.

The repercussions? Kidder said Jett was solely responsible for the debacle and fired him. Kidder's parent company, General Electric, booked a $210 million charge against earnings and sold most of Kidder to Paine Webber. Jett later testified that he was being made a scapegoat and that his superiors knew all about his trading strategy.

If they didn't know, they should have. There's no excuse. His boss, Edward Cerullo, had been fined and censured in 1991 by the National Association of Securities Dealers for not properly supervising a trader. In Jett's case, the SEC suspended Cerullo from the securities business for twelve months. (Cerullo ran fixed income and was also on the management committee and executive committee.) In May 1996 the SEC began hearings on fraud charges against Jett; while Jett himself continues to assert his innocence and is fighting to clear his name: "I will fight my accusers until my dying breath." In his view he did not commit fraud because all his trades were entered into the accounting books, which were available for inspection.

TOM RYAN IS now president of the American Stock Exchange. Part of his job when he was with Kidder Peabody was to manage risk:

"The scenario is always the same. Whether it was Hamanaka or Iguchi or Leeson, the denominator is common. They all had relatively free independence and little or no supervision. One way to do it is to look at their inventory. Everybody has overnight inventory, so you should know what it is in the morning. And every trader is only given so much authority to trade certain things in certain amounts. If he is going to exceed those bounds, he needs permission.

"Traders have losses. That's part of the business. Markets are volatile and relationships change and so there are going to be losses. Just like there are profits. But when you have off-the-wall losses, then it comes down to their being given too much independence and too little supervision."

Thoroughly vetting a trader before you even hire him is something that Linda Strumpf does as chief investment officer at the Ford Foundation, even if they have been in the markets for a long time:

"I remember when I first got here and I had to hire a senior trader. The first thing that I did was to call up the major firms that we did business with and I said, 'Who do you think would be good for this organization? It has to be someone with the utmost integrity.'

"There have been some trading scandals. Basically the traders on the buy side are not paid what the traders on the sell side are paid. And there were all kinds of shenanigans going on where they were getting kickbacks, or they were getting personal allocations on deals, or they were committing trading volume to a certain firm. If you don't have the controls in place—as we've seen with Leeson and Kidder—which most people don't have, to monitor what the traders are doing, how would you know if your trader was channeling business to somebody just because they were good buddies, or somebody was giving them cash on the side?

"It comes down to your personal judgment, and that you hire and retain people so you know they have the good of the institution at heart. I don't think a lot of people who are supervising the trading desk really know what is going on. No one ever likes to admit that they don't understand what somebody working for them is doing. So they say, fine, go ahead, as long as you are making money, that's okay."

No one can ever guarantee absolutely that such scandals couldn't happen again. But the difference will be to what degree. It is within the reach of financial institutions to limit amounts traded, to monitor the positions on the trading desk every night, and to have backup risk management systems in place. With greater use of information technology you can prevent a great deal. You can minimize damage and not allow problems to grow so large. The focus that firms have given to obtaining the fastest and most sophisticated trading systems has so far been at the expense of obtaining the same level of sophistication in the back-office systems, which keep track of what is going on out front on the trading floor. The checking systems haven't been up to the level of the trading done.

A common factor in the Leeson, Iguchi, and Hamanaka cases was that the trader was also responsible for the settlements or bookkeeping. Normally these are kept separate, which provides an independent check on the trader's activity. If the bookkeeping function were distinct, traders would not be capable of maintaining a separate set of books and hidden accounts.

How do traders get into this kind of bind? Frankly, they fear never being able to look their peers in the face again if it was found out they had made a stupid bet. They'll backtrack and try to cover up. Some have hidden tickets in their drawers and have mismarked the market, waiting until it turns in their favor. At some point they admit their mistake, take a loss, and go on to trade another day. Or they swerve off the tracks and do something to cover it up for as long as they can.

How do firms get into this kind of bind? Contributing factors are lack of supervision, lack of effective internal controls, not asking enough questions, and willingness in some cases to turn a blind eye to what the trader is doing as long as he's making a profit. Cynics would tell you that some traders in these blowups are scapegoats for management.

In the future, there is more likelihood of problems occurring in emerging markets than in mature ones. They are the growth areas for financial firms to expand. Newly emerging and third world markets are being taken into the fold before they can stand, and international banks and investment houses have rushed in to stake their claim on the territory. In 1994 trading volumes in emerging markets were almost $2.8 trillion. In an effort to professionalize the market, the Emerging Market Traders Association developed a code of conduct in 1992, which is now used as the industry standard for voluntary self-regulation and orderly market development in those areas.

Whenever markets expand geographically, or at the beginning of a cycle for a financial product, when market participants are using it but have not yet become sophisticated users; when the hype is at its most intense; when the promise of big profits masks the possibility of equally big losses; and when everyone is jumping on the band-wagon—the likelihood is that mess-ups will happen. Having new instruments in the hands of the inexperienced in new markets increases risks. There will be problems because not everybody understands what they are doing. The real control has to be from the management of the firm, to ensure that the people are knowledge-able and capable of handling whatever they are responsible for.

The derivatives that Nick Leeson was using were "plain vanilla" futures and options traded on a regulated exchange. There was noth-ing complex about them. Yet senior management at Barings was later blamed for not understanding well enough what he was trading.

Allen Wheat, CEO of Credit Suisse First Boston and one of the first to construct derivatives, said that since then:

"There has been a sea change in the ability of senior manage-ment at banks and firms to understand how risk really works. Ten years ago, nobody senior had a clue. They were completely ignorant. But that's all changed. Senior management understands risk, sys-temic risk, all sorts of risk. They have put into place all sorts of processes, computer reports that break it down to all levels. But there's always the possibility that the rogue trader could lose a lot of money—that's always there."

Externally, regulators are looking at how a trader, or a possible conspiracy between traders, could cause a disaster to happen that would pose a systemic risk to the system. The rivalry that existed between the Singapore and Osaka exchanges resulted in a lack of information between the two that many believe made it easier for a person like Nick Leeson to be deceptive. The problem is, each coun-try with a schoolbook boundary has one or more regulatory agen-cies, yet the world financial markets have no boundaries. Efforts in the past to regulate the financial markets in one country have resulted in the business flowing to another without those regula-tions. We saw that with the genesis of the Eurodollar market.

Closer coordination and information flow between exchanges offer one answer. And giving the regulatory authorities bigger bud-gets for better technology and better talent is another. One of the problems with regulatory bodies and rules is that they were created in a different era. They never seem to be able fully to understand the market intricacies of the current market well enough to keep up or be a step ahead. With the financial markets utilizing the best technology and buying the best talent, the regulatory authorities are at a disadvantage and tend to be reactionary or out of touch.

I'm not saying that they should slap on restrictions and freeze the markets during a crisis. That usually causes the crisis to spread and escalate. One of the worst things you can do in that situation is to dry up liquidity. But rather, by enabling regulators with the best technology and encouraging them to communicate with one another and agree on a uniform global strategy that supersedes lines drawn on a map, you would be giving them the tools necessary to abort a crisis before it grows into a catastrophe. Not in the traditional sense, but more as a collegial effort to coordinate, educate, inform, and guide.

That, hand in hand with the 1997 Group of 30 recommendation that the private sector self-regulate, would be encouraging. The group's recommendation is that the fifty largest financial intermediaries in the world get together to create a set of standards that they will adhere to, that crosses borders and crosses functions. It would be for the financial system as a whole, not just the banking system—which already has the supervisory net of the Basel Committee beneath it—but also the capital markets.

Carolyn Jackson feels strongly that formal regulation wouldn't work, and looks at her own market as an example:

"The reality is that there is nothing that you can do with a derivative that you couldn't do in the cash market. So even if they regulated the derivative market, people could do it through the cash market. And the only time you will see somebody use a derivative rather than cash is because it was more economically viable for them, which meant that they got a better price. Everybody benefits from that. They are saving their company money that they can redeploy. In fact, Myron Scholes makes the point that in some cases, people may come full circle and find that they can do a lot more things more cheaply in the cash market than in the derivative market."

Add in tighter internal controls at securities firms and banks, and eventually a lot of the laxness that existed previously should be eradicated. No system will ever be foolproof; someone will always find a way to tear a whole in the fabric. But there will be fewer of them because of the legacy of the Leesons and Iguchis. The stakes are so high that managements have stepped up their surveillance and put in risk controls.

For example, now when a trader at Fidelity Investments exceeds his trading limit or tries to do something outside of the parameters he is allowed, an alarm goes off on his computer screen that is visually communicated to him as a burst of red flames. When that happens, a report is automatically sent to the compliance officer of the firm. Another example is traders using the Tradepoint screen, because they are limited by the software from stepping over their limits. The head of the trading desk can at any time call up on his screen what individual traders are doing.

There's significantly less concealment possible now. With information technology, there is no reason other than the fault of management for not monitoring traders closely enough. For all or most traders in the markets, the understanding is clear. There's so much money to be made legally, they wouldn't think of bothering to be illegal.

The trading scandals of the mid-1990s were clues to what needed to be fixed in the trading world. They were also a reminder that when terms like *wizard, magic, king of the market, cowboy, star,* or *sorcerer* are believed, they are but temporary myths. A solitary trader breathtakingly raking in astounding amounts of money is a great story, but it is highly unlikely, because no one person can move a market other than for a short period of time. And he certainly cannot do it alone, without management's compliance.

Gary Lapayover has faith as well:

"Every industry has its bad eggs in it. Everyone knows of people who are less than scrupulous, who have a lack of ethics. Actually, I think we do an excellent job of weeding out and finding the bad guy, better than most industries and certainly better than Congress."

PART III

LOOKING FORWARD

12 QUANTS

THIS IS A HIGH-RISK GAME AT THE FRONTIER OF MATHE-
MATICS, PHYSICS, AND FINANCE. MANY CORRELATIONS
EXIST AMONG SECURITIES AT DIFFERENT POINTS IN TIME,
AND SOLVING THE OPTIMIZATION PROBLEM THAT IMPLE-
MENTS A SUCCESSFUL MARKET STRATEGY INVOLVES THE
SAME TOOLS THAT WE USE FOR GUIDED MISSILES. YOU'RE
TRYING TO HIT A MOVING TARGET.

ANDREW LO, MIT PROFESSOR

Mechanized trading is emotionless. That's a chilling thought. It means that the intuition and gut reaction most traders depend on is eliminated in favor of letting computers trade instead. New technology has sparked the imaginations of a different breed of trader that believes that information overload, moods and emotions, and the slower form of manual trading hinder the chances of beating the markets—or even coping with them.

The "quantitative" approach to trading, using mathematical models, has a growing following and has drawn people into finance who otherwise would be more at home in a research lab or engineering facility. They are changing the face of finance.

* * *

I WAS MEETING with David Shaw, secretive private fund trader and founder of D.E. Shaw in New York.

In his offices, serene surfaces and vital forces merge. It is no ordinary place. There are no details for the eye. Just smooth white walls with bands of yellow and green light forming an architectural impression. The space was included in an important architectural exhibit at the Museum of Modern Art in New York. It looks sort of SoHo.

All I could think of was megabytes and money. David Shaw is a quant. He generates rich returns for his investors by using a quantitative approach, sophisticated mathematical models to search with computers for minuscule price differences between international markets. Basically he is doing arbitrage—looking for something selling lower in one market, buying it and selling it higher in another market, doing both trades simultaneously. This is statistical arbitrage, or looking at thousands of tiny discrepancies and inefficiencies in the markets that may be caused by a variety of factors that happen at the same time concerning currencies, interest rates, paired trading relationships—anything can go into their program.

Like sifting sand to find treasure, his team monitors more than one hundred markets around the world twenty-four hours a day. Trading like this is very different from what other private investment funds do. Shaw is not at all trying to predict the direction of a currency or stock or interest rate or market, and his group is not particularly interested in picking individual stocks, or knowing about the companies that they trade. What he is doing is "market neutral," finding tiny price discrepancies and taking advantage of them without taking a position on a direction. That's where he's made his money.

As for megabytes, Shaw's brain is loaded with them. Armed with a Ph.D. in computer science from Stanford University, he went on to become an assistant computer science professor at Columbia University while he conducted research on massively parallel supercomputing and its application to artificial intelligence—or neural networks. He shifted to Wall Street in 1986 to join a "top gun" group at Morgan Stanley doing quantitative analysis, working under Nunzio Tartaglia, one of the top quants in the business. Tartaglia was applying his interest in trading with computers using algorithms to do proprietary trading for the firm.

Shaw was so fascinated at what he learned could be amazing opportunities using his knowledge, and what he was discovering about the financial markets at Morgan Stanley, that he left just a year and a half later to start his own hedge fund. But it was a hedge fund in the old-fashioned sense of the word. It was hedged for risk. By comparison, many private pools of money that are referred to as "hedge funds" today are actually hedged very little, but rather use leverage to make big one-way bets.

Shaw's hedging strategy paid off in 1994, when some of the best-known hedge funds were up only slightly or not at all because they were not fully hedged and had made the wrong bets on the direction of interest rates and currencies. In contrast, Shaw's market-neutral fund had a gross return to its investors of 30 percent. In the decade since he founded D.E. Shaw & Company, the annual returns on his fund have averaged more than 20 percent. In those ten years, the original fund of $28 million has grown to more than $1.3 billion. It's been reported that Shaw's trading volume can reach up to 5 percent of the total volume on the New York Stock Exchange, and can be upwards of 10 million shares a day. He explains:

"One of our other businesses is basket trading. We'll bid on, say, a basket of as many as 100 or 200 different stocks. We'll buy them for our own portfolio from an institution and bid a price, which we try to make more than competitive with what Wall Street is able to offer. We're able to do that by using some of the same computer technology as we use in our proprietary trading. We've routinely bid on trades that could be $250 million or $500 million. We've given indications higher than a billion."

As I sat across from him at his desk I had to shade my eyes. The sun was beaming in and the desk, shaped like a huge airplane wing and made of polished aluminum, was deflecting light directly into my face. At forty-seven, David Shaw is a thoughtful and polite financial and engineering genius. A bundle of controlled energy. He is not only immersed in a project for President Clinton but is at the same time running his business and busy launching new ones. Shaw has acted as a policy adviser to Clinton since 1994 on the increased use of computers in education, and has written strategy position papers for Clinton's Advanced Technology Program. In 1997 he completed a report on computers in schools to help promote the president's $2 billion effort to have every U.S. classroom connected to the Internet by the year 2000. Both men feel strongly about getting children ready for the new software-and-knowledge economy.

As for finance, Shaw is excited about the future:

"Right now, the financial world is at the beginning of what looks like a fundamental transformation. People are trying to figure out different ways technology can be used to do a lot of things that humans have been doing, and do it in a more systematic way."

He's already there. One of the business offshoots he developed is a "third market" operation, becoming an off-exchange market maker in stocks listed on the New York Stock Exchange and the American Stock Exchange. With his technological expertise he is able to do it cheaper and faster, pulling order flow away from the traditional exchanges.

His radical view of the future look of Wall Street has led him to use his knowledge of trading and take it up several notches—to one where he is building a new-age investment bank on the Internet. He's crazy about the Internet. And he believes it is through that medium that he can transform the very traditional industry of finance, using information technology:

"We're trying to find areas that are going to be fundamentally transformed by computers. Not just made slightly more efficient, but where the whole industry is going to be turned on its head."

With the some of the firm's capital being invested in small start-up companies specializing in products for the Internet, Shaw is actively lining up a launch pad of missiles ready for cyberspace.

His first foray into this universe was with the launch of Juno Online Services, which offers free e-mail to anyone on the Internet and presently has over 4.6 million subscribers. The software and the service are free, providing users with folders for holding mail, a spell-checker, and an address book. Profits come from the advertising on the Juno screen. The service eliminates the need to be a paying member of an online service like CompuServe or America Online. You order the software from Shaw, then dial an 800 number and connect directly to him through your modem.

FarSight is his second missile, an online, real-time financial services operation that is offered exclusively on the World Wide Web to retail customers, both directly and through other financial institutions. FarSight was the first online financial services firm to integrate brokerage functions with services traditionally offered by banks, such as checking, debit cards, and electronic bill payment. It enables customers to simplify their financial lives through an intuitive point-and-click screen, accessible at any time, from anywhere.

"We'd like you to be able to do pretty much everything you want to do with your money with us. Maybe we will try to find some way to tie into taxes. The real thrust is to try to make a system that you would want to use to manage your own finances.

"Most people would really like to have one system where they don't have to get four different reports every month and copy the numbers down, at the end of the year compile them, and write them into their tax returns. You just want a system that knows about all of that stuff and allows you to do it very, very easily. Maybe one that has some educational component that can explain to you how mutual funds work."

Shaw talked to me openly about wanting to change the financial world as we know it, and spoke out against what he considers archaic Wall Street practices:

"Frankly, I think too much money already goes to Wall Street for the services that they actually provide to retail investors. Retail investors pay such a hugely larger fraction of each trade to a broker-age firm compared to what an institution pays, and in many cases there is not really any solid evidence that they are getting much value. With brokerage recommendations, there is not much evidence that they outperform the market. I think they might be better off just investing in a Vanguard, low-fee index fund."

He thinks computers should be used to eliminate what he sees as wasteful and time-consuming functions. His philosophy goes as far as embodying the concept of letting the customers connect with each other in the financial area. That extends to the belief that an Internet exchange could develop that would take traditional market makers and financial firms out of the transaction altogether—out of the middle, between the customers, allowing them to "cross" their trades with each other by themselves.

Shaw's entrepreneurial streak was perhaps unwittingly encour-aged when he was quite young by his stepfather:

"He was a professor of finance at UCLA. But I learned a lot more than just finance from him. A lot about how businesses work. Since I was a teenager he would bring me along to board meetings with him, which nobody did. Or if he was giving a talk somewhere he would bring me along. If we'd walk by a store, I'd say, 'Why are they selling that?' He'd say to me, 'Well, I don't know that business very well, but that store probably makes most of its money on this sort of thing, and if they paid this, they'd never get anywhere.' With a million little case studies like that I started to get a feeling for it. I think I am able to do the right-brain kind of stuff. I am by no means a perfect businessman, but some of the stuff I think I am better at than the average person.

"I had a very successful company when I was in graduate school. I decided to sell off the pieces, and went back to school to finish my Ph.D. because I had some ideas. And I really wanted to do some research. Then I was a professor, because I really love doing that. I've been really fortunate. It's been a lot of fun at every stage."

Taking a tour around his offices, I noticed that we were back to the old offices-with-doors-to-shut philosophy of business, so unlike the philosophy of the rest of the trading world. Then I realized that this is not at all the same. People don't trade here: computers do. People think here, and they need peace and tranquillity to do it. Instead of hiring the people that other investment houses hire, Shaw searches the world for "rocket scientists"—the finest engineering and mathematical brains—then teaches them what they need to know about finance.

The culture is totally different from other investment firms. It's located nowhere near Wall Street. People wear jeans and sneakers. The gifted prodigies are given as creative an environment as Shaw can provide them with. He told me:

"We are not typical Wall Street types. We're more like an academic department. We have eight or nine people writing novels, one of which is getting a huge amount of attention and getting rave reviews. We have several serious musicians. We have people that run theater companies in their spare time. So the conversations that you hear in the hallway are not what you would hear at a typical firm. It just has a different tone."

DOYNE FARMER AND Norman Packard were once professional gamblers who used computers slipped into their shoes to try to win at the roulette table. They are also physicists. Utilizing chaos theory built into mathematical models, they sell software that gives traders signals when to trade. Their company, Prediction Company, is run out of Santa Fe, New Mexico, and it is marketing the software as a way to predict the direction of financial markets and products. They're not on the cutting edge, they're on the bleeding edge.

Blair Hull Company, one of the largest independent trading firms in the United States, accounts on any given day for up to 7 percent of the total number of index options traded there, and 3 percent in equity options.

Programmers with backgrounds in physics develop mathematical models for their computers to try to beat the markets. Blair's traders in the pits of the Chicago Board of Trade then use handheld computers to receive information from their firm, and execute trades. Blair himself is a student of blackjack. Along the same lines as Shaw, his computers search for price imperfections while at the same time developing hedging strategy so there is minimum or no risk in the trading.

"Walk into our trading room, and you'll see a couple of people watching a single screen. That computer is trading 1 percent of the entire New York Stock Exchange."

At the Santa Fe Institute a group has developed software using algorithms to create an artificial intelligence program that trades. Trading rules are input about how to react to news events and changes in market characteristics, and the programs actually "learn" by judging the outcome of each of the trades the computer does, then adjust to try for better results.

All over the United States small boutiques are popping up with quantitative software that they either sell to traders or trade with themselves, the more unusual ones using things as random as sunspot activity to generate mathematical models. Delving into artificial intelligence and programming computers to mimic what a human being would do has been a successful endeavor for some. With mathematical models they can write programs to recognize patterns of human thought.

Hughes Research Laboratories, a defense contractor in Malibu, California, tried to do just that. It developed a software package that will trade bonds based on work done with Christine Downton at Pareto Partners in London. For two years researchers tracked her thought processes in analyzing, reasoning, and making decisions in the bond market. Pareto Partners is now using the bond-trading software to run a $500 million portfolio. The most important benefit they have found is that it has given them more time, because the program can process huge amounts of information quickly.

Quantitative analysis coupled with advances in technology is cutting a wide swath into the way traders work. As their tools are changing, the way they trade changes. Their concept of time and risk changes. For instance, traders who used to do a "program" trade manually can now do it electronically. Before, they would write out and call in orders for up to hundreds of different stocks for people on the floor to execute at the same time. Now the computer can value a "basket" of a hundred or more stocks, worth hundreds of millions of dollars, and buy or sell them in one go. It's more efficient, faster, and risk can be factored in when the computer does the quantitative analysis on valuing the basket.

Arbitraging between markets is greatly speeded up using quantitative analysis and computers to find discrepancies that may last only minutes, even seconds, between the prices in two markets. Programming computers to arbitrage automatically, taking into account currencies and trading costs, allows traders to do it swiftly and continuously, and to monitor many markets and variables at once.

Depending on events, correlations may happen between seemingly disparate securities—two stocks or a bond and a currency—as quickly as a flash of lightning. Neural networks can pick up on the patterns instantly and automatically trade on them. There's no way a human could sift through hundreds of markets as efficiently or as fast.

Traders can program with stochastic calculus to deal with the randomness or unpredictability of prices, trying to predict what prices of commodities or securities will be in the future using certain variables as parameters. They can also use it to determine the risk characteristics of a portfolio if certain interest rates exist. A mathematical concept called dynamic programming can be used to try to determine how to time the selling of a huge block of stock. If there are millions of shares to be sold, and selling them all at once would knock the price down when it hits the market, a trader can estimate how to slice up the portfolio and when to sell off its pieces to minimize the price effect.

Some develop programs to search the markets for undervalued

securities, others to pick up and track securities that have escalating and unusual volume, or where the price is rising quickly. In even broader terms, traders as well as others in the markets are using quantitative techniques and computers to do things that humans have been doing in order to achieve them in a more efficient way. They are looking for a way to eliminate error and paper where they are thought unnecessary and time consuming. The mistake could be to become too dependent on robotic trading, or to substitute it for human common sense. As a tool, it is a miracle. Mind, money, and computer work very well together, better than each one alone.

In London, the movement toward quants is lagging behind New York. There are a few who stand out. The pioneers committed to bringing the gospel to their community were speakers at a conference in London in October 1996. One was Stanley Ross, founder of Tradepoint in London and one of the senior figures in the capital markets around the world. He was formerly a managing director at Deutsche Bank Capital Markets, and was reportedly responsible for trading the very first Eurobond. He started trading in 1951, and had been aggressively pursuing the evolution of computers as a tool for decades.

In 1979 he formed his own company called Ross and Partners, and became the first to use the newly available screens to post gray market prices in Eurobonds. The screens immediately displayed visible two-way trading quotes where previously they had paid the issue price. All of a sudden traders saw they could save money. His pages were shown on Reuters, and in 1980 they were the most widely accessed of any on the Reuters network. He was at the conference to announce a link-up with Bloomberg that would allow electronic trading on the Tradepoint exchange via the Bloomberg system.

Wedged into the roster of conference speakers was a young quant working in the London markets named Marcus Hooper. Unlike his U.S. peers, Marcus has no advanced degrees in engineering or computer science or physics. He was eighteen when he started in the City.

"I joined the stock exchange, and I did have a small background in computing beforehand. Just home computing and stuff, because I used to toy around with computers at home, which I loved. I absolutely loved computers."

He worked at the stock exchange as a programmer on Talisman, its settlement system. He had been there a year when a chance to become a trainee junior dealer opened up at Hill Samuel. That was 1986.

"There certainly weren't any PCs in the area before I got there. We had an internal system, but it wasn't very advanced. We brought PCs in and used them a lot more. We used them for things like program trading and for internal control of orders. Not very sophisticated stuff. After six years on the dealing desk, I transferred internally and joined the quant team. It was a somewhat unusual situation. The quant team was rather independent within the organization. They were given rather free rein."

Marcus developed trading routines and built a stock-management program to control what was going on in the quant area:

"I'd take a portfolio and adjust for risk to get the lowest possible level I could. And we would tilt portfolios toward different factors to outperform various factors over a period of time. And we were moving between factors over time. We were using analytical tools to do that."

He moved again, this time to Sun Life, where he perceived the chance to work with a dealing team where there weren't any preconceived ideas of how a dealing desk works.

Marcus was one of the first to jump onto Tradepoint because, he said, it was leaps and bounds ahead of anything else that existed at that time. The screen interface was part of what excited him:

"You see, the biggest problem we have with some of the computer systems is that they are inflexible. They do their own set of functions but nothing else, and you can't interact with them very well. The whole structure of this is changing. We are seeing how Windows has changed the world in terms of connectivity of programs. You can get information freely between environments, and that was the thing that was lacking in financial systems, and still is in many areas at the moment. What you need is a pipeline to the information backward and forward. That's all it comes down to. Now some systems do have some kind of pipeline to do that."

He uses INSTINET and thinks it is a good system, but points out that it is still too self-contained. He has found that its ability to interact with the outside world is not up to what other systems have. There is a degree of import and export capability. It can import text into its automated management system, but it is not a live connection. It is an upload or download kind of function. You respond to it, rather than it responding to you. What he wants is to be able to interact with the system:

"I'm talking about getting the information flows backward and forward, getting the instruction into the machine and getting the reports back. Online, live, electronic information. INSTINET can provide that, although it is packaged within their own systems so you have to comply with the way their system works. Whereas with Tradepoint, there is the difference that it has Excel, a spreadsheet, which is easy to communicate with in a variety of ways, using Windows as an environment.

"It is a communication issue that is really foxing everyone at the moment. It depends really on how people want to use electronic trading in the future. I would like to have machines doing things for me, and that just doesn't mean telling me I've got to trade. The reason I need the Excel pipeline is because these are not simple decisions. If it was just, okay, this price has moved up two pence today, I want to sell it—I want to go beyond that. The obvious thing is to take that a step further. We have seen, mainly on the sell side over here, people toying with the idea of using neural networks."

A neural network is essentially a program that supposedly thinks. It is actually pattern matching. At least if we are in a position to say to the computer, spot this for me and do something about it when it happens, then we are way ahead. That means we have to have very sophisticated programs behind the connectivity. That's going to take years before people really get into it. You have to write the algorithms and the programs to actually identify it in the first place, identify millions of variables.

Despite Marcus's quant orientation to trading, he, like Bloomberg, believes that computers won't get rid of people:

"Does it feel right? Only people can know if it feels right. We still need that, it is essential. And you still have to think up a strategy of how you are going to work or run big orders. If you take a good trader, and say, 'What is your strategy for this order?' he will say, 'Well, I think maybe it is going to go down a bit so I will wait and buy some if it comes down, and I will sit and wait, and wait again.' That's all strategy, it's just that he can't express it. The fact that he is saying that's how he feels at the moment is great. That's the human part, the part you can't get rid of, and that's why the computer can't dispose of that person."

The problem on a dealing desk is that it is the head trader who knows the markets inside out, has experience, and he will be the one to strategize and work the big orders. It is possible for the computer to take over the small orders, the ones that used to be worked by the junior dealers on the desk trying to learn the business. So the question becomes, how do young traders learn if increasingly the small order flow is pushed through computers?

It may be that the junior dealers will be assimilating different skills in the beginning. They'll feed in the appropriate information, spend time thinking about it, and communicate ideas to the head trader. They'll have more time to pick up the phone and keep a constant flow of information on the markets and players coming in to the desk, in the meantime learning where to go and where prices are developing. The job would be more that of an information manager, managing all the key data, whether it is research information, news headlines, technical charts, a liquidity piece of information from a broker, or a feeling of who was trading a stock yesterday. And they'd have more time to watch the head trader.

The shift toward quantitative techniques in the United States is much more pervasive than elsewhere, a reflection of the move toward recruiting at science and engineering schools as well as at business schools. In 1997 MIT noted that 19 percent of the companies that recruited their graduates were financial firms. As technology becomes a competitive weapon in the financial arena, knowledge of computers, how they are designed, and math- and science-related problem solving is being seen on Wall Street to be as valuable as a business degree.

13 MIND, MONEY, AND MACHINE

As at any auction, trading in person is exhilarating. The human interaction involved within a crowd of people creates an adrenaline-pumping kind of trading. You can see your competition, hear the noise, and feel the energy and the momentum build. Advocates of this form of trading believe that the markets would suffer from the loss of the floor trader's enthusiasm for making a market, and from a loss of the liquidity they provide.

On the other hand, opponents point to the obvious benefits of computerized trading—lower cost, the capacity to handle higher volumes faster, the liberation from having to go to a certain location in order to trade, and the ability to access markets from a PC or lap-top from anywhere in the world.

Outside of exchange trading, screens provide traders with information. After viewing prices and news, and manipulating data on their screen, the majority will then trade over the phone—still linking in by voice, intellect, personality, and emotion to others in the market. The camaraderie and foreplay still exist.

When you strip that away you have pure electronic trading,

where you buy and sell directly on the screen, much like playing chess against the computer. Sound boring? Not really. Winning and losing still provides a thrill.

There's no doubt about the excitement I feel walking onto the floor of an exchange or a large brokerage where people are aggressively trading. But I also feel excitement when I see on the computer that the price of a stock I bought has gone up $6. Victory for me in having made the right assessment against others in the market brings satisfaction that's both personal and monetary.

Mind, money, and machine are the future. The question is how far we will take it. Would purely electronic markets provide the needed liquidity? Or do we opt for the best of both worlds—screen and scream?

Which we choose and how far we take it will make a huge difference. Consider the social implications of how it will affect traders and how we view the markets.

For traders, the ones who have economics degrees and are more comfortable with screen trading could completely push out the traders on a floor who use intuition and personal skills to bring a market to life. The barriers to entry to the trading profession could become higher. Now on most exchange floors, there are few barriers to entry other than being smart.

For the rest of us, think about this. If we go to a world of electronic trading where no exchange floors exist, there would be no visual connection anymore to the excitement and vibrancy of the financial markets. We wouldn't be able to "see" the markets. Would that make a difference? It's a hard question. The next generation may not need that. They already opt for screen life.

"THE BIG UPGRADE on the New York Stock Exchange floor came in 1987 after the crash. That was when the Star Wars look came in. The ticker tape now has the capacity to carry 2.3 billion shares. They spent a lot of money on technology. With the kind of volume we do today, if we had to do everything by hand, nobody would ever go home. We would have two shifts.

"I come from that era when we did everything by hand. Everything.

"Just think, when I started down here, most of the business was retail, transacting 100 shares, because you didn't have the computer system. People were transacting 100 shares, 500 shares, 200 shares. And that was the bulk of it.

"I mean, when you saw one million shares go across the tape, people would start screaming and applauding. It's not like that now. One million on the tape is nothing new."

That was Gail Pankey remembering what it was like before the exchange automated.

The New York Stock Exchange is spending $200 million in 1998 upgrading its systems and software technology. Orders still reach the exchange by being phoned in to the floor, but almost 85 percent reach the specialists' posts electronically through the SuperDot system. Member firms can enter orders on the computer and they appear on the specialist's electronic workstation for execution. In 1997 the SuperDot system handled a trading volume of 109.5 billion shares. So the New York Stock Exchange has evolved into a successful blend of both electronics and a live auction market.

Down the street on the American Stock Exchange over 70 percent of orders reach the floor electronically. The exchange will have a system of wireless computers that traders will walk around the floor with. Buy and sell orders will come in directly from anywhere in the world and be displayed on the screen in their hand. Traders will be able to write on these little handheld boxes, use touch, and possibly speak into them. And they will interface with the other systems that the exchange plans to provide.

Floor trading on the American Stock Exchange is expected to be augmented with the computerized trading of NASDAQ when the two combine, providing traders with both screen and scream trading. The NASDAQ market for over-the-counter stocks has operated since 1971, linking brokers and dealers to a main computer center that records and transmits the prices and information. They are working on a new and improved computer trading system that they hope will not only offer an electronic bulletin board—where buy and sell offers are displayed—but also incorporate automated crossing, where traders can input a range of possibilities they would be interested in pursuing, and institutions on the buy side could enter their orders as well, the new system automatically matching them.

Advanced technology is being layered in to all the markets in order to accommodate the huge growth in money pouring in to be invested and to contain costs.

Futures exchanges in America are opting for the "hybrid" route for now, by keeping their floors while at the same time offering an electronic platform. The Chicago Mercantile Exchange's new electronic trading system, GLOBEX2, operates parallel to trading on CME's floor, offering traders customized screens, more ways to trade, and the ability to trade from anywhere in the world. The benefits are that these exchanges preserve the existing liquidity produced on the floor while ensuring that they offer an electronic route into their market.

But according to Leo Melamed, the futures markets are bound to move even further in the direction of electronic trading platforms:

"All the new markets that have been developed since 1987 have been electronic. I personally have no doubts about the direction of the business. I think it is going electronic. Whether the futures markets of 'open outcry' want to admit it or not, the world is moving in that direction. Probably in the next ten or fifteen years, there is going to be a complete shift to electronic trade.

"I am hoping that I can be a provocateur of change toward placing more of the world of futures on to the screen. I really believe that is the direction we have to go."

At this point, Melamed is not advocating turning out the lights on the futures exchange in Chicago, but rather integrating electronic trading to work hand in hand with the traders on the floor. The inauguration of the E-mini S&P futures contract, which is traded electronically, was one of the first steps in that direction.

In June 1998, the London Financial Futures and Options Exchange (LIFFE) voted to move away from face to face "open outcry" trading to electronic trading of all contracts by the end of 1999. Despite an initial reluctance to move in that direction, it was the competition from Frankfurt's all-electronic DTB (Deutsche Terminborse) futures exchange that proved too strong when the DTB started gaining market share from them. The bulk of futures trading in German bunds had been on the floor of LIFFE, but by the first quarter of 1998 DTB had attracted 80 percent of the trading from London onto its electronic system. And Matif, the futures exchange in Paris, began electronic trading in June, which it was thought would run parallel to the floor for a while. But after only seven weeks everyone had switched over to the electronic system and the floor was closed down.

In Europe, exchanges have moved swiftly and with open arms toward electronic trading—without floors—and toward forming mega-exchanges. EuroNM is an electronic linkage between markets in Paris, Brussels, Amsterdam, and Germany for the shares of small or new companies. Eurex merges DTB and the Swiss futures exchange, SOFFEX, into one electronic trading system on one screen. EURO Alliance is a convergence of the German, Swiss, and French stock exchanges with Eurex into one electronic trading system. EURO Alliance wants to become the largest derivatives market in Europe. The London Stock Exchange and the Frankfurt Stock Exchange announced they were linking, although it may take a while to blend into one electronic trading platform.

And alternative electronic systems like Bloomberg, INSTINET, POSIT are building a loyal following among adherents of screen trading.

Peter Jenkins estimates:

"Currently, 35 to 40 percent of the market trades through INSTINET first. This seems to be the up-and-coming market structure. An entrepreneur went out there and created a technology that competes with the exchange, a dealer market structure. And it has done a very good job. Made it more efficient."

One example of how traders use INSTINET, the electronic broker/dealer screen, is when they are nervous about a stock and want to trade it after hours, after the traditional market closes in New York at four P.M. or in the hour or two in the morning before the market opens. If they are in a hurry to get out of a stock because big news has come out on a company after hours, they can punch in an offer to sell. The number of shares and the price desired are immediately visible on the screen for another trader to "hit" if it is attractive to him and he wants to buy. You have to be fast, though, if it is a very active stock.

INSTINET is also an interesting way to monitor what other buyers and sellers are moving in and out of in a big way, and therefore may affect the following morning's prices when the market opens. The *Wall Street Journal* noted that on one day in July 1996 it was possible to see more than two hundred traders on INSTINET working off positions in U.S. Robotics after hours, which in this case was a reflection of momentum players trying to unload the stock.

Investment Technology Group's POSIT, the computer-based

equity matching system, holds "calls," or auctions, four times a day. A huge amount of liquidity is gathered at one time, eliminating the specialist as the go-between. Institutions trade at one price, and they are charged a low commission for doing that. You might get five hundred institutions electronically downloading everything they want to buy and sell at the POSIT crosses. POSIT puts all the information into the computer, which has an algorithm built in to match as many buyers and sellers as it can. It is basically a tool for inactive stocks, those that are harder to trade. With ITG's QuantEx system, an institution can electronically transmit orders to a wide choice of locations, including the NYSE and AMEX; can participate in POSIT crosses; and can view at any time its trading lists—what has been traded, where, and at what price.

Ray Killian at POSIT explains one of the advantages of the system:

"Each individual stock has a nonlinear kind of characteristic to it. It trades in a fashion peculiar to that stock. Now, you can imagine if I tried to sit down and trade one hundred different stocks and say, oh yeah, stock 3, that has a characteristic that says I ought to be trading more aggressively between ten-thirty and eleven in the morning, because that is when most of the traffic historically hits—you just couldn't do it. You've got to automate the process. You've got to get the computer to think hundreds of thousands of times faster than you think in order to use the same thoughts, but with faster calculation.

"You can see why [these trading systems] are successful because they perform a real economic function. They take the middleman out. They disintermediate the specialist. Instead of paying the specialist for that service of standing there and selling you the stock at a quarter, you are pricing in the middle. So the economics drives the success of the system, it's not the genius of the system. Like most products, if they are good, they earn their place in the marketplace."

Big brokerages are linked up electronically to trade among themselves. Merrill Lynch, Salomon Brothers, Morgan Stanley, Paine Webber, and others, as well as institutions like Fidelity and systems like POSIT, can use a computer-based network to transact trades as well as clear them and do the accounting back-up.

In the bond market, Coredeal is an around-the-clock electronic trading system for Eurobonds, with a group of ninety banks participating.

In the currency markets, where the first breakthrough in trading computer to computer was achieved on the Reuters system, there is the EBS (Electronic Broking System), which was created by a group of primarily U.S. banks. With the touch of a key, traders can "hit" a displayed bid or offer, resulting in a trade and a printed ticket. And there is the Dealing 2000–2 electronic trading system, which has become one of the largest forex brokers in the world. This system allows traders to "call" each other from their screen and type in a conversational, two-way negotiation where they agree on a price. Then the computer automatically prints out a ticket.

Many in the foreign currency markets feel these systems provide greater liquidity and price transparency, or the public dissemination of prices out in the open. Voice brokers are still part of the market, but the electronic brokerages have become a significant force as well.

"THE HISTORIAN, BARBARA TUCHMAN, said that men will not do what does not fit their prearrangements. In other words, status quo is what they want. Because that is where they have made their money, and that's how they have made their money, and why change?"

So commented Leo Melamed on the resistance of some traders to technological changes in the marketplace.

Although many easily accept, indeed welcome, electronic trading, examples exist not only of it not working, but of traders actively opposing it.

After Big Bang in London in 1986 many traders were left feeling as if an old friend had shut a door in their face. The institution that had been a part of the belief in "forever" was shut down. People were picked off the floor of the stock exchange and hired on to trading desks. That generation is maturing. They've done their trading the same way for the past ten years, and now things are changing at a rate some of them are not willing to accept. The London Stock Exchange switched Footsie 100 share trading over to a computer screen order book, and it has been a hard transition, because the way of working that they've always known is changing.

It was like being told one day that you had to conduct all your business from now on in Italian. It is understandable that you would feel unease, if all you knew was how to say *ciao bella*. A new generation of computers and a new generation of traders will eventually dominate the market. The period of transition will be hardest for those not willing to learn Italian.

When Steve Wilson was introducing some London traders to the new Tradepoint trading system, he was amazed at the attitudes he came across. While computerized trading came in as a gradual evolution in New York, in London it felt for some more like a revolution, especially in the equity market. The majority of traders in London sit in front of a computer screen to watch prices and information flows, then they trade over the phone. The idea of executing trades directly on the screen, or programming the computer to trade without human intervention, is something different and is taking longer to catch on. Steve pointed out:

"Pretty much everyone had grown up trading on the floor or trading on the phone. So to actually say to someone, 'What I want you to do is, put an order on a screen using a mouse, pointing and clicking'—it was kind of a leap of faith. A massive cultural leap.

"It was age and experience. Those over a certain age find this very difficult to accept as a concept. For anyone below a certain age, who has grown up with a PC, knows Windows, and speaks fluent spreadsheet, this is something that they tend to like because they are comfortable with it. They see this is the way trading is going to happen."

The first step was when the exchange took trading off the floor and put it onto a screen billboard system called SEAC. Rather than brokers quoting the price of a stock face-to-face, they'd put it up on a screen. They would negotiate over the telephone, using the price on the screen as an indication. If a trader saw a price that he liked, he would phone up the name on the screen and deal.

This method still exists except for the Footsie 100, which has gone to a new SETS (Stock Exchange Electronic Trading Service) screen order book. Brokers input their bids and offers, and if a bid matches an offer, a trade is done and it disappears from the screen. Those remaining become the new bids and offers. It's like a blotter or bulletin board.

How long will traders be willing to wait to get a match? Will they decide instead to deal over the phone and find a more immediate match and money?

There had been high hopes that SETS would bring greater speed, visibility, transparency, and efficiency to equity trading in London. But a lot of trading there still goes on by telephone. The dealer market is viable and important in terms of providing immediacy, the ability to move stock when you want to, and in terms of liquidity. It could well be that electronic trading takes a while to catch on, especially with the established British houses.

Marcus Hooper, an advocate of electronic trading, expressed serious concern about the SETS trading system.

"The volume that goes through SETS is incredibly low. There are a variety of ways that market makers can figure out who is actually doing what in the marketplace. And as soon as they think it is a client order, they will corrupt the prices. It is very hard to put an order on SETS and not get price corruption. My bid will go up there at 251. Within seconds a few hundred shares will go up there at 251 and a half or 252 bid. My order would get jumped. Not a bad thing, because that is part of the price formation mechanism. The problem is, you don't expect it to happen 90 percent of the time. It is very hard for me to maintain the best bid on the screen. It is virtually impossible.

"What has happened from my point of view is that the principal traders now have a very strong understanding of how this market works. They want to get the principal orders flowing back through. What they are doing is trying to maintain the sort of attitude that is still prevalent in London, which is demanding immediacy. There is absolutely no logic at all in going to the order book, when you can get larger size from the principal traders. Most people now are just demanding capital. That's why SETS isn't taking off. The system is not attractive from an investor point of view."

In a survey by Reuters that was sent to trading desks of the largest fund managers in England, 90 percent of the traders reported that SETS is slower, 83 percent said it was worse than the previous system, and 46 percent said that they found prices were actually worse than before. Colin Taylor said the failure of SETS was due to its lack of depth, and its failure to provide anonymity or a central counterparty.

Only about thirty stocks show liquidity on the system at any one time—out of one hundred on the order book. So London has electronic trading that is supposed to be cheaper and faster, but they are not enthralled with it. Is this a cultural reluctance or a failing of the system? It is a bit of both.

Marcus continued with the thought:

"There is a big problem in this marketplace with institutional investors. They have not gotten used to the idea of trading with an order book. They are just not up to speed yet. It is very very frustrating. The orders are just being phoned up, same as before SETS. They just phone in an order for X million and say, 'Work it as best you can.'

"When I speak to American traders, they have a different approach to the way they do things. They are much more open to new ideas, much more open to exposing themselves to the risk of what is going on, as opposed to passing the risk on to the broker. The traders here in London are quite happy to blame a broker for getting it wrong, but they are not prepared to take the risk and get it right themselves.

"Whereas we should be running the orders on SETS. And that, under the current market structure, is not feasible because of price corruption. And also because the ability to get things into and out of the order book is just not there."

Phil Nathan, trader at Charles Stanley in London, views the SETS system with cynicism:

"The big push was to get rid of the brokers' touch, the buying and selling price. That's why we went to an order-driven system. That was the American push. And the belief is that it will become like the U.S. markets. It will create liquidity and it will create easier and speedier trading. At the same time we are bringing in paperless trading. So it will be an interesting couple of years. I think there will be a few mistakes.

"The stock exchange has been trying to force this on us for a while, and they won. But the exchange is traditionally well known for getting it wrong. They spent God knows how many millions on Taurus, and then had to pull the rug on it. Traders lost a lot of faith.

"One day there might be a big enough group that wants to start a trading floor again. It depends. You could get a rebellion. And there could be a trading floor again, for small companies or something. As soon as Tradepoint came in, the stock exchange panicked to an order-driven system."

Tradepoint is the alternative exchange in London, which is automated and open to the buy side. Anyone in the world with a Bloomberg computer terminal can have access to trade on Tradepoint electronically as well as on the Tradepoint screen.

Marcus was an early user of the Tradepoint system:

"It's amazingly frustrating and staggering that people aren't using the Tradepoint system. I find it beyond belief."

Steve Wilson explained the Tradepoint process:

"There is scope to automate the trading process from inception of the order idea, the point at which you have a wish to trade in a particular stock, all the way through order generation. Through to order entry. Through to public disclosure of that order. Through to order execution, trade confirmation, settlement message routing, and final settlement of monies and delivery of stock."

Tradepoint has some very sophisticated-looking software. The screen is easy to use and has all sorts of features attached to it. But it may be indicative of the reluctance in London to trade this way that Tradepoint's trading volume is also still quite low.

EASDAQ, a computerized trading exchange in Europe, offers pan-European stocks. It is focused at the entry-level, venture-capital end of the market, providing a way for companies to come to market, to raise capital, and to achieve visibility.

Both systems are providing more vehicles for traders to find the best price and market available at the time they want to trade. Getting traders to use the systems is another matter.

In Paris, electronic trading has been accepted for some time in equity trading. M. Belgarde of the Paris Bourse explained the advantage he sees with the CAC (Cotation Assistée en Continu) system:

"You can use any software to use our system. You can ask for a screen built by one of the software houses in Paris. And you have brokers that have built their own screens. So you do not have only one view of the market. There is no official view of the market. You have to put the buy orders on one side and the sell orders on the other side. But otherwise you can put in your own colors. You can decide to see ten different orders or only one. It is up to you. So at each broker you may see a different screen.

"Everyone can access our market from anywhere in the world. We do not have any kind of middleman in the markets. Buy orders and sell orders cross and trade directly on the system. The trades go through a broker, but it is much less expensive than in London. Or even in New York, where you have the specialists on the New York Stock Exchange that take a fee on trades. Here, no one takes any fee."

However, over at Matif, Paris's futures exchange, and at LIFFE in London, some traders at first opposed the move toward electronic trading. Locals, or day traders speculating with their own money, staged a strike in protest to Matif's planned introduction of electronic trading, which would parallel open outcry trading. Many French locals voted with their feet, and crossed the channel to London to trade instead on the floor of LIFFE. Shortly thereafter LIFFE experienced pressure from some of its large international members to move toward electronic trading in order to compete with the electronic European exchanges, and a political battle ensued for months between that group and the locals in London who opposed it before LIFFE finally committed to electronic trading.

Despite some traders' resistance to the electronic systems, in order to survive the escalating competition from Europe and elsewhere, exchanges have to either transfer wholeheartedly to an electronic universe, or at least consider it as an added parallel function. Before 1985 most of Europe's stock exchanges were still open outcry and were private memberships. After Big Bang in London in 1986, most of the European exchanges as well as the rest of the world moved directly into electronics. If the single euro currency successfully comes into play, there will be less of a difference between European exchanges, which is prompting them to merge and link so they are all accessible on one screen. The attraction of this, rather than traders having to trade on several different screens for different markets, is obvious.

Ultimately, the deciding factor will be whether trading entirely on an electronic system, although it is cheaper and more flexible, can replace floor trading entirely in terms of volume and liquidity—the ability to buy and sell quickly when you want to at the price you want. So far the SETS system in London isn't liquid. Mouse-challenged traders will gain faith once system designers produce a workable and fair electronic trading system for the London equity market.

THERE ARE REASONS the proponents of change toward computer-driven trading are so confident. Higher trading volumes are available when you trade this way. It would be impossible to accomplish today's high volumes in the United States without the use of technology. Electronic trading is significantly cheaper, especially for straight, commodity-like trades. For instance, on a U.S. Treasury bill, you know the coupon, you know the issue date, you know the issuer. It's as near as you can get to a perfect market. All the information is provided to the market at the same time, and the price is the summation of all the information in the marketplace. On that basis, there is no reason electronic trading cannot be used to push a product around in the marketplace.

But you obviously are still going to need traders to take positions based on their understanding of changes in the political environment, monetary policy, or news. You need them to think. It won't totally eliminate the need for a human touch. Peter Jenkins at Scudder, Stevens & Clark commented:

"We can handle buying and selling more with the same number of traders to keep margins up. The more traders there are—obviously, they are expensive—the more it is going to cost your firm. What you want to do is, as your assets grow you want to trade in bigger size but have the same amount of traders. The only difference is that they will be trading bigger quantities rather than smaller quantities."

Then there is the speed factor, which is a huge advantage. You can use the computer to spot trade opportunities and let the computer go ahead and trade for you. It is faster than you could be. You won't miss the opportunity, and you will gain by being ready to pick up the next one. Electronic trading strategies save you from staring at the computer screen all day trying to spot an opportunity when you could be doing analytics and strategy.

Business schools have been getting the next generation ready for electronic trading in simulated trading environments. In the basement of the business school at MIT in Boston is a world-class 3,000-square-foot electronic trading classroom under the supervision of Professor Andrew Lo. It is paved with Reuters and Bloomberg feeds and Quantex boxes. Students do simulated trading against the computers in a room fitted out with an electronic ticker, news panels, and computer workstations. Ticker data goes back twenty years so that they can build a trading strategy on Quantex, then run it against the simulation to see if it actually works. They are not alone. Carnegie Mellon University students have been training in a computerized trading laboratory for years, and Wharton began offering mock trading classes on computers in 1993.

Michael Bloomberg and software vendors are rushing to provide these students with the tools they will need, and indeed will expect, when they emerge from the basement to work on trading desks for real.

Some traders who prefer trading in person reject screen-based trading because they have a hard time conceiving that the skills they have developed are transferable to the screen. One of those skills is what traders call "color"—what they glean from being with other traders physically in the same place: information from looking another trader in the eye, watching the intensity of the bidding in a crowd on an exchange floor, or recognizing the people in the crowd and making a judgment about how much they might be trading and why.

Can you get "color" from a computer screen trading system? Color does comes from a screen, but it involves a totally different process of taking in information. You see the markets blinking. You see their price and volume changes. You see their ebbs and flows and unusual movements, which tell you something. The screen talks to today's traders the same way the tape used to talk to Bob Mnuchin. People who claim they don't get color from trading on screens usually miss hearing things: hearing the noise on the floor build, hearing the voice of the person on the other end of the phone and trying to guess what they are thinking or are about to do in the market. But screen color can be learned.

Quants can be so comfortable with a mathematical model that they let computerized trading happen without human intervention at all. Ray Killian told me about traders he knows who use ITG's Quantex machine this way:

"You run the mathematical model on the Quantex box, which is designed to interface with the New York Stock Exchange electronic system. So it sends orders electronically to New York. You program your system to formulate your orders. You tell it how to do it. If your model is good enough, you can have the model generate the orders, drop it onto the Quantex system electronically, and have it automatically go to the floor and execute according to a set of rules. Like the Ten Commandments. Without any human intervention at all.

"We have one guy that has eight Quantex boxes linked, and sends orders all day long like that. David Shaw could tell you the same thing, but it depends on your own personal philosophy. Some people want to have a human being between the automation and the button."

There's a growing group of traders that use the color from the screen alone to trade. They simply watch numbers, like the old tape watchers who used to trade based on what they read being printed on the paper ticker coming out of a machine. These traders have little interest in what the company does. Although many traders blend their interest in and knowledge of companies with this kind of number watching and trade, the "bandits," as they are called, watch a stock for a big spread between bid and offer, and if they see the stock is moving, they trade inside the spread and take a small profit. Sometimes their trades only last minutes.

There are more than two thousand independent traders like these, trading NASDAQ stocks inside the quote. As of April 1998 they accounted for over 12 percent of NASDAQ volume.

They make trades in smaller fractions than the brokers, squeezing inside the traditional spreads market makers normally earn, willing to make less on each trade, but counting on making more of them. Fast new technology allows them to do that. New trading software gives them all the information they need, as well as access to NASDAQ's system. Island network software allows them to view NASDAQ market makers' quotes and transact within those quotes for only $1 per trade.

As a result of their trading, spreads on NASDAQ stocks are narrowing, making it harder for the traditional big market makers to make money.

As freelance day traders working through an electronic medium, they can trade from anywhere. This has brought into being a new kind of dealing room which is populated by traders dealing for their own account on computers and software supplied by small brokerages. For a small commission, they can trade all day or not show up. The rooms are usually sparten and quiet. Electronic trading has liberated traders in London as well, where clearing firms have converted unused office space into trading rooms filled with computers for day traders who come in to trade derivatives on their own account.

As FAR AS computers and trading goes, we have climbed the first set of stairs: organizing mountains of information into comprehensible databases, having it available to everyone at the same time, and developing electronic order books, electronic bulletin boards that post prices for everyone to see. But the application of data processing goes only so far. Right now, the most effective trading tool for most of the world is still the telephone. But very soon telephones may become obsolete in their present form, the way the ticker tape went from paper to digital. The marriage of the computer and the telephone will change everything. There could be trading systems with built-in phones where you talk to the screen and the screen talks back. There could be built-in videophones. Trading from a computer will become more straightforward and screens more user friendly.

Chris Keith of Wit Capital in New York once developed a system based on this concept. Today with your telephone you offer to trade with one person at a time. But what if you could have the power to show your issue of 75,000 shares, and show it differently, to two hundred people at the same time? Selective lists could be generated that would categorize traders "called" into groups, some by relationship, some by the fact that they are risk arbitrageurs, some because they are passive index funds; and the product displayed would be at a different price to each group. The product may even be shown in different variations or pieces to different groups, all at once, instantly, online.

The computer would display the data, and the telephone function within the system would enable the trade. The screen could be big and split up into a patchwork of windows, enabling you to watch multiple displays at once. It could be mounted on the wall, on a large panel at your desk or built into your desk. It is inevitable that everybody will be going to big flat screens, mainly because of the radiation levels that emanate from a cathode ray tube. Electronic trading will permeate the industry, with the next generation of computers and software uniting into one platform not only advanced features but the trading and settlement functions as well. It will be a much faster, more flexible business.

One trader in New York said he looks at ten or twelve screens now:

"I'll tell you, I might be willing to look at an entire wall, maybe forty or fifty screens. I would love to sit and have the entire conference room wall filled with screens. Once we get flat screens I am really going to go full-time. You actually don't want one keyboard, as crazy as it sounds. The reason is, you need two or three keyboards sometimes. Because you want to be flipping all the different things at the same time to look at the relationships in all kinds of things. You want them side by side. You've got to have everything displayed simultaneously so you can take it all in simultaneously. And I would like sound from a trading floor."

What lingers is a confusion about how far computers and electronic trading are going to take us. It is possible to conceive of a totally computerized market where no human intervention is necessary. But still, realistically and even philosophically, most of the world's markets are far away from that. And there are advantages to both forms of trading.

There will always be instances where a mismatch is taken up by the brokerages, providing capital to their clients. There aren't always buyers for sellers at exactly the same time for the same amount and price. So the human element will always be needed.

Stanley Shopkorn sees both sides, especially for stocks:

"It doesn't mean that I've always agreed with the New York Stock Exchange. But I will tell you that I think the physical auction market system is probably the strongest and deepest market that there is. Even though there is electronic interface in the marketplace today, the larger orders are generally handled by the two-dollar brokers, by the specialists.

"There is a form of give and take, human interaction, which allows the trust factor. I think the human interaction with electronic additive is probably the best market system in the world."

14 TRADING ON THE FUTURE

THE PUBLIC IN GENERAL IS BECOMING MUCH MORE
COMFORTABLE WITH ELECTRONICS, AND A LOT OF
PEOPLE REALLY ENJOY ACTIVELY TRADING IN THEIR
ACCOUNT. AND IF THEY CAN DO IT AT THREE IN THE
MORNING WHILE THE BABY IS UP CRYING, AND THEY
CAN HOP ON THE NET AND TRADE A FEW STOCKS,
WELL, THAT'S WONDERFUL.

HOLLY STARK

You're on the Internet. Click Yahoo! finance. Then look at Inside
Trading Reports, go to Associated Press Business Wire to check the
latest news on companies you are interested in, click Quotes to see
where individual stocks are currently trading, then click and read the
morning's *Financial Times,* or the *Wall Street Journal,* or the *Singapore
Business Times.* Click *Fortune* or *Forbes* magazine, and read the latest
issue.

   Click and order reports from Wall Street's top analysts. Drop
into the trading and investing forums like Silicon Investor to read

what thoughts and rumors people are talking about in the market. Click on a company or the investor relations person or leave a note for the treasurer to respond to. Click news.com/investor for stock charts and earnings estimates. Click Edgar to read the latest SEC filings, click the Bloomberg Personal page to scan quotes from financial markets around the world. Click Wit Capital for access to initial public offerings, or Fidelity for mutual funds. Then click on Datek, Charles Schwab, or E*Trade and trade for your own account effortlessly, accessing the markets and knowing the outcome of your trades within minutes of their being put through.

Schwab has nearly 50 percent of the online do-it-yourself trading market, with over $112 billion in online asset accounts. It offers company news and information from Dow Jones, Business Wire, and Newsbytes News Network, free, updated every fifteen minutes. It also offers Market Buzz, access to stock, company and market information from CNN Financial News, MarketEdge, and First Call. Muriel Siebert offers free research by fax within five minutes, compiled from independent sources like Standard and Poor's, First Call for earnings estimates, and Argus Research.

There are well over thirty cyber-brokers available on the Internet, providing price quotes, technical graphs, links to the news wires, analysts' reports and bookkeeping, and the ability to buy or sell a security with the click of a mouse. Escalating price wars between discount brokers to win your account means you benefit from ever lower trading costs.

One of the major Internet search engines, Lycos, reports that business topics and stock trading are among the top ten topics people request from them. And it has been reported that the Motley Fools Web page, an investment site, has the most hits of any site in the entire World Wide Web.

People who trade on the Internet know it is much cheaper. They feel they have more control. They consider they know some companies pretty well, even if it is just because they have always bought and loved their products. And they can research their stocks online and talk to their own sources without the interpretation of a salesperson from a securities firm who is trying to sell them something.

This kind of electronic trading has democratized trading activity. Anyone anywhere can do it for themselves, student, business person, or grandparent. And in a way, it has become a sort of entertainment, become more Hollywood. Watch CNBC, which reaches households and businesses around the world. It takes its cues from TV sitcoms—the guy who looks like Robert Redford at the trading desk breathlessly telling you what is happening in the markets, his eyes sparkling with excitement; reports direct from the floor of stock and futures exchanges around the world; *Power Lunch*, a segment where you meet the celebrities of the business world and watch reporters question them the same way a professional portfolio manager would, all presented with more than a hint of glamour and intrigue. It's a new world.

Could finance, the old yawn of cocktail party conversations, actually be capturing the imaginations of people everywhere, sitting transfixed before their computers, diving in for hours of activity? Is it because we are doing it in front of screens, and in the future will do it through our TV, that our perception of it as entertainment and something akin to a hobby has taken hold? Or is it because those of us who grew up with computers find it a natural extension of our everyday lives?

Before, average investors were to a large extent passive, captive to the opinions of their brokers. Now they've been coached by experts, by Peter Lynch with his book *One Up on Wall Street*, stubbornly on the best-seller lists for years. Or by a slew of similarly friendly books encouraging investors to do it for themselves, probably better than the professionals can anyway.

Now cyber-trading is approached with equanimity and calm, with a glass of wine after work or school, for an evening of leaving messages for the president of Virgin Airlines, or tapping into the latest conversational news group discussing the possibility that Home Depot may come back in price and why, or a discussion in another news group about how employees are noticing problems at their company and warning investors online to take care.

This is interesting. It is person to person. You can read an online regional newspaper and learn local information on a company there from reporters on the scene. You can even question those reporters by leaving e-mail for them to answer. You have power. You are empowered. Do-it-yourself online investing/trading has tremendous appeal compared with being a recipient at the end of the telephone listening to a broker's scripted monologue, or with passively dropping your money off with a mutual fund.

There has never been a better time for the individual investor, who now has unprecedented access to more research and information, better prices, and drastically lower commissions. The gates are open. Where information was controlled before, now it is available to everyone. It's completely changed how we invest and what we pay for it.

Forrester Research Inc. in Cambridge, Massachusetts, predicts that online investing will grow from the 3 million acccounts at the end of 1997 to 14.4 million accounts by 2002, with $688 billion in assets. It believes: "The potential shift is huge. The Internet investor will be the cream of the crop. . . . "

In the first three months of 1998, almost half of all trades put through Charles Schwab were online. Deeply discounted trading commissions are one of the forces driving people to the screen. We're talking about a huge transfer in power from the traditional market professionals on the sell side to individual investors at their computers. The probability is that once investors have traded online they will stay online, even as their assets grow.

The American Stock Exchange conducted a survey in 1996, which revealed that people between the ages of twenty-five and thirty-four, whom it nicknamed "NextVestors," have very different characteristics from the previous generation of baby boomers. They are more likely to own a computer at home by a two-to-one margin compared to the public as a whole, and 29 percent of them have Internet access, compared to 8 percent of all households. Half surveyed said they prefer to do their own research before investing, and only 39 percent use brokers.

Forrester Research forecasts another major shift, away from both traditional brokerages and discount brokerages. It foresees the evolution of a "mid-tier broker" that will provide, online, most of the services of a full-service broker at a much lower price. "Mid-tiers" will provide investors with analytic models that can evaluate portfolios and help with asset allocation. These models will also allow investors to scan for companies looking only for certain criteria. There will be research, trading, news, and Internet investing assistants.

Changes in demand and preferences will shape the new financial system. Wall Street will inevitably change as retail customers increasingly find new trading avenues through their computers, which includes trading through discount brokerages that cost up to 90 percent less than full-service brokers.

Smaller regional brokerages could take on a more collegial look, where brokers will educate and counsel. And they will need to be willing to do that online by e-mail, right to customers' homes, to earn their business away from the alternatives lining up. If they are a constant, friendly presence that is unobtrusive and unaggressive, they may appeal to the new investor. Although change is difficult, and will more than likely mean the loss of jobs for some stockbrokers, it presents tremendous opportunity for increased business if traditional brokerages realign their function and their thinking to anticipate the demands of the new market.

At present, brokerages are reacting to the market, but still viewing it in a traditional light. They ask with trepidation, who is going to educate the consumer? Who is going to protect them? Like stunned Catholic clergy who disbelievingly watch their congregations dwindle out the door to find their own spiritual path, traditional brokerages too will lose practitioners, especially because they don't think they will. Another objection the brokerages raise is the specter of con artists and scams on the Internet. But investors are never totally protected from unscrupulous brokers or promoters. It will be in the self-interest of market participants to find ways around that problem.

Howard Kramer, senior associate of the Securities and Exchange Commission's market regulation division, said in relation to retail Internet trading:

"We look at the growth of online trading not as problematic, but as promising. It's opening up a whole new avenue for the use of technology to increase investor services and disseminate information."

David Shaw sees the passing of traditionally defined brokerages this way:

"Money simply collected for inefficient paper processing will pass. As things get more automated there will be fewer middlemen. You would expect to see costs come down. And the nice thing about a free market is that it will mean automatically those savings will get passed on to customers, just through competition. So right now the deep discount brokerage firms offer these dramatically low commissions, stunningly lower than they were ten years ago, because of cutting out a lot of middlemen, including the New York Stock Exchange.

They all go to the third market. And what they are doing is going through a much smaller chain of human beings, using computers much more, with fewer mistakes, and that saves money. That is getting passed on to the customers. We will see much more of that."

It would be a mistake to underestimate the intelligence of the retail investor worldwide. Demographics, age, and technological innovation are radically changing the way the average person perceives the act of investing. Financial/business television will be the engine that pushes individual investor interest to new levels, and will be prominent on the screen we will be interacting with when television, telephone, and computer merge. It will be the life force of the financial Internet hub to which we connect.

There is a television sitcom in Canada centered around life on a trading desk; such a show could easily spawn similar, and better, sitcoms that pick up on the excitement and reality of trading, and these could fire the imagination of the television viewing public that presently has no interest in this aspect of their lives. Today when you go to the visitor gallery's interactive center at the New York Stock Exchange, what hits you is that the masses of visitors are so young, that they are asking questions, and that they are watching the educational video with rapt attention, using the touch-screen kiosks, exploring real-time trading information on the rows of computer terminals, and staring transfixed at the scene on the trading floor.

Ray Killian of Posit told me:

"Generation X is not really interested in talking to brokers. There is always going to be that segment of the investing public that needs a lot more help. There will always be a firm like Smith Barney that provides good solid research to a high net individual. The CEO of some company is too busy to do the analysis himself. But I think that business is going to be more the retail kind of buyer, the sell one hundred shares kind of guy, that has more time on his hands, and that loves going on the computer."

A national survey conducted for the NASDAQ market by Peter D. Hart Research Associates found:

"A 49 percent plurality say they prefer an investment approach based on 'learning a lot about investing so you can manage your own investments well' over an approach that focuses on 'having an advisor whom you can trust to manage your investments well.' We see a real generation gap among investors on this question, with

Generation X and baby boom investors both preferring the self-management mode . . . what it means is that today's investors—particularly young investors—will want advisors who can educate and empower them, not make decisions for them."

Investment clubs have taken off. It's do-it-yourself investing. The National Association of Investors Corporation of America reported that in the first quarter of 1998, there were more than 1,100 new clubs forming each month. Currently the association guides 36,872 clubs across the nation by providing information and advice, as well as maintaining an active Web site. And investment forums, or online message boards, are growing at a phenomenal pace. Motley Fools, Silicon Investor, and America Online attract the lion's share, with millions of people sharing their opinions and information.

NAIC's Ken Janke noted:

"An awful lot of people want to have control of their future by selecting their own securities, and they are willingly taking on far more risk. They are enjoying it."

Let's hope that they are taking on more risk prudently, with disposable income only.

The first step into the water for individual investors was a wholesale mad rush into mutual funds. Investors have paid attention and are reading the financial and business pages. It would be a natural progression to take the next step toward doing some or all of it themselves. Pundits worry about the risk inherent in that, but pundits are also writing a lot of books exploring the "risk-taking" orientation that has developed in the population at large. Vested interests claim that the public taking risks is a bad thing. But in truth, educated risk taking is a positive force that could produce not only better and more prudent returns for the individual but more business for the brokerages. It will just be a different kind of business.

There is also the worry that individual investors have historically plowed into the markets and taken on added risk at market tops. That's true. Short-term market tops and crashes are a concern if individual investors need to get their money out of the market during the period of the crash. In the long term it makes less of a difference. If anything was learned from the last crash it was that there were some excellent buys to be made while the mutual funds were cashing in on the market out of fear. Peter D. Hart Research Associate's Survey among Stock Investors found that, if there were a significant drop in the market:

". . . only 8 percent would sell stocks in order to avoid further losses. The largest portion (54 percent) of investors anticipate that a drop would not lead them to make any major changes in their stock investments."

The public segment that is interested in the financial markets and wants to become personally involved in their investments/trading is finding different ways to derive their research. One approach is to research and invest in local companies that they know or use. Another is to do research on the Internet, which often yields information that is fresher and more valuable than reading an annual report written months before about historical data on a company. Annual reports are prepared merely to satisfy accounting requirements and give only a snapshot of what the numbers were for the company on a particular day. And they are unabashed propaganda brochures to market the products and services of the company. Furthermore, traditional analysts' reports from brokerages are first and foremost meant to sell stocks for the firm. Online investors exhibit a pronounced skepticism about the motivations of Wall Street analysts and "off-the-rack" commentary from brokers.

Online investment clubs research quarterly financial reports on companies, study the NASDAQ home page and online investment newsletters, and monitor Bloomberg Personal. Sometimes the members come from all over the world, so they can report to the others on companies doing well in their local areas and do the research for other members. Some come together to talk about and study only high-tech companies. Software developers and engineers take part in Silicon Investor's online discussions. As of October 1997 it was the largest discussion group on the Web, and one of the top three financial sites in terms of traffic. Some groups are just interested in health care companies. They share information with each other willingly because they've quickly learned that they will get a great deal in return. These investors are harvesting live, current information to spot opportunities and potential. Granted, this segment of investors is tiny compared to the overall market. The point is, it is growing. And it uses the Internet to derive information and as an order-routing system.

Stanley Ross noted that a recent survey found that the average investment manager visits 240 companies a year. He wondered what the point of their going was, since they are not allowed to glean or utilize anything that is not immediately available to everybody else.

He wondered how a quick trip could tell them something valuable. And he wondered how they could make a decision to own shares in a company or not, simply by poring over reports the company gave them that held stale information.

His point of view is unique, but it is a tenet of the new investor, who will increasingly be fed the same information the fund manager gets by the companies themselves online. The one difference is that the local investor might actually know people at the company or drive by the factory every day and notice the activity level, which is more than a professional money manager can do in a one-day or one-hour visit. Already, the online investor can access multimedia company "road shows" and download their prospectuses. They have access to sophisticated, free analysis to determine risk/return, value, and volatility on their portfolios—in any stock, in any currency.

In the U.K., public awareness of stock trading has expanded tremendously relative to what it was before, with new flotations and the attendant publicity. To service the new investor, there are a host of do-it-yourself share-trading services that are user friendly and inexpensive. You can pick up a phone and deal directly through Dealwise, Yorkshare, City Deal, and Hargreaves Lansdown. Or you can trade on the Internet directly through Charles Schwab or Barclays Stockbrokers. You can walk into a National Westminster Bank and buy or sell shares through the NatWest Instant Share Dealing service, whose business at times has been as much as one out of ten of the retail shares traded on the London Stock Exchange. The success of the concept and trend of direct purchase in the U.K. can be observed at Direct Line, which markets insurance by telephone, or at Richard Branson's Virgin, which sells pensions over the telephone.

By contrast, in France, although individuals can buy as little as one share on the Paris Bourse online through Minitel (the computer terminal that everyone in France can receive with their telephone), there is still not much interest in do-it-yourself.

The Merrill Lynches of the future world of investing will have extensive and deep home bases on Internet television, or whatever we call it then. They may even have an announcer. Or they may link up into a separate financial intranet, a hub of financial institutions, all linked electronically to offer the individual the penultimate source for ease of transactions, security, and information. Banks, central banks, brokerages as they might look in the future, new forms of stock exchanges, commodity auctions and real estate auctions, financial databases, financial newsletters, newspapers, magazines, financial think tanks and professors, and live seminars will all be connected. An individual's bank accounts, taxes, stock accounts, real estate holdings—all this information will be interrelated and accessible in easy report form. Credit links will allow and facilitate in seconds the transactions they may want to make.

There will be instant access to the global financial marketplace: Mexico, Singapore, Germany, all markets and markets in all products will be available, including software to compare and analyze them—then help you to buy them. The Internet could become the preeminent order-routing system that will bring individual investors' order flow into the traditional and nontraditional exchanges of the world. A type of INSTINET will develop for the retail trader, just as it exists now for the buy-side professional trader, matchmaking trades directly between between individuals.

Twin forces, the home trader and the buy-side trader, are driving changes in the workings of the financial community that will shape the future. Interestingly, the balance of power between the home do-it-yourself trader and the buy-side trader representing funds may tip in either direction at different points in future market cycles. Laszlo Birinyi at the research firm that bears his name confirms that more people than ever want to have control over the stocks they own rather than relinquishing that choice to anonymous fund managers.

This is natural in an up market. But when there is a down market, people could pour back into the perceived havens of managed money, tipping the balance of power back toward the buy-side trader. There is no doubt that now the buy-side trader and pension funds rule the market. And to compare the two forces in terms of size would be ridiculous. Online traders at home make up but a small percentage. However, that percentage is growing at an astonishing speed, and like buy-side traders, will be a motivating factor shaping the future of the business.

WHAT WILL THE future marketplace look like for professional traders? In New York it will evolve in pace with the evolution of technology and changes in end-user preferences. Managed money funds are growing so quickly, and there are so many of them, that intense competition is driving them to become more efficient, more cost conscious and profitable. One way to become more efficient is to become more electronic.

What will the sell side do? The electronic revolution that is driving the industry is squeezing profit margins. Sell-side traders will be transacting in a marketplace that expects different things from them, or less from them, than before. So they will be driven to add value through technology and quantitative approaches. The attrition in sell-side jobs will be because firms will have to cut their transaction fees and find other ways to get their research paid for. Proprietary trading will take on added significance as a revenue producer. The securities markets will continue to open up to nonmembers, to all financial institutions, as the balance of power shifts in favor of the end customers. There undoubtedly will be a loss of jobs because continued consolidation in the industry will inevitably mean streamlining and layoffs.

A new market structure is already taking shape, full of different markets, rather than a few traditional centralized ones. Alternative markets are disintermediating orders away from traditional markets because they are seen as offering advantages to the end user and could well become major "exchanges" themselves.

Overdevelopment on the selling side in London in all markets spells attrition as well. Michael Paull related what is happening:

"On top of the London market you have an overlay of tremendous capacity from the U.S. providers. If you wanted to do a Eurobond transaction, there are fifteen or twenty houses you could go talk to straight off. For a medium-term note program there are probably thirty medium-term note-dealing desks in London with dedicated functions. Then the Japanese provide capacity as well. You have BZW providing capacity, the Swiss, UBS, Crédit Suisse, Swiss Bank—there is vast overcapacity.

"Now overlay on that the move toward a European currency. If that happens, you will have whole areas which are specialized on a particular currency focus now, the French franc desk, the deutschmark desk, which will all be merged into an EMU desk. Which means people will feel very nervous about their jobs."

Periods of transition cause turbulence and unusual opportunities for traders. John Heiman, former U.S. comptroller of the currency, thinks that the transition period will be a quiz:

"During interregnum, are all currencies going to be traded? Will governments switch as quickly as they can to the euro? Will they convert existing debt to the euro? Will they keep it in the present currency? So there are enormous side effects on this. That creates great opportunities for traders as it shakes itself out, and clearly the arbitrage possibilities that are going to exist and the dislocations that are going to exist, they are just bound to happen."

The currency markets will become vastly different than they look today if Europe achieves a lasting monetary union. Leo Melamed's vision of the future of the European Monetary Union is that it will happen, in time. He sees the world as forming into three major currency blocs—the dollar bloc, the yen bloc, and the euro bloc—and the instruments of trade would evolve around those major blocs.

"We are not going to be so much playing a given currency as we are going to be trading a bloc of currencies. So that there will be a great deal of shift between the bloc in Europe, the bloc in the U.S., and the bloc in Asia. I don't think what I am seeing is a move toward a static world. I think there will be continuous opportunity between blocs and between nations and all kinds of financial change. I think it will be different. It will be highly sophisticated and very competitive."

Gary Lapayover is not so convinced it will happen, and if it does, there will be problems:

"Take the new EMU contracts. Try and play that one against all the currencies. Banks here and individuals must have loads of money tied up in all those foreign countries. The manufacturers that do lots of business with those countries have investments in them because that is protection for their product sales on the differences in U.S. costs and selling there. That will be an amazing one to try and figure out if and when they unwrap those contracts. A lot of people have contracts out and agreements out under variances of different currencies with one another and different interest rate plays. How do they go flat? How do they meld them? How do they match them all up against dollars and yen?"

When the EMU is in place, the market should become relatively calm. It could shrink currency trading by as much as 8 percent, which will in turn shrink the number of currency traders needed.

Traders in stocks and bonds and other securities should enjoy a surge in trading business if the European Monetary Union stays together. Anyone who has a euro fund will have to come down to the market's weight. It means that the core countries of the euro will be big buyers of their neighbors. And domestically they will be big sellers of the natural markets. For instance, Crédit Lyonnais Asset Management will reduce its weighting of French stocks in its portfolios to add to the weighting in the core euro equities, or bonds, or whatever. That initial surge in trading volume would subside back to normal once portfolios are normalized to become euro portfolios.

Susan Ollila thought that one effect might be to "foster the development of a corporate bond market in Europe. Right now, we don't have much of a corporate bond market there. So you would begin to liquefy markets. Once you have reduced that volatility, you are able to create markets that have greater depth in them. I suspect if you create less volatility at the core, then people start to look at peripheral markets. They will develop, and I am thinking of the Eastern European bloc. The whole nature of the portfolios that we have today would be different."

Which of the European futures markets wins the business for a new EMU market is up in the air, but they are in a fierce battle to be king of the hill. The resulting decline in demand and business will mean only one will thrive. London's LIFFE futures exchange would have a good chance of becoming the European center for trading euro-denominated interest rate futures, or euro derivatives, simply because it already has various product lines and good liquidity.

Even if the U.K. isn't part of a currency union, being the financial center would be advantageous to London in that it would be outside of the bureaucracy of Brussels. It would be free to do what it likes, free to move more rapidly and flexibly to changes in the market environment. London has all the infrastructure to maintain a financial services sector, and has a long tradition of doing so. It is already the largest foreign exchange market, a true international banking center with a time overlap with Asia and New York and Europe. There are 565 foreign banking institutions in London, and it has 30 percent of the global foreign exchange business and 75 percent of secondary market trading in the international bond market. And it has a culture and language that are comfortable for other cultures to live with.

In London buy-side traders will catch up with those in New York. The funds will be bigger and salaries will be higher; they are already moving into more responsible positions. Trading desks on the buy side will have to become much more sophisticated and more technology dependent as they trade larger volumes of shares.

The brokerages of the future—or however we will define them—will become larger entities, and probably fewer of them will operate as small independent securities houses. The amalgamation we are seeing in the financial services industry between big banks, insurance companies, brokerages, and fund management firms is bound to continue. The resulting superinstitutions, along with the webwork of electronic information providers and exchanges, will shrink the traditional cost structure, bringing to the top of the power pyramid a smaller number of muscular, worldwide institutions. There are tremendous advantages in this—more efficient distribution, seamless liquidity—but it will mean a loss of jobs during the transition.

The screens on most traders' desks will enable them to tap into wherever in the world they want to buy something, dependent solely on cost or preference for a certain trading system, liquidity, or the tax environment in a certain country. If a trader wanted to buy Danish stocks on the Frankfurt Stock Exchange because he liked that system, and Frankfurt listed that Danish stock, then he could choose to trade in Frankfurt. His trading business will flow to the exchanges or systems where he perceives better value or less market impact when he trades. It will be his choice to go where he can keep his trading costs down and therefore improve his performance and value to his firm or client.

There will be a constellation of places to trade, competing pools of liquidity. It could well be that entities like Bloomberg, Reuters, INSTINET, POSIT, EASDAQ, and unforeseen others will at some point have to talk to each other and make their systems work with each other. As the alternatives continue to proliferate, they are going to have to offer greater connectivity and integration between electronic trading systems, information systems, and analytical systems, which traders are talking more and more about wanting to see. One way this could happen is chaotically, not by design. The impetus may come from the end users, their clients, who will say, "I am a big client of yours. I want you to make your system talk to this guy's system, because I am also a big client of his. So the two of you get together and make it happen."

Significant disintermediation has happened in the marketplace with these new kinds of trading mechanisms. In addition to using electronic alternatives, major multinational corporations trade among themselves. IBM and DuPont, for example, are sophisticated in trading securities, have information access, and get a "first call" from the brokers. They start to look a lot like the broker/dealers themselves, which looks a lot like the clients are becoming competitors to the broker/dealers.

The challenge is for the traditional broker/dealers and traditional exchanges to face what central banks, governments, and the financial establishment as we know it are having to face: a loss of power, if they think power lies in remaining within outmoded definitions of themselves. They are increasingly impotent in the face of the evolution of technology and its democratizing impact on business and the individual, who through technology can supersede them. Distribution channels are changing dramatically: institutional investors and traders are connecting directly without necessarily going through a salesman. Some are linked electronically; alternative systems are providing new markets; individuals are dealing directly, channeling their orders through the Internet; companies are accessing the end investor directly with their Initial Public Offerings (IPOs) through the Internet to raise money.

Artificial barriers created by traditional exchanges and regulatory agencies are likely to break down under the weight of opposition from the buy side, as well as from competition from nontraditional electronic exchanges and information providers. Commercially operated investment exchanges will eventually be open to all viable financial institutions, although there are a lot of regulatory barriers to this happening quickly.

As competition escalates for business that used to flow to traditional sources, trading fees will be forced down—great for the customer, but not so great for the brokerages and traditional exchanges.

James Shapiro at the New York Stock Exchange disagrees:

"We may see INSTINET or Bloomberg or someone figuring out a way to trade stocks, link up everybody around the world, and kind of bypass the major exchanges. It is certainly conceivable. It may not be the most likely. There are lots of practical problems. There are lots of regulatory issues, like clearing and settling a stock. And there are inertia issues—it is hard to take stock trading away from the New York Stock Exchange. And there's lots of political issues. The French don't care how good the Bloomberg system is. They still want trading on the Paris Bourse. So I don't think that by any means it is an immediate possibility, but it is something that has a certain logic to it."

Not yet, but maybe sooner than one would think.

Considering the future of the New York Stock Exchange, Holly Stark commented that most of the world's stock exchanges are electronic now. Although the New York Stock Exchange has made tremendous changes in the last five years as a result of technology, Holly wondered if the floor was really needed in a physical sense:

"I guess if you want the physical presence of the specialist there, yes, you want the physical floor. Could he be sitting in a room at a terminal of his own and having his auction come to him electronically? I don't see why not. Is it going to happen anytime soon? I don't think so."

There's an us-versus-them theme here: old stock exchanges versus new electronic versions; old-school traders versus new computer-assisted traders; old regulations versus new regulations. Many young traders think the old order will be turned upside down. There's been a generational shift, and some of the young traders are rising to positions of power on trading desks. They are very comfortable with electronics and computers. They are not convinced that writing an order on a pad of paper and running around with it is the only way trading can be done. To them it looks like Pilgrims carrying relics.

But consider this. The New York Stock Exchange has proven to be a formidable survivor. It has evolved in a way that has integrated different markets. It is an order-driven system, with orders sent in to the floor, most of them through the electronic SuperDot system. It has been able to operate very successfully with both a dealer market doing the big institutional orders and an auction market. Over ten thousand U.S. institutions use the NYSE market. It provides tremendous liquidity not found anywhere else in the world. An average of $28.2 billion flows through the NYSE every day, and this figure is growing. Before 1995 there were only eight days where daily share volume reached or exceeded 400 million shares. In 1998, 626 million shares is a normal day.

The overwhelming majority of U.S. companies list on the NYSE, more than 2,716; as do more than 350, and counting, major foreign companies. In total, more than 3,060 companies list 217.3 billion shares valued at over $12.5 trillion dollars on the NYSE. For all intents and purposes, the exchange will continue to go from strength to strength as a market that combines the best of floor trading and new technology.

And let's talk about something abstract and intangible. Traditional exchange trading, most especially New York Stock Exchange trading, has a value to it that goes beyond the benefits of a totally electronic system without a floor. The stock exchange is a cultural institution generating emotional attachment. The New York Stock Exchange floor is the symbol and heart of U.S. capitalism. For me that is an important reason for it always to be there in its physical form, and sufficient reason for over three thousand people to crowd its visitor gallery every day—seven hundred thousand a year—and tens of millions to view its activity on televisions around the globe.

Bill Johnston has no fears about the continuing existence of the New York Stock Exchange as it has been evolving:

"Hell, I've been crucified and dead and buried more times in my life than I can even think about. We were dinosaurs. We were outmoded. The exchange had no ability to exist. But look, in the first quarter of 1998 we were averaging 626 million shares a day. When I started in the business, 4 million was a big day. In 1990, 100 million was a big day."

Richard Grasso, the chairman of the New York Stock Exchange, has a vision of the exchange, as it becomes more global and lists more foreign stocks, opening up to an extended trading day. Members of the exchange would be given four badges. One would be good for trading between 9:30 A.M. and 4:00 P.M.—the normal hours. Then one would be good for trading between 4:15 and 9:15 P.M., another from 9:30 P.M. to 1:00 A.M., and another for trading between 1:15 and 7:00 A.M. Members would have the ability to trade during any of those sessions, or lease out their badge for the sessions they do not want to attend. Not a twenty-four-hour market, but close to it.

The opposite side of the coin is what the rest of the world is moving toward. Look at Asia. Hong Kong is an electronic exchange. All or most of the countries in the emerging rim have electronic stock exchanges. Ray Killian of ITG said that people from Australia, Malaysia, Japan, and Sweden have come to him to develop their routing systems and trade-related technology using electronics. If you wanted to build a new exchange and didn't have the culture, tradition, and existing liquidity of a mature exchange like the NYSE, you would build an electronic marketplace based on modern technology.

For the futures markets, Gary Lapayover has a radical vision of the future:

"If I believe in science fiction, and I do, it is very possible that one day all the trading we do today in one physical location will migrate into a network where you don't necessarily have to be physically present. It might evolve in another strange way. It might one day become virtual reality. You'll all think you are in the same room, but you'll actually be trading in your closet wearing your little gear, and the rest of it will be electronically processed. It will be a wider network of individuals that will be able to have access to do it. You'll just have different means of ascertaining somebody's ability to meet their obligations."

Although some of the really big, mainstream futures markets are open outcry markets with physical floors and hustling traders in crowded pits, what you are seeing more and more are overnight systems and electronic linkages with other exchanges. For instance, while the New York Mercantile Exchange closes for the day at 3:10 P.M., its electronic trading system begins at 4:00 P.M. and runs until 8:00 the next morning. There are terminals in the U.S., London, Sydney, and Hong Kong. So Sydney has the ability to trade New York Mercantile Exchange products in its daytime, when New York is asleep.

Linkages between exchanges around the world will mean a worldwide flow of orders twenty-four hours a day. Each exchange's products will be traded on other exchanges that exist in other time zones. Exchange-to-exchange linkages seem at this point to be the way that the world futures markets want to operate. Yet some believe there is more liquidity in the physical pits, execution can be faster, and some traders just prefer it. Time will tell.

One of the first steps toward global linkage is happening between countries in the European time zones, where most of the stock markets are linked electronically. Sweden, one of the most advanced, eliminated its physical trading floor in 1989 and went electronic. Then in 1993 it promoted membership for brokers and financial institutions from other countries. With that head start, it now has more nondomestic members than any other stock exchange in Europe. EASDAQ offers pan-European stocks. Tradepoint offers both U.K. and non-U.K. stocks. Others are merging their systems.

The move toward cross-listing stocks on the exchanges of different countries is the beginning of a continuous cross-border market. Because more and more people want to diversify across borders and across currencies, markets that formerly were purely regional are reaching out for that business by offering those choices. American companies list their stocks in Hong Kong. Japanese stocks trade on the London Stock Exchange. Even though access is increasingly available in other time zones, globalization will take a while to occur because the bulk of money tends to stay in domestic markets. It will eventually happen, nevertheless.

The continuation of computer and software refinement will push trading to new frontiers and will create more opportunity for business globally.

Stanley Shopkorn has a theory about this:

"Computers have allowed what I call a long wave to develop, which the United States is involved in right now. What it means is a space in time where the moon and the stars and the sun line up to give you superior return for a very particularized reason.

"We saw a long wave in Japan in the 1950s because after the Second World War we rebuilt their factories. They had cheap labor and they were able to develop their factories to be more efficient than the U.S. They experienced a thirty-year economic wave, which ended in disaster. In the industrial revolution in England in the 1800s, we saw the same thing. In our present long wave, the worker is nervous that he can be replaced by a machine. So he doesn't push very hard for raises, so we have no wage inflation.

"The chief financial officer that is in charge of a multifaceted corporation today, twenty-five years ago had no idea where all his stores of copper were. Today he can just push out a software package and he knows exactly where his copper is. So rather than buy more copper he just moves copper from one factory to another. That holds down labor costs. The technology in mining and discovering commodities today is so much better than it was that the supply of the underlying material that is around is in surplus and not in excess demand.

"So we are experiencing a period, which is a very sweet period, which will not last forever. People have learned today to stay on one side of the market and you can only be right if you own them. But there will be a point in time when markets will go back to what they were before. And that's markets that trade up for a year or two, and down for a year or two.

"Technology has played a very important part in what is an economic long wave, and the rest of the world is understanding it. Europe is beginning to pick it up and is restructuring. I think we may sit in this sweet period for a period of time, but then again, if you look back in history, everything changes all the time."

That's one thing you can bank on.

TRADE$PEAK

A SOMETIMES IRREVERENT GUIDE TO TRADERS' TERMINOLOGY

Note: Terms used only in certain markets are identified

2-by-2s: As in a two-year employment contract, with a guaranteed annual compensation of $2 million. (U.S.)

2-by-4s: As in a two-year employment contract, with a guaranteed annual compensation of $4 million. (U.S.)

AMEX: American Stock Exchange. One of the primary central auction markets for stocks in the U.S.

Arbitrage: The purchase of a security in one market and the simultaneous sale of the same security in another market to make a profit from the price differential that may exist. From the French word "to estimate."

Arbitrageur: A speculator who takes on risk and adds liquidity to the market.

Alternative Trading System (ATS): These are not exchanges because they do not list securities. They allow customers to buy and sell securities on their systems. Some alternative trading systems are in-house, between broker/dealers, customers, and market participants. INSTINET is an example of an ATS.

Ask: An offer to sell at a certain price.

Auction market: Where buyers and sellers come together and, through the process of supply and demand, prices are continuously being "discovered." The participants form a "market."

Bargain: *See Trade.* (U.K.)

Basis point: One hundredth of one percent (0.01 percent). 100 basis points = 1 percent.

Bear market: A market where prices are on a declining trend.

Bid: An offer to buy at a certain price.

Big Bang: Refers to October 1986 when the London Stock Exchange abolished fixed commissions and dealing went off the floor to traders in offices using computers and phones. Firms that had been jobbers or brokers became broker/dealers, and ownership of a member firm by an outside corporation was allowed. Big Bang altered the shape of the market and resulted in many City of London firms being bought by foreign banks and securities firms, which changed forever the feel of the City. It created U.S.-style investment banking firms, combining merchant banking activity with stockbroking activity. It also cranked up competition as a result of new foreign money flowing in and negotiated commissions. (U.K.)

Big Bang 2: The changeover of the U.K. equity market in 1997 from a quote-driven (market maker) pricing system to an order-driven one. (U.K.)

Bond market: The market where corporate or government debt issues are bought and sold.

Breaking out: A term from technical analysis. Refers to a price moving above a previous high, or below a previous low, which is considered a sign that it will continue in that direction.

Bretton Woods: The now defunct 1944 international agreement to fix exchange rates.

Broker: A person who acts as an agent for customers, providing them with the ability to buy and sell. Brokers charge a fee for the service. They also trade/deal (latter U.K.) for their own account.

Bull market: A market where prices are on an upward trend.

Buy side: Refers to the money management institutions that buy from the brokers who sell.

CBOT: Chopped balls on toast. (No relation to the Chicago Board of Trade!)

Call market: A market where prices are "discovered" at a particular time. All orders are put together one or more times a day and "crossed," or matched.

Capital markets: Where individuals, companies, and institutions meet to invest or trade for a return, or to raise capital.

Cash market: The market for a cash commodity where the actual physical product is traded.

Central bank: The overall governing bank in each country. They inject money into the financial markets, or pull back the supply of money as needed; they set interest rates; and they supervise the banking system. They are looked to as "lenders of last resort" to bail out banks and avert a systemic risk of panic in the financial markets.

Circuit breakers: Temporary trading pauses that are deliberately put into place. On the NYSE, circuit breakers are put into place if the Dow Jones Industrial drops 10 percent, 20 percent, or 30 percent.

Collar: When used in reference to the New York Stock Exchange, "putting a collar on" relates to Rule 80A, which restricts the ability of computer trading programs to engage in trading when the Dow is up or down 50 points from the previous day's close. It was put in place in 1990 to dampen the volatility in the market, which results when there are big moves. In 1994 it was triggered 30 times; in 1995, 29 times; and in 1996 the collar was triggered 119 times. The more you see it, the more it indicates volatility in the market.

Corner: Temporarily owning the available supply (float) of a stock or commodity with the result that anyone wanting it has to come to you to pay your price.

Cover: To liquidate a position.

DCM: Don't come on Monday; i.e., you're fired!

Dealer: A person engaged in buying and selling securities for his own account. A dealer provides liquidity by acting as a market maker.

Dealer market: Where you as buyer or seller must trade with the dealer. The dealer is making the market, he is the "market maker." On the NYSE, the specialist in certain instances is the dealer, risking his own money to make the market.

Derivative: A contract that changes in value depending on the price movement of the underlying instrument or index.

Dictum meum pactum: Stock exchange motto (My word is my bond . . . if it suits).

Discretionary trading: When you have the authority to trade without the prior approval of a client.

Disintermediation: In the context of this book, business flowing away from traditional markets and market participants, toward nontraditional markets, away from middlemen toward direct investor-to-investor trading—a challenge that traditional broker/dealers and exchanges are having to face.

Dow, the: Dow Jones Industrial Average (DJIA), the oldest and most popular stock price indicator, made up of thirty companies' stocks.

Downtick: The minimum price movement down in a market.

EASDAQ: A pan-European stock market based in Brussels for young growth companies.

ECNs: Electronic Communication Networks. Private trading systems that match buyer and seller, with no middleman. Island and Bloomberg's Tradebook are examples of ECNs.

ECU: *See EMS.*

EMS: European Monetary System.

Equities: Stocks or shares of companies.

Exchange: An organized and regulated body that provides a marketplace for the auctioning of commodities or financial instruments. Membership is private, although Stockholm, Sydney, and Copenhagen are examples of exchanges that are ceasing to be members' clubs.

Financial futures: Contracts to buy or sell a standard amount of a certain financial instrument or index at a future date and agreed-upon price.

Floating exchange rate: When a currency is free and allowed to "float" to find its own value in the marketplace.

Flipper: Short-term speculator. (U.K.)

Floor broker: Someone who is a member of an exchange and who trades for clients.

Floor trader: Someone who is a member of an exchange and who trades for his own account.

Flutter: *See Speculation.* (U.K.)

Footsie: A game played under a table. Or the FTSE 100, an index of one hundred of the largest U.K. companies, which is the basis for futures and traded options listed on the London International Financial Futures and Options Exchange (LIFFE).

Foreign exchange (FX): A market where the buying and selling of different currencies takes place. The price of one currency in terms of another country's currency is called an exchange rate.

Fourth market: Institution-to-institution trading in the United States that is primarily electronic and is favored by users who are technology friendly.

Fucking: "Fucking this, fucking that." As in "Do it now! I mean it!"

Futures: An agreement reached on price and delivery of a commodity or instrument at a specified later date. You have to take delivery of the underlying commodity or instrument if you hold the futures contract until its expiration date. If you are a seller, you have to deliver the commodity.

Gilts: U.K. government bonds issued to fund shortfalls between government revenue and expenditure. (U.K.)

Having balls: As in having guts. More testosterone language.

Hedge: Protection against uncertainty and loss. A position in a futures or options contract that is intended to protect the value of the underlying security.

Hedge funds: In the old-fashioned sense of the word, a private investment pool of capital that was fully hedged. Now, any private pool of capital, no matter how much risk it takes, is called a hedge fund. Usually refers to a fund with fewer than one hundred investors that can be more aggressive in trading.

Illiquid markets: Recognizable by infrequent trading, accentuated volatility in prices, and wide spreads between the bid and the ask price. Hard to get in and out of at the price and time you want.

Immediacy: The ability to execute your trades right away; i.e., block traders use their capital to buy blocks of stock from funds, so the funds get immediate cash. Otherwise, they'd have to wait until a natural buyer or buyers appeared in the market to be able to execute their trade.

Index: A group of weighted securities used as a performance indicator. You can buy an index representing a group of securities faster than you could buy each individual security at the price you want, and for a fraction of the money down. Basically a quick way to participate in the market and get your money working.

Index arbitrage: The purchase or sale of a basket of stocks in conjunction with the sale or purchase of a derivative (stock index future) with the intent of making a profit from the difference in price between the two.

Indication of interest (IOI): A bid or offer sent between brokers and clients using an electronic system/information provider.

Information providers: Bloomberg, Reuters, for example. You can see prices, financial data, and news on their screens. You can trade/deal (latter U.K.) on some of them. Markets are interlinked through the information providers.

INSTINET: A "broker/dealer," electronic trading service, owned by Reuters. Allows institutions to trade electronically between each other. Advantages to an institution include lower costs and anonymity. The disadvantage is that you have to be patient, because the other side of the trade may not always be available when you want it.

Inverse floaters: Derivatives designed to pay off when interest rates fall.

Institutional investors: Mutual funds, pension funds, banks, insurance companies. They invest for the public or themselves.

Jobber: Middleman or broker. (U.K.)

Junk bonds: High-yield, low-grade or no-grade bonds. Used to be called "fallen angels" or "bonds of distressed companies."

Leverage: Putting a little money down to control a large amount of value. The higher the leverage, the greater the risk/reward ratio.

LIFFE: London International Financial Futures and Options Exchange.

Like a bishop's prick: "Firm but idle," referring to the state of the market. (U.K.)

Liquidity: Where there is enough activity in a market or security that you can easily buy or sell. In recent history, with order flow up, demand for liquidity has increased . When huge institutional blocks slam into the market you see sharp price moves because the market is under pressure for liquidity when they all want to buy or sell at once. If it were easy to trade, either buy or sell, in a large number of stocks, the market would be liquid and "deep."

LSE: London Stock Exchange.

Margin: Small down payment of cash or securities to control a larger monetary amount of a security.

Market: Companies are listed and quoted on a market, e.g. London Stock Exchange, NYSE. All members have common trading rules that they abide by.

Market maker: A broker/dealer who is willing to buy or sell securities and make a market in them. He provides a two-sided (bid and ask) market and greater liquidity.

Mark to market: The price of an investment at current prices.

Men in sandals: Arab traders. (U.K.)

Momentum: This is essentially a measure of rate of change. When a market has upward momentum, the rate of change in price and movement forward over a period of time are increasing; downward momentum, the opposite. "Momentum players" in the market are money managers or traders who buy and sell when they identify a market or security gaining or losing momentum.

Money market: A market where money is borrowed and lent between banks, companies, governments, and individuals.

NASDAQ: Began in 1971. A screen-based inter-dealer quotation system that allows the trading of over-the-counter and exchange-listed securities. Electronically links market makers around the U.S.

NYSE: New York Stock Exchange, organized in 1817. The dominant primary market for stocks in the United States. The advantage is that it is a deep, liquid, continuous auction market that offers immediacy.

Off: If a market maker is waiting for a client to respond to a price quote, and the price moves against the market maker, the terms may be withdrawn. The market maker is "off." (U.K.)

Open outcry: The traditional method of trading in a physical area of an exchange, which combines shouting and hand signals.

Opening/to open: To establish whether a client is a buyer or a seller by offering unbalanced bid and offer terms. (U.K.)

Options: An interesting dilemma. You have the option to buy or sell for a certain period of time something at a specific price. Sound good? Wait until it entails a multitude of embedded features. A call option gives you the right to buy the underlying instrument, a put option the right to sell the underlying instrument.

Order book: Bids and offers, which are input by brokers, displayed on a computer screen. Sort of like a bulletin board.

Over-the-counter market (OTC). It's huge. Two or more parties deal by telephone or computer in a security or instrument that is not traded on an organized exchange.

Pink slip: Notification that your services are no longer required. (U.S.)

Pit: A circular area on a commodity exchange where traders congregate to participate in a continuous auction for a specific commodity, e.g. the sugar pit, the gold pit, the pork belly pit.

POSIT: Portfolio System for Institutional Trading, started in 1987 by Investment Technology Group (ITG). An alternative to organized exchange trading for institutions that want to trade directly with each other. A confidential computer-based equity matching system between institutions, used mainly for inactive, harder-to-do stocks.

Price and size: "A cock and hen" equals 10,000, a "pony" equals 25,000, "nifty" equals 50,000, a "ton" equals 100,000, a "quarter" equals 250,000, and "half a bar" equals 500,000. (U.K.)

Print: Any transaction in listed stocks is "printed" on a recognized exchange or consolidated "tape" to ensure public disclosure of prices arrived at.

Program trading: Computerized trading by big institutions that is the simultaneous purchase or sale of at least fifteen different stocks with a total value of at least $1 million. On an average day, program trading can constitute at least 10 percent, if not more, of activity on the NYSE.

Proprietary trading: Trading the firm's own money with the intent of making a profit. Or trading for your own account.

Protection: A verbal agreement between a market maker and a client. The market maker underwrites the client in an order at a certain price, often with a possibility of price improvement. This trade does not "print" until the protection is removed and the order is then officially recognized. (U.K.)

PTSs: Screen-based proprietary trading systems for institutions and broker/dealers, e.g. INSTINET, POSIT.

Punter: *See Speculator.* (U.K.)

Quant: Short for "quantitative." Person who uses a quantitative method to trade or invest, normally via the computer.

QUOTRON: An electronic information system owned by Reuters.

Rally: An advancing price movement after a decline in a market.

Risk: Uncertainty, the unpredictable. Both are risks to the value of assets, the bottom line or cash flows.

Risk arbitrage: Betting that a company will be taken over by buying the stock and hoping that it will go up in value and that you will make a profit.

Risk/reward curve: A ratio between a calculated potential loss or profit depending on how much risk you take.

Running round: Dealing with more than one market maker in rapid succession. (U.K.)

S&P: Standard & Poor's 500 Stock Index, a broad-based index of five hundred companies used as a benchmark indicator of how the market is doing.

Seat: Membership on an exchange. Members used to have assigned chairs during the auction of stocks, which they called a "seat." Having a seat permits a member physical or electronic access to the trading floor.

Sell side: The brokers who sell securities to the buy side.

SETS: Stock Exchange Electronic Trading Service (London). An order-driven system for the Footsie 100, inaugurated in October 1997.

Short selling/sell short: When you are betting against the crowd and have the opinion that a stock will go down. The opposite is a long sale, when you have a bullish opinion and think a stock will go up. To sell short is to sell a stock you don't own (broker arranges for you to "borrow" it) and pocket the money from the sale, hoping the stock will go down so that you can buy it back cheaper and make a profit.

Specialist: Stocks on the New York Stock Exchange are sold through one person, called a "specialist," who has a membership on the exchange. He can trade for his own account after trading for the public, but first and foremost must maintain an "orderly and continuous market" in those stocks he has been assigned by the exchange.

Speculator (U.S.)/**punter** (U.K.): Someone who takes a calculated risk that he will make a profit if he buys or sells something by anticipating price movements.

Speculation (U.S.)/**flutter** (U.K.): Taking a calculated risk.

Spread: The difference between the bid and offer price.

Stock market: Smaller than most other markets, it is the most visible and understandable of the financial markets, where pieces of direct ownership in companies are bought and sold.

Strike price: The price for which you buy an option on the underlying security or commodity.

SuperDot: An electronic system that transmits orders from member firms to the specialists on the New York Stock Exchange trading floor, and reports confirmation of their trades back to the member firms. Orders that need special handling are sent via SuperDot by the member firms to their brokers on the floor, who then go to the post to execute the trade.

Swap: Literally, a swap, or exchange. A derivative in which parties agree to exchange either a stream of payments over a period of time, or a price where they swap currencies.

T-bills: Treasury bills; short-term government instruments.

Third market: Over-the-counter trading of securities.

Tick: The smallest change in price, up or down.

Ticker tape: A digital stream of stock symbols and their prices disseminated as soon as trades are done from the floor of the exchange.

Touch: The bid and offer price in a quote-driven market. (U.K.)

Trade (U.S.)/**bargain** (U.K.): In the context of this book, a sale by one person and a purchase by a counter-party that can be executed either verbally or computer to computer

Tradepoint: A recognized investment exchange in London, which does not list stocks, but rather offers a secondary market to trade them. Works on an order-driven basis using both real-time trading and call auctions.

Transparency: When information about prices, volume, and trades is disseminated immediately to everyone in the marketplace. Ensures fairness and efficiency.

Two-dollar broker: The term used to refer to independent brokers on the floor of the stock exchange who trade for large brokerage houses.

Up and down like a whore's drawers: Volatile. (U.K.)

Uptick: The minimum price movement up in a market.

Volatility: Prices moving up and down, not stable. Volatility is a trader's best friend. He can make money with volatility.

Volume: The number of shares or contracts traded during a particular period of time.

You are wearing those: As in "I believe I wish to sell these securities to you at your price." Often abbreviated to "yours!" (U.K.)

NOTES

CHAPTER 1: MILLIONS A MINUTE

Page 3

"It was a big adrenaline rush," from an interview with Gary Lapayover.

Page 4

$1.5 trillion traded in the world currency markets, at approximately 252 trading days a year, equals over $300 trillion traded a year. Figure of $1.5 trillion from *Business Week*, January 12, 1998, p. 32.

Page 4

Approximately $15.6 trillion of stocks traded a year on the world's stock exchanges, from the Fédération Internationale Des Bourses de Valeurs, Paris, June 1997.

Page 4

Approx. $27.5 trillion of bonds traded a year, from the Fédération Internationale Des Bourses de Valeurs, Paris, June 1997.

Page 8

CME has two trading floors on 70,000 square feet, from CME Web site, April 1998.

Page 8

NYMEX on new 25,000-square-foot trading floor, from interview with Nachamah Jacobovits.

Page 12

"The only newspaper I read is the *National Enquirer*," from Victor Niederhoffer (1997), *The Education of a Speculator*, New York: John Wiley & Sons, p. ix.

CHAPTER 2: MY WORD IS MY BOND

Page 19

"Traders exist in a world," from Alan Rubenfeld (1992), *The Super Traders*, Chicago: Probus Publishing, p. xii.

Page 21

"John Maynard Keynes," from speech given at the University of Virginia, "Investor Education: Disclosure for the 1990s," November 1995.

Page 21

Jay Gould and Jim Fisk research from John Steele Gordon (988), *The Scarlet Woman of Wall Street*, New York: Weidenfeld & Nicholson, pp. 153–206.

Page 21

U.S. House of Representatives determined it was not illegal to corner nation's gold supply, from Dana L. Thomas (1967), *The Plungers and the Peacocks*, New York: G.P. Putnam's Sons, p. 46.

Page 21

Bernard Baruch research, from Robert M. Sharp (1989), *The Lores and Legends of Wall Street*, Homewood, Ill: Dow Jones-Irwin, pp. 201–3.

Page 21

Joe Kennedy research, ibid., p. 212.

Page 21

Billy Durant research, *The Plungers and the Peacocks*, pp. 144–81.

Page 21

Daniel Drew research, *The Scarlet Woman of Wall Street*, pp. 8–160.

Page 23

Marines invade NYMEX, from the *Herald Tribune*, December 17, 1996, p. 15.

Page 27

Salary amounts from interview with Gary Goldstein of the Whitney Group, New York.

Page 28

"Mike worked away trading securities," from Glenn Yago (1991), *Junk Bonds*, Oxford: Oxford University Press, p. 21.

Page 28

Milken earned $550 million, from Fenton Bailey (1991), *The Junk Bond Revolution*, London: Fourth Estate.

Page 28

Bloomberg was proud to be a "Salomon man," from Michael Bloomberg (1997), *Bloomberg by Bloomberg*, New York: John Wiley & Sons, p. 19.

CHAPTER 3: FREE-MARKET WARRIORS

Page 36

There used to be 1,600 commodity exchanges in the United States and cat pelts traded in St. Louis, from "Why do they need to yell and make funny gestures?" New York Mercantile Exchange, p. 4.

Page 36

Three exchanges in the U.K. and forty in the world, from FT.com Directory, April 1998.

Page 38

Day traders can account for up to 50 percent of the volume on NYMEX, from interview with Nachamah Jacobovits.

Page 41

Aggressive traders and Michael Steinhardt, from the *Washington Post*, "Wired into Wall Street: Tough Trader Steinhardt Brings Wealth to Clients, Attention to Himself," December 1, 1991, p. 1.

Page 42

Marty Schwartz called "one of the world's best traders," from Jack D. Schwager (1993), *Market Wizards*, New York: HarperBusiness, p. 279.

CHAPTER 4: FROM ANALOG TO ALGORITHM

Page 45

Information on Bob Mnuchin's hotel from Relais & Châteaux Guide (1996), p. 588.

Page 45

Kennedy Crash and the tape ran late that day, from interview with Muriel Siebert.

Page 45

Dow shed 100 points over eight days, 40 points over three hours, from Robert Sobel (1986), *Salomon Brothers 1910–1985*, New York: Salomon Brothers, p. 106.

Page 46

Gus Levy credited with inventing the block trade, from John Brooks (1987), *The Takeover Game*, New York: E.P. Dutton.

Page 48

Dow rose 45 percent from 1963 to 1967, from *Forbes*, "My Story," March 16, 1992.

Page 48

Firms on Wall Street could earn 30 cents a share, from interview with Chris Andersen.

Page 49

"I learned firsthand," from speech at the Bloomberg Conference in London, November 1996.

Page 50

Burnham & Company installed its first computer in 1962, IBM mainframe in 1966, from *Institutional Investor*, article on Bill Tuite of Burnham & Company, June 1987.

Page 50

Late 1960s NYSE developed automated block trading system, from Robert Sobel (1996), *Salomon Brothers: Advancing to Leadership*, New York: Salomon Brothers.

Page 51

From 1969 to 1970 stocks fell 35 percent, from *Forbes*, "My Story."

Page 51

Recession 1973–74, from Tim Carrington (1985), *The Year They Stole Wall Street*, Boston: Houghton Mifflin, p. 88.

Page 51

Inflation 1978–79, ibid., p. 110.

Page 52

"The biggest thing at work," from *Institutional Investor*, June 1987, p. 216.

Page 55

Lewis Ranieri and Robert Dall thought up packaging of mortgages into securities, from *The Takeover Game*.

Page 56

NYSE $24 million technological upgrade, from Richard Teweles, Edward Bradley, and Ted Teweles (1992), *The Stock Market*, New York: John Wiley & Sons, p. 117.

Page 57

Traders generated most of the profits for brokerage firms, from Tim Metz (1988), *Black Monday*, New York: William Morrow, p.18.

Page 61

Program trading accounted for almost 16.8 percent of share volume every day in 1997, from Kimberly Williams, NYSE media relations, April 22, 1998.

CHAPTER 5: BIG CIGARS AND RED SUSPENDERS

Page 71

"You are fair game," from *Crisis*, "Arrogance Thy Name is Media," February 1996, pp. 12–13.

Page 71

"Too often the media," ibid.

Page 71

"The capital-raising process," from *Traders Magazine*, November 1996, pp. 16–22.

Page 72

CNBC reaches 65 million homes, from Mary Cutter, CNBC London.

Page 72

CNN reaches 8.7 million homes, from Caroline Villiers, CNN London.

Page 74

Tiger Fund runs charitable foundation, from *Financial World*, July 6, 1993, p. 38.

Page 74

Paul Tudor Jones does fund-raising for the inner city, ibid.

Page 74

Soros gave away $1 billion to Eastern Europe, from the *New Republic*, "The Speculator: A Trip with George Soros," January 10, 1994, p. 19.

Page 75

"It was right after the Watts riots," from Milken Investment Institute literature.

Page 75

Milken giving math classes to inner-city kids, from *Fortune* magazine, "What to Make of Mike," September 30, 1996, p. 96.

Page 75

"I've always strived," *Profit* magazine, Sept./Oct. 1993, p. 13.

Page 76

Bloomberg donated $65 million to Johns Hopkins University, Baltimore, Maryland *Daily Record*, October 2, 1995, p. 3.

Page 76

Bloomberg donated computer terminals to United Negro College Fund, from *Black Professional* magazine, Summer 1994, p. 14.

Page 77

Each managing director has to give away 4 percent of salary, from *Fortune* magazine, January 5, 1987, p. 94.

Page 77

Siebert giving half of company's profits on new securities underwriting to charity, from the *Los Angeles Times*, May 28, 1995, Business Sec., p. 5.

CHAPTER 6: THREE VISIONARIES

Page 81–82

Bloomberg career information, from *Bloomberg by Bloomberg*, pp. 1, 12, 13, 18–19, 122.

Page 83

"I owe a great debt," from *Bloomberg by Bloomberg*, p. 7.

Page 84

"We give our clients," ibid., p. 53.

Page 85

"If you buy data from Reuters," from speech given at the Bloomberg Conference in London, November 1996.

Page 90

Background information on Melamed from Leo Melamed (1996), *Escape to the Futures*, New York: John Wiley & Sons.

Page 90

The idea for financial futures, ibid., pp. 170–74.

Page 90

"The most significant financial innovation," from *Escape to the Futures*, p. 331.

Page 90

Volume of futures contracts grew from 37 to 216 million, from *Escape to the Futures*.

Page 90

$12 billion in currency contracts traded every day, from the *Wall Street Journal*, April 10, 1995, Sec. C, p. 1.

Page 91

"I think from that day forward," from *Institutional Investor*, June 1987, p. 311.

Page 94

E-mini S&P futures and options contract fastest-growing index contract CME ever launched, from CME Web site, April 1998.

Page 94

"With the E-mini S&P contract," from PR Newswire, September 3, 1997.

Page 96

I was told I would be unable to interview Milken, from conversation with Glenn Yago.

Page 96

"Milken had a sense of decorum," from Jesse Kornbluth (1992), *Highly Confident: The Crime and Punishment of Michael Milken*, William Morrow, New York.

Page 96

Milken wasn't really liked in the beginning, ibid.

Page 96

How Milken was viewed within Drexel, from *The Junk Bond Revolution*, pp. 25–27.

Page 97

"When I was growing up," from a study paper by Michael Milken, "Fueling America's Growth."

Page 98

First Investors Fund converted into one devoted to low-quality bonds, from Diana B. Henriques (1995), *Fidelity's World*, New York: Scribner & Sons.

Page 98

First Investors Fund top in U.S. 1974, 1975, and 1976, from interview with Chris Andersen.

Page 99

564 companies that were investment grade, leaving 21,000 that were not, from *Junk Bonds*, p. 21.

Page 99

1977–87 Milken raised $93 billion, ibid., p. 25.

Page 100

"MCI challenged," "Economic Growth and Job Creation," p. 26. Published by the Milken Institute for Job and Capital Creation in Santa Monica, CA, 1994.

Page 100

Milken-MCI junk bonds raised $2 billion, from the *Los Angeles Times*, November 2, 1996, p. D1.

Page 101

"What are your hopes," ibid., p. 25.

Page 101

"Despite later perceptions," *Junk Bonds*, p. 27.

Page 101

"A full 73.7 percent of the proceeds," ibid., p. 36.

Page 101

Milken paid fines and was sentenced to ten years in jail, from the *Los Angeles Times*, February 18, 1996, Business Sec., p. 1.

Page 102

Milken's idea about real estate, from the *Washington Post*, June 8, 1994, Sec. F, p. 1.

Page 102

"I believe that access to capital," from "Economic Growth and Job Creation," p. 82.

CHAPTER 7: CRASHING THE PARTY

Page 105

Gerry Tsai gave Muriel the idea of buying a seat, from *Institutional Investor*, June 1987, p. 89.

Page 105

"I couldn't get sponsored," ibid., p. 90.

Page 106

NYSE asked for guarantee from her bank, from the *Los Angeles Times*, May 28, 1995, Business Sec., p. 5.

Page 106

"controversial," ibid.

Page 106

Not until 1970 was another woman admitted, from Leonard Sloane (1980), *The Anatomy of the Floor: The Trillion Dollar Market at the New York Stock Exchange*. New York: Doubleday.

Page 106

Siebert told by doorman to go through kitchen, from the *Los Angeles Times*, May 28, 1995, Business Sec., p. 5.

Page 111

Louise Jones found in telephone booth, orphaned, from the *New York Post*, "Adoptee and Her Dad Trade Gifts of Love," December 20, 1991, pp. 2, 24.

CHAPTER 8: STATELESS MONEY

Page 125

"When speculators profit," from George Soros (1995), *Soros on Soros*, John Wiley & Sons, p. 84.

Page 126

Over a 1 trillion dollars trade in a day, from *Business Week*, January 12, 1998, p. 32.

Page 127

$300 trillion of transactions in a year, from the *Chicago Tribune*, March 5, 1995.

Page 131

"Statistical tests were performed," from the Federal Reserve Board of San Francisco Economic Letter, "Models of Currency Speculation: Implications and East Asian Evidence," Ramon Moreno, No. 96-13, April 19, 1996.

Page 131

Maurice Obstfeld on currency speculation, ibid.

Page 132

"dynamic disequilibrium in the ERM," from *Soros on Soros*, pp. 79–82.

Page 132

Soros allegedly reaped $1 billion in trading profits, from the *Washington Post*, "Billionaire Bettor," October 1, 1995.

Page 132

Soros said funds would bet against irrational investment decisions, from the *International Herald Tribune*, January 13–14, 1996, p. 17.

Page 133

1992 peseta dropped 25 percent, others weakened against the mark, from *Business Week*, "Hot Money," March 20, 1995.

Page 133

Chirac calls currency speculators "AIDS of our economies," from the *Wall Street Journal*, June 19, 1995, Sec. A, p. 11.

Page 133

Mexico peso devaluation 1994, economic predictions relating to inflation and investment, from *Time* magazine, "A Case of Nerves," Michael S. Serrill, April 1995.

Page 134

Japanese yen discussion, from *Business Week*, "High Yen, Low Anxiety," Robert Neff, March 27, 1995.

Page 134

Currency crisis in Thailand, ibid.; and Asiaweek Online, "Eye of the Storm," Ricardo Saludo and Antonio Lopez, August 1997.

Page 135

IMF steps up endeavors to ward off potential currency crisis, from the *Washington Post*, "When Signs of Trouble Go Unheeded," Paul Blustein, August 17, 1997, p. H01.

Page 136

Malaysian currency and stock market crisis background, from the *Financial Times*, August 29, 1997, pp. 1, 5.

Page 136

Malaysian ringgit falls 30 percent, from the *Herald Tribune*, October 18–19, 1997, p. 15.

Page 136

Mahathir banned *Schindler's List* as "Jewish propaganda," from *Business Week*, "Malaysia's Mahathir," April 25, 1994.

Page 136

"Currency trading is unnecessary," from the *Observer*, "Unnecessary, unproductive and immoral," William Keegan, September 28, 1997.

Page 137

Mahathir blamed George Soros, from the *Times*, "Asian Tigers face return to law of jungle," January 2, 1998.

Page 137

Stock markets fall in October, from the *Daily Mail*, October 29, 1997, p. 6; and the *Sunday Times*, November 2, 1997, p.6.

Page 137

General background on Asian crisis, from *The Economist*, March 7, 1998.

Page 137

Soros "a moron," from *The Economist*, "Dr Mahathir and the Markets," September 6, 1997.

Page 137

Mahathir "has a point," from the *Observer*, "Unnecessary, unproductive and immoral," William Keegan, September 28, 1997.

Page 137

"Financial markets are inherently unstable," from the *Observer*, "Unnecessary, unproductive, and immoral," William Keegan, September 28, 1997.

Page 138

Japan financial scandals at Yamaichi, Sanyo and regional banks go bust, from the *Financial Times*, November 24, 1997, pp. 1–2, 23.

Page 138

Indonesian currency lost 70 percent of its value from March 1997 to March 1998, from the Sunday *Times* (London), June 14, 1998, page 26.

Page 141

Federal Reserve independent, founded in 1913, from William Greider (1987), *Secrets of the Temple: How the Federal Reserve Runs the Country*, New York: Simon and Schuster.

Page 141

James Baker as catalyst of crash of 1987, from Victor Neiderhoffer (1997), *The Education of a Speculator*, New York: John Wiley & Sons, pp. 303–4.

CHAPTER 9: DERIVATIVES—THE GOOD, THE BAD, AND THE UGLY

Page 146

Black and Scholes publish paper, from *Derivatives Strategy* magazine, March 1997, pp. 20–21.

Page 147

1972–83 prime rose from 5 to 10 percent, 1977–81 long-term interest rates doubled, prime lending rate tripled, from Lorraine Spurge (1991), *An American Renaissance,* Encino, CA: Knowledge Exchange, p. 15.

Page 147

IMM introduced first currencies futures contracts, ibid., p. 17.

Page 149

Seven interest rate hikes in a twelve-month period, from *Futures* magazine, "The Sound and Fury of Derivative Losses," October 1995, p. 84.

Page 149-159

Citibank, Bankers Trust, Chase Manhattan, J.P. Morgan income from derivatives 1993–94, from *Business Week*, "Derivatives: Alive, But Oh So Boring," January 30, 1995, pp. 76–77.

Page 150

Background on Orange County derivatives, the *New York Times*, January 18, 1995, p. D1–6.

Page 150

Orange County bankruptcy, sustained $1.7 billion loss, from *Business Week*, March 13, 1995.

Page 150

$7.4 billion portfolio of Orange County leveraged up to $20 billion, from the *Wall Street Journal*, "Before the Fall," January 18, 1995.

Page 150

Citron was betting interest rates would stay low, from *Forbes*, January 30, 1995, p. 138.

Page 150

Citron was sentenced to one year in jail, from the *Wall Street Journal*, November 20, 1996, p. B8.

Page 150

Orange County sued Merrill Lynch for $3 billion, from the *Wall Street Journal*, January 13, 1995, p. 1.

Page 150

Citron was "imperialistic and dictatorial," from the *Wall Street Journal*, January 18, 1995, p. 1.

Citron thought he knew better than industry professionals, from *Risk* magazine, March 1995, pp. 27–33.

"It includes inverse floaters," from *Risk* magazine, "Orange on a Banana Skin," January 1995, vol. 8, no. 1.

Orange County was 300 percent leveraged, ibid.

"Those things were just bad speculation," from *Futures Industry* magazine, November/December 1994, p. 5.

Metallgesellschaft hedged with short-term oil derivatives, from *Natural Gas Focus* magazine, December 1994/January 1995, p. 52.

Bankers Trust discovered from listening to internal tapes, from *The Economist*, "Bankers Trust's Dirty Linen," February 11, 1995, and *Risk* magazine, "Blow for Bankers," February 1995.

Bankers Trust hid losses for two years, Gibson's lost $20 million, Bankers Trust paid $14 million to Gibson, from the *New York Times*, January 3, 1995.

Bankers Trust paid $10 million fine, from the *New York Times*, January 20, 1995.

"lured people into that total calm," from *The Economist*, October 7, 1995, p. 135.

Bankers Trust hit with staff defections, client lawsuits, and plummeting morale, from *Business Week*, "What is Bankers Trust Waiting For?" March 13, 1995, p. 82.

Bankers Trust hired new CFO, stepped up training programs, from *CFO magazine*, January 1996, pp. 38–42.

Bankers Trust set aside $423 million for potential losses, from the *Financial Times*, January 20, 1995.

Page 152

Procter & Gamble did diff swap, from *Natural Gas Focus* magazine, December 1994/January 1995, p. 54.

Page 152

Procter & Gamble thought German interest rates not likely to increase, from *Treasury & Risk Management* magazine, March–April 1995, p. 27.

Page 152

Treasurer signed swap contract without reading it, didn't tell boss, from *Derivatives Strategy* magazine, November 1995, p. 11.

Page 152

Traders earning $1 million to $1.5 million in 1993 were earning $500,000 to $700,000 in 1995, from the *New York Times*, "D is for Doghouse As Well As Derivatives," April 30, 1995.

Page 153

"I used to say, 'I'm in trading,'" ibid.

Page 153

New SEC rules regarding value-at-risk (VAR), *Derivatives Strategy* magazine, March 1997, p. 12.

Page 153

SEC adopts derivatives disclosure rules, from the *New York Times*, January 29, 1997.

Page 153

Futures and Options Association guide, from the *Financial Times*, June 8, 1995.

Page 154

Andrew Crockett's opinion on not regulating derivatives, from the *Financial Times*, "Top Banker," January 31, 1995.

Page 154

Group of 30 recommendation that top fifty financial institutions self-regulate, from interview with John Heiman, board member of the Group of 30.

Page 154

"There are yet unknown dangers," from *Futures Industry* magazine, November/December 1994, p. 5.

Page 154-155

Officials from the Government Finance Officers Association testified to Congress regarding derivatives salesmen, from the *Wall Street Journal*, January 9, 1995.

Page 155

ISDA reported first half 1997 OTC outstandings at $28.7 trillion, from

International Swaps and Derivatives Association news release, January 12, 1998.

Page 156
Securities firms voluntarily report on risk to SEC, from the *Wall Street Journal*, March 9, 1995, Sec. C, p. 1.

Page 158
Emanuel Derman heads quant team at Goldman Sachs, from *Derivatives Strategy* magazine, March 1997, p. 57.

Page 158
40 percent of Goldman Sachs' trading profits in 1992 were related to the use of derivatives, from *Forbes*, March 29, 1993, pp. 62–67.

CHAPTER 10: THE RISE OF THE BUY SIDE

Page 161
$4.8 trillion in assets, from the Investment Company Institute, Washington, D.C., February 1998.

Page 161
Unit trust and investment trust totaled $380 billion, from the Association of Unit Trusts and the Association of Investment Trusts, London, February 1998. Personal correspondence.

Page 162
In 1940, fewer than eighty funds, from the Investment Company Institute, Washington, D.C., August 1997. Personal correspondence.

Page 163
In 1987, 2,000 mutual funds, from the Investment Company Institute, Washington, D.C., August 1997.

Page 163
More than 7,500 mutual funds to pick from, from the Morningstar Fund report, first quarter 1998.

Page 163
"The difference between the number one and the number two," from interview with INSTINET in New York, August 1996.

Page 170
Sell-side commissions fell from 40 cents to 10 cents to 5 cents, from interview with Peter Jenkins.

Page 171
Merrill Lynch employs 38,000 in private client area, has over $750 billion in assets, double size of Bank of England reserves, from interview in London with Colin Taylor and associates.

CHAPTER 11: BLACK SHEEP

Page 174

Leeson/Barings information from the *Financial Times*, September 20, 1996, p. 12 and September 21/22, 1996, p. 7.

Page 175

Five peerages for Baring family, from *Time* magazine, March 13, 1995.

Page 175

Governor and directors of the Bank of England, from the *Daily Telegraph*, February 27, 1995, p. 21.

Page 175

Diana, Princess of Wales, had Baring in bloodline, ibid.

Page 175

Barings helped finance Louisiana Purchase, from John Orbell (1985), *Baring Brothers & Company, Limited: A History to 1989*, London: Baring Brothers, pp. 15–16.

Page 175

Barings finance trade around the world, ibid.

Page 175

Bank of England's emergency meetings, from the *Independent*, March 5, 1995.

Page 175

Queen Elizabeth and Prince Charles clients of Barings, from *Newsweek*, March 13, 1995; and the *Independent*, March 3, 1995.

Page 176

Barings thought its arbitrage business was risk free, from Bank of England report on the collapse of Barings, Sec. 3, para. 3.41, p. 45.

Page 176

Long position in Nikkei 225 futures, from the *Independent*, March 5, 1995.

Page 176

He was concealing losses in an error account, from Bank of England report, Sec. 5, para. 5.2–5.3, p. 78; and Sec. 5, para 5.21, p. 82.

Page 176

1993 loss of £23 million, 1994 loss of £208 million, February 1995 loss of £827 million, from Bank of England report, para. 1.69, p. 13 and Sec. 4.

Page 176

Leeson doubled his bets, from *Newsweek* magazine, March 13, 1995.

Page 176

Leeson held over 60,000 futures contracts, from Bank of England report, Sec. 4, para. 4.18, p. 59.

Page 177

His losses brought the bank down, from *Business Week*, March 13, 1995.

Page 177

"From Nick and Lisa" fax identification, from the *Financial Times*, September 21/22, 1996, p. 7.

Page 177

Leeson hired as settlements clerk, from Nick Leeson and Edward Whitley (1996), *Rogue Trader: How I Brought Down Barings Bank and Shook the Financial World*, Boston: Little, Brown, p. 22.

Page 177

Sent to Singapore in 1992, from *Time* magazine, March 13, 1995, p. 42.

Page 177

His group accounted for 20 percent of the firm's profits, from *Business Week*, "Lessons from the Barings Fiasco," April 17, 1995.

Page 177

Reported $30 million profit, from the *Daily Telegraph*, March 7, 1995, p. 7.

Page 177

Morgan Stanley and Goldman Sachs morning wires, from the *Financial Times*, September 21/22, 1996, p. 7.

Page 177

Leeson charges and prison sentence, *Rogue Trader*, p. 265.

Page 178

Leeson cast about for someone to blame, ibid., pp. 5, 6, 65, 73, 104, 185.

Page 178

"I was a fraud and a cheat," ibid., p. 165.

Page 178

Worked from 6 A.M. to 7 P.M., from *Time* magazine, March 13, 1995.

Page 178

He was doing unauthorized trading, ibid., pp. 70, 71, 108, 112.

Page 178

He allegedly did not use pricing models or risk management systems, from Bank of England report on the collapse of Barings, Sec. 4, para. 4.76, p. 71.

Page 178

Incurring big losses, from *Rogue Trader*, p. 7.

Page 178

Losses big enough to cause Barings' collapse, from Bank of England report, Sec. 5, para 5.2, p. 78.

Page 178

Leeson saw nothing wrong in making up his own rules, from *Rogue Trader*, pp. 152, 155, 166.

Page 178

"Lies and lies," ibid., p. 171.

Page 178

All the warning signs had apparently been ignored, from Bank of England report, Sec. 7, para. 7.15, p. 121.

Page 178

One trade four times over his limit, from the *Financial Times*, September 21/22, 1996, p 7.

Page 178

Trading limit of 200 Nikkei futures, ibid.

Page 180

"Mr. Five Percent," from the *Wall Street Journal*, November 18, 1996, Sec. A, p. 8.

Page 180

$2.6 billion losses, from the *Wall Street Journal*, December 20, 1996, Sec. C, p. 1.

Page 180

Hamanaka controlled 70 percent of copper at LME warehouse, from the *Wall Street Journal*, June 17, 1996, Sec. A, p. 1.

Page 181

President of Sumitomo revealed, from the *Wall Street Journal*, "Sumitomo Debacle Is Tied to Lax Controls," June 17, 1996, Sec. A6.

Page 181

Secret bank accounts, from the *Wall Street Journal*, November 18, 1996, Sec. A, p. 8.

Page 181

Threlkeld letter, ibid.

Page 181

Hamanaka confessed to his superiors, ibid.

Page 181

Copper prices fell 10 percent, ibid.

Page 181

Hamanaka to serve eight years in prison, from *Sunday Business*, March 29, 1998, p. 5.

Page 181

Lax supervision and lack of control, from the *Wall Street Journal*, June 17, 1996, Sec. A, p.1.

Page 182

LME annual metals trading of $2.5 trillion a year, from the *Wall Street Journal*, "Sumitomo Debacle Is Tied to Lax Controls."

Page 182

90 percent of all copper trading done on LME, from Reuters Business Wire, "British Fraud Investigators Head for Japan."

Page 182

Juan Pablo Davila of Codelco, from the *Wall Street Journal*, "Sumitomo Debacle Is Tied to Lax Controls."

Page 182

Sumitomo's new trader rotation system, from Dow Jones Wire Service, "U.S. Copper Trader's Death Is Probe," June 24, 1996.

Page 183

Iguchi information from Reuters News Wire, "Pay re-think Could Deter Rogue Traders," September 27, 1995 and the *Wall Street Journal*, November 29, 1995, Sec. C, p. 1.

Page 183

Iguchi sent to prison for four years, Daiwa expelled from New York and fines, from the *Wall Street Journal*, December 17, 1996, Sec. B, p. 11.

Page 183

Daiwa's alleged cover-up, not telling banking authorities for two months, from the *Wall Street Journal*, November 29, 1995, Sec. C, p. 1.

Page 183

Jett educated at MIT and Harvard, from *USA Today*, "Intense Trader Played to Win," April 25, 1994, p. 3.

Page 183

SEC alleged Jett showed false profits of $348 million to hide losses of $83 million, from the *Washington Post*, January 10, 1996, Sec. G, p.1.

Page 183

SEC filing information regarding Joseph Jett, from U.S. Securities and Exchange Commission Release no. 7252 and Release no. 36696, January 9, 1996.

Page 183

Kidder's lax oversight, supervisors never understood Jett's activity or apparent profitability, from *USA Today*, August 5, 1994, p.1.

Page 184

Anomaly in accounting system and trading of strips and reconstitutions, from U.S. Securities and Exchange Commission Release no. 7252 and Release no. 36696 on January 9, 1996, Administrative Proceeding file no. 3-8919, Cease and Desist proceedings against Jett and Melvin Mullin.

Page 184

Jett's promotion, from *USA Today*, "Intense Trader Played to Win."

Page 184

Jett received $9 million bonus, from *USA Today*, "Wall Street Ethics Again Face Scrutiny," May 8, 1994, p. 1.

Page 184

Award for being firm's top money-maker, from *USA Today*, "Intense Trader Played to Win."

Page 184

Jett fired, from the *Washington Post*, January 10, 1996, Sec. G, p.1.

Page 184

Kidder said Jett solely responsible and fired him, from *USA Today*, "Wall Street Ethics Again Face Scrutiny."

Page 184

GE $210 million first quarter charge against earnings, ibid.

Page 184

Jett contended superiors knew all about his trades, from the *Washington Post*, January 10, 1996, Sec. G, p. 1.

Page 184

Edward Cerullo fined and censured in 1991 by NASD, *Black Enterprise* magazine, January 8, 1994, vol. 25, p. 28.

Page 184

Cerullo accepted one-year suspension, from the *Washington Post*, January 10, 1996, Sec. G, p.1.

Page 184

In May 1996 the SEC began hearings on fraud charges, from *USA Today*, "Former Trader Gets to Tell SEC his Side," May 20, 1996, p. 5B.

Page 184

"I will fight my accusers," ibid.

Page 186

Emerging market trading volume 1994 $2.8 trillion, from speech by Nicolas S. Rohatyn, managing director, J.P. Morgan & Company, cochair of the Emerging Markets Traders Association, December 12, 1995.

Page 186
Emerging Markets Code of Conduct guidelines, ibid.

Page 187
"There has been a sea change," from *Derivatives Strategy* magazine, March 1997, vol. 2, no. 3, p. 23.

Page 189
Fidelity Investments' red flames, from the *Wall Street Journal*, Wednesday, November 29, 1995, Sec. C, p. 1.

CHAPTER 12: QUANTS
Page 193
"This is a high-risk game," from *Wired*, "The Phynancier," January 1997.

Page 194
Shaw's office design in exhibit at Museum of Modern Art, from *Fortune* magazine, "Wall Street's Kind Quant," February 5, 1995.

Page 194
Shaw worked under Nunzio Tartaglia at Morgan Stanley, from *Institutional Investor*, "Computational Finance with David Shaw," March 1994, vol. 28, p. 92.

Page 195
Shaw's fund had a 30 percent return in 1994, from the *Wall Street Journal*, "D.E. Shaw Pockets Profits Other Hedge Funds Sag," September 20, 1994, Sec. C, p. 1.

Page 195
Annual returns of 20 percent, fund up to more than $1.3 billion, Edith Kealey, D.E. Shaw, May 1998.

Page 195
D.E. Shaw trading volume 5 percent of the volume of the New York Stock Exchange, from *Fortune* magazine, "Wall Street's King Quant," James Aley, February 5, 1996.

Page 195
"One of our other businesses," from *Bloomberg Personal Finance*, August 1995, pp. 55–56.

Page 195
Shaw appointed adviser on technology by President Clinton, from *Crain's New York Business*, "Street Computer Whiz Takes Mega-Bite of Tech Start-Ups," October 30, 1995.

Page 196
"Right now," from *Technology Review* (MIT), "An Engineer Goes to Wall Street," January 1996.

Page 196

Shaw believes in Internet possibilities, from *Investment Dealer's Digest*, "Reprogramming D.E. Shaw," September 4, 1995.

Page 196

"We're trying to find areas," from *Wired*, "The Phynancier."

Page 196

Juno has more than 4.6 million subscribers, Edith Kealey, D.E. Shaw, May 1998.

Page 197

"We'd like you to be able," ibid.

Page 198

Prediction Company, from *Fortune* magazine, February 5, 1996.

Page 199

Blair Hull trades 7 percent total index options and 3 percent equity options in United States, from *Fast Company*, April/May 1997, pp. 85–87.

Page 199

Santa Fe Institute, from the *Guardian*, July 31, 1997.

Page 200

Basket trading background, from *Traders* magazine, November 1996, pp. 24–27.

Page 201

Background information on Stanley Ross from speech by him at Bloomberg Conference in London, November 1996.

Page 204

MIT noted 19 percent of companies recruiting in 1997–1998 were financial firms, from Carole Ferrari at MIT Graduate Recruitment Office, May 1998.

CHAPTER 13: MIND, MONEY, AND MACHINE

Page 208

In June 1998 Matif moved to electronic trading and LIFFE voted for electronic trading, from the *Financial Times* (London), June 10, 1998, p. 1

Page 207

NYSE spending $200 million on technology in 1998, spent $190 million in 1997; SuperDot trading volume of 109.5 billion shares in 1997; almost 85 percent reach the specialists re SuperDot, from New York Stock Exchange Press Media Relations Office, April 22, 1998.

Page 207

American Stock Exchange wireless handhelds, from interview with Ralph Rafaniello at the American Stock Exchange.

U.S. Robotics stock unloaded on INSTINET, from the *Wall Street Journal*, July 26, 1996, Sec. C, p. 1.

Brokerages have set up own electronically linked network to trade, from Associated Press, "12 Brokerages Form Electronic Trading Network," June 15, 1997.

Dealing 2000-2 allows traders to "call" each other, from *Euromoney*, "When Is a Market Like Treacle?" July 1996, p. 155.

Marcus Hooper's comments on SETS from interview in London, April 1998.

Reuters survey on SETS, from *Sunday Business*, "SETS Gets a Big Thumbs Down," April 26, 1998.

Information on MIT's electronic trading classroom, from interview with Ray Killian.

"Bandits" information from *Forbes*, "Day Trading Dudes," April 6, 1998.

Future could have trading system that shows product to two hundred people at once, from an interview with Chris Keith.

CHAPTER 14: TRADING ON THE FUTURE

Schwab has $112 billion in online accounts asset, from the *New York Post*, April 28, 1998.

Thirty brokerages for online trading, from the *Sun-Sentinal*, Ft. Lauderdale, FL, November 13, 1996, p. D1.

Lycos reports business and stock trading in top ten of topics requested on the Internet, from the *Wall Street Journal*, June 25, 1996, Sec. C, p. 1.

Motley Fools Web site most hits on the Web, from the Minneapolis-St. Paul *City Business*, vol. 14, no. 9, August 2, 1996, p. 24.

Page 225

Online investment accounts will grow from 3 million at the end of 1997 to 14.4 million by 2002, or assets of $688 billion, from *Business Week*, December 8, 1997, p. 112.

Page 225

In first three months of 1998, almost half of all trades put through Charles Schwab were online, from the *Financial Times*, April 18–19, 1998, p.10.

Page 225

American Stock Exchange survey re: "NextVestors" from Gannett Suburban Newspapers, Business Sec., September 8, 1996.

Page 225

New "mid-tier" brokers on line, from the *Forrester Report*, vol. 2, no. 1, September 1996, p. 8.

Page 226

"We look at the growth of online trading," from *Wired* Magazine Business News Online, "The SEC Tries to Learn New Tricks," September 18, 1997.

Page 227

Peter D. Hart Research Survey results, from "A National Survey among Stock Investors," conducted for the NASDAQ Stock Market, by Peter D. Hart Research Associates, February 1997, p. 6.

Page 228

More than 1,100 new investment clubs each month, total of 36,872 clubs, National Association of Investment Clubs, April 13, 1998. Personal correspondence.

Page 228

"An awful lot of people," from the *Los Angeles Times*, April 1996, p. D1.

Page 229

". . . only 8 percent would sell stocks to avoid further losses," ibid., p. 5.

Page 229

Background on Internet investment clubs from the *New York Times*, "Investment Clubs Flock to Internet," July 7, 1996.

Page 229

As of October 1997, Silicon Investor was largest discussion group on the Web and one of the top three financial sites in terms of traffic, from Yahoo! Internet Life page, August 1997.

Page 229

Stanley Ross's comments about investment managers, from his speech given at the Bloomberg Conference in London, November 1996.

Page 230

Do-it-yourself share dealing services in the U.K., from the *Observer*, November 3, 1996, p. 13.

Page 233

EMU could shrink volume of trading by 8 percent, from the *New York Times*, February 2, 1997, p. 12.

Page 234

There are 565 foreign banking institutions in London. London has 30 percent of global forex business, and has 75 percent of secondary market trading in international bond market, from the *Times*, April 8, 1998, p. 32.

Page 237

Before 1995 only eight days daily share volume reached or exceeded 400 million shares; in first quarter 1998 daily average of 626.4 million; 3,060 companies total, of that 350 foreign companies listed on the NYSE; average of $28.2 billion flows through NYSE every day; more than 3,060 companies list 217.3 billion shares valued at over $12.5 trillion on the NYSE, from Kimberly Williams, NYSE media relations, April 22, 1998.

Page 238

Richard Grasso's vision of NYSE extended trading hours, from Global Investment Technology, vol. 4, no. 19, June 26, 1995, p. 5.

Page 240

Japanese equities on the London Stock Exchange, from Sir Paul Newall (1996), *Japan and the City of London*. London: Athlone Press, p. 96.

BIBLIOGRAPHY

An American Renaissance (1991). Los Angeles, CA: Knowledge Exchange.

Arbel, Avner and Albert E. Kaff (1989). *Crash: Ten Days in October.* New York: Longman Financial Services Publishing.

Auletta, Ken (1986). *Greed and Glory on Wall Street: The Fall of the House of Lehman.* New York: Random House.

Bailey, Fenton (1991). *The Junk Bond Revolution.* London: Fourth Estate.

Bank of England Board of Banking Supervision (1995). "Report of the Board of Banking Supervision Inquiry into the Circumstances of the Collapse of Barings." London.

Bank of International Settlements (1996). "Central Bank Survey of Foreign Exchange and Derivatives Market Activity 1995." Basel, May.

Bloomberg, Michael (1997). *Bloomberg by Bloomberg.* New York: John Wiley & Sons.

Brooks, John (1987). *The Takeover Game.* New York: E.P. Dutton.

Buck, James E. (ed.) (1992). *The New York Stock Exchange: The First 200 Years.* Greenwich, CT: Greenwich Publishing Group.

Carrington, Tim (1985). *The Year They Sold Wall Street.* Boston: Houghton Mifflin.

Chernow, Ron (1990). *The House of Morgan.* New York: Atlantic Monthly Press.

Christensen, Donald (1994). *Surviving the Coming Mutual Fund Crisis.* New York: Little, Brown.

Cook, Timothy and Robert LaRoche (eds.) (1993). *Instruments of the Money Market.* Federal Reserve Bank of Richmond, Virginia.

Davis, William (1976). *It's No Sin To Be Rich.* Nashville: Thomas Nelson Publishers.

Delamaide, Darrell (1984). *Debt Shock: The Inside Story of the Crisis That Threatens the World's Banks and Stock Markets.* London: Weidenfeld and Nicolson.

Dreman, David (1980). *The New Contrarian Investment Strategy.* New York: Random House.

Duffee, Gregory R. (1994). *On Measuring Credit Risks of Derivatives Instruments.* Washington, D.C.: Federal Reserve Board, Division of Monetary Affairs Study.

Eckes, Alfred E. (1975). *A Search for Solvency: Bretton Woods and the International Monetary System, 1941–1971.* Austin: University of Texas Press.

Economic Growth and Job Creation (1994). Santa Monica, CA: Milken Institute for Job and Capital Creation.

The Economist (1996). "Technology in Finance Survey." October 26.

Fadiman, Mark (1994). *Market Shock.* New York: John Wiley & Sons.

Federal Reserve Bank of New York (1995). "Survey of Foreign Exchange Market Activity in the United States." April. Revised October 6.

Ferris, William G. (1988). *The Grain Traders.* Lansing, Michigan: State University Press.

Finnerty, J. D. (1990). "Financial Engineering in Corporate Finance: An Overview," *The Handbook of Financial Engineering.* New York: HarperBusiness.

Fischel, Daniel (1995). *Payback: The Conspiracy to Destroy Michael Milken and His Financial Revolution.* New York: HarperBusiness.

Fisher, Alfred A. (1989). *Wall Street Women.* New York: Alfred A. Knopf.

Fisher, Kenneth L. (1993). *100 Minds That Made the Market.* Woodside, California: Business Classics.

Gardner, David and Tom Gardner (1996). *The Motley Fools Investment Guide.* New York: Simon & Schuster.

Geisst, Charles R. (1990). *Visionary Capitalism: Financial Markets and the American Dream in the Twentieth Century.* New York: Praeger.

Goodwin, Doris Kearns (1987). *The Fitzgeralds and the Kennedys: An American Saga.* New York: Simon and Schuster.

Gordon, John Steele (1988). *The Scarlet Woman of Wall Street.* New York: Weidenfeld & Nicholson.

Graham, Benjamin (1973). *The Intelligent Investor.* New York: Harper & Row.

Grant, James (1993). *Minding Mr. Market: Ten Years on Wall Street with Grant's Interest Rate Observer.* New York: Farrar Straus Giroux.

Greider, William (1987). *Secrets of the Temple: How the Federal Reserve Runs the Country.* New York: Simon and Schuster.

Hamilton, Adrian (1986). *The Financial Revolution.* New York: Free Press.

Harrod, R. F. (1969). *The Life of John Maynard Keynes.* Augustus M. Kelley Publishers.

Henriques, Diana B. (1995). *Fidelity's World.* New York: Scribner & Sons.

Institutional Investor (1988). *The Way It Was: An Oral History of Finance: 1967–1987.* New York: William Morrow.

International Monetary Fund (1998). "ABCDE: Tenth Conference Address," by Stanley Fischer, Washington D.C., April 20.

Jubak, Jim (1996). *The Worth Guide to Electronic Investing.* New York: HarperBusiness.

Kindleberger, Charles (1978). *Manias, Panics, and Crashes: A History of Financial Crises.* New York: Basic Books.

Kindleberger, Charles (1981). *International Money: A Collection of Essays.* London: George Allen and Unwin.

Klein, Frederick C. and John A. Prestbo (1974). *News and the Market.* Chicago: Henry Regnery Company.

Kolb, Robert W. (1993). *Financial Derivatives.* Englewood Cliffs: New York Institute of Finance.

Kornbluth, Jesse (1992). *Highly Confident: The Crime and Punishment of Michael Milken.* New York: William Morrow.

Landrum, Gene N. (1996). *Profiles of Power and Success.* New York: Prometheus Books.

Leeson, Nick and Edward Whitley (1996). *Rogue Trader: How I Brought Down Barings Bank and Shook the Financial World.* Boston: Little, Brown.

Levitt, Arthur (1995). Remarks at the Second Annual Symposium for Mutual Funds, United States Securities and Exchange Commission, Washington, D.C., April 11.

Levitt, Arthur (1995). "Professional Standards: The Next Competitive Frontier." Speech at the New York Stock Exchange Ethics Conference, February 9.

Lewis, Michael (1989). *Liar's Poker: Rising Through the Wreckage on Wall Street.* New York: W.W. Norton.

Lucas, Henry and Robert Schwartz (eds.) (1989). *The Challenge of Information Technology for the Securities Markets: Liquidity, Volatility and Global Trading.* Homewood, Illinois: Dow Jones-Irwin.

Luft, Carl F. (1994). *Understanding and Trading Futures.* Chicago: Probus Publishing.

Lynch, Peter and John Rothchild (1989). *One Up on Wall Street: How to Use What You Already Know to Make Money in the Market.* New York: Simon and Schuster.

Lynch, Peter and John Rothchild (1993). *Beating the Street.* New York: Fireside.

Mandel, Michael J. (1996). *The High Risk Society: Peril and Promise in the New Economy.* New York: Times Business Books.

Mayer, Martin (1988). *Markets.* New York: W.W. Norton.

Mayer, Martin (1992). *Stealing the Market.* New York: HarperCollins.

Melamed, Leo (1993). *Leo Melamed on the Markets.* New York: John Wiley & Sons.

Melamed, Leo and Bob Tamarkin (1996). *Escape to the Futures.* New York: John Wiley & Sons.

Metz, Tim (1988). *Black Monday.* New York: William Morrow.

Millman, Gregory J. (1995). *Around the World on a Trillion Dollars a Day.* London: Bantam Press.

Mitchell, William J. (1997). *City of Bits: Space, Place and the Infobahn.* Boston: MIT Press.

Naisbitt, John (1995). *Global Paradox.* London: Nicholas Brealey Publishing.

Newall, Sir Paul (1996). *Japan and the City of London.* London: Athlone Press.

Niederhoffer, Victor (1997). *The Education of a Speculator.* New York: John Wiley & Sons.

Orbell, John (1985). *Baring Brothers and Company, Limited: A History to 1939.* London: Baring Brothers.

Pring, J. Martin (1985). *Technical Analysis Explained.* New York: McGraw-Hill.

Revell, Jack (1973). *The British Financial System.* New York: Barnes & Noble.

Rubenfeld, Alan (1992). *SuperTraders: Secrets and Successes of Wall Street's Best and Brightest.* Chicago: Probus Publishing.

Schwager, Jack D. (1993). *Market Wizards.* New York: HarperBusiness.

Securities and Exchange Commission Administrative Proceeding against Orlando Joseph Jett and Melvin Mullin (1996). File no. 3-8919, January 9.

Securities and Exchange Commission, Division of Market Regulation (1994). "Market 2000: An Examination of Current Equity Market Developments." January.

Security Traders Association Institutional Committee, Buyside Trading Survey (1996). "What If It Were Your Market Instead of the Brokers'?" November.

Sharp, Robert M. (1989). *The Lore and Legends of Wall Street.* Homewood, Illinois: Dow Jones-Irwin.

Sloane, Leonard (1980). *The Anatomy of the Floor: The Trillion Dollar Market at the New York Stock Exchange.* New York: Doubleday.

Smith, Roy C. (1990). *The Money Wars: The Rise and Fall of the Great Buyout Boom of the 1980s.* New York: Truman Talley Books, Button.

Sobel, Robert (1986). *Salomon Brothers 1910–1985: Advancing to Leadership.* New York: Salomon Brothers.

Sobel, Robert (1996). *Salomon Brothers: Advancing to Leadership.* New York: Salomon Brothers.

Soros, George (1995). *Soros on Soros: Staying Ahead of the Curve.* New York: John Wiley & Sons.

Tamarking, Bob (1993). *The Merc: The Emergence of a Global Financial Powerhouse.* New York: HarperBusiness.

Teweles, Richard J., Edward Bradley, and Ted Teweles (1992). *The Stock Market.* New York: John Wiley & Sons.

Thomas, Dana L. (1967). *The Plungers and the Peacocks*. New York: G.P. Putnam's Sons.

Thomsett, Michael C. (1993). *Getting Started in Options*. New York: John Wiley & Sons.

Volcker, Paul A. and Toyoo Gyohten (1992). *Changing Fortunes*. New York: Times Books.

Welles, Chris (1975). *The Last Days of the Club*. New York: E.P. Dutton.

Yago, Glenn (1991). *Junk Bonds: How High Yield Securities Restructured Corporate America*. New York: Oxford University Press.

Ziegler, Philip (1988). *The Sixth Great Power: A History of One of the Greatest of All Banking Families the House of Barings, 1762–1929*. New York: Alfred A. Knopf.

INDEX

U.S. dollar and 1996 budget agreement, 134; world markets, annual revenue, 4

Daiwa, 180, 183
Dall, Robert, 18, 55
Dalton, Greiner, Hartman, Maher & Company, 24, 108, 165
Dalton, Tim, 108
Davila, Juan Pablo, 182
Derivatives, 144–59; currency futures, 147–48; flex options, 157; OTC, 155–57; regulation, 153–54, 156, 188; -related disasters, 149–53, 174–83, 187;
  software packages for, 158; technological revolution, 146; transaction sizes, 154; types of, 145
Derman, Emanuel, 158
D. E. Shaw, 9, 40, 194, 195
Dillon Read Capital, 108
Dillon Stanley, 57
Downton, Christine, 199–200
Drexel Burnham Lambert, 18, 27–28, 96–97, 99, 101
Druckenmiller, Stanley, 131

EASDAQ, 71, 215, 235, 239
Education of a Speculator (Niederhoffer), 12
Electronic trading, 8, 9, 92, 94–95, 166–68, 172–73, 193–221; business school programs, 217; versus floor/manual trading, 85, 197, 205–21, 236–41
Elsevier, 65–66
Emerging Market Traders Association, 186
Emerging markets, 186–87
ERISA (Employee Retirement Income Security Act), 51, 161
Ethics, 83; "code of conduct" for OTC derivatives, 156; "my word is my bond," 19–22, 109;
  partnership ethos, 28–29
European Banking Company, 128
European Central Bank, 141
European Exchange Rate Mechanism, 131

European Monetary Union (EMU), 13, 142, 232, 233–34
European trading: EASDAQ, 71, 215; electronic, 208–9, 215–16, 238–41; Eurex, 209; EURO Alliance, 209; Eurobond, 201, 210; Eurodollar, 156, 187, 232;
  Euro market, 6; EuroNM, 209; future of, 232

Farmer, Doyne, 198–99
Federal Reserve Bank, 130, 140–41
Fidelity Investments, 189, 210
Financial markets. *See* Currency
Fink, Larry, 56
Finkle and Company, 105
Finkle, Davey, 105
"First calls," 160
First Investors Fund for Income, 98
Fisher, Richard, 56; and brother, 58
Flanagan, Michael, 25
Ford Foundation, 112–14, 185
Forex brokers and Dealing 2000–2, 211
Forrester Research Inc., 225
France: CAC, 215; currency trading, 129–30, 133; electronic trading, 215–16, 236–37; EMU, impact of, 234; individual trading, 230–31; Matif, 208, 215–16; Paris trading, compensation, 27
Free market economy, 139–40, 147
Friedman, Milton, 90–91
Futures, 37, 145; annual amount traded, 4; common good of, 92–93; copper trading, 180–83; electronic trading, 208, 215–16; E-mini, 94, 208; foreign exchange, 81, 90–93, 147–48; future of, 239–41; OTC market, 157; trading floors, 39
Futures and Options Association, 153

General Electric, 184; Pension Fund, 113
George, Eddie, 174
Germany: currency trading, 132; DTB (Deutsche Terminbose); futures exchange, 208; Frankfort-London linkage, 209
Gibson Greetings, 149, 152

108, 153, 165; retail Internet trading, 226; shortened filing times, 56
Security Pacific, 25
Security Traders Association, 165, 168
Sell-side traders, 164, 169–73; attrition, 232–33; buy-side versus, 58–59, 107–10, 115, 163–64; future of, 232–33; proprietary, 164
Shank, Susan, 107
Shapiro, James, 236
Shaw, David, x, 155, 194–98, 218, 226–27
Sheinberg, Eric, x, 7, 29, 64–68, 69, 74, 142, 171, 180
Shelf registration, 56–57
Shopkorn, Stanley, x, 33, 52–54, 56, 58, 59, 70, 76, 83–84, 95, 221, 240
Siebert, Brandford, Shank & Company, 107
Siebert Entrepreneurial Philanthropic Plan, 77
Siebert, Muriel, x, 17, 51, 103–7, 129–30, 131, 139, 161–62, 223
Siebert OnLine, 107
Silicon Investor, 228
Simon, Bill, 71, 75
Singapore International Monetary Exchange (SIMEX), 176, 177
Smith Barney, 45, 227
Smith, Cliff, 118
Smith, Lionel, 52, 53
Smith Newcourt, 65
SOFFEX, 209
Soros, George, 18, 41–42, 74, 125, 131–32, 137
Specialization, 31, 41–42, 59–62, 121–22, 168, 207, 237
Speculation, 14–16, 38–39; bad, 151; common good and, 17, 128–29; currency, 126–28, 131–36; derivatives, 146
Stark, Holly, 24, 73, 107–10, 165, 167, 171, 222, 237
Stearns, Bear, 83
Steinhardt, Michael, 41
Stock exchanges: alternatives to, 196, 205–21, 232–41; annual amounts traded, 4; trading floors, 39
Strauss, Tom, 16, 54, 95
Strips and reconstitution, 184

Strumpf, Linda, 19, 171, 185–86
Suharto, President, 138
Sumitomo Corporation, 180–83
Sun Life, 11, 71–72, 84, 202
Sun Microsystems, 4
SuperDot system, 207, 237
Swaps, 116, 145, 148–49, 156; currency, 148; diff, 152; interest rate, 148, 158

Takeovers, and junk bonds, 101
Tartaglia, Nunzio, 194
Taylor, Colin, 9, 24, 213
Telephone trading, 166, 212–13; merger with computer/TV, 220, 227
Television: business, 72–73, 81–82, 85–88, 227; global markets and, 72–73, 87; merger with computer/telephone, 220, 227; on NYSE, 72, 120. *See also* Bloomberg Business News; CNBC; CNN
Texaco, 56
Threlkeld, David, 181
Ticker tape, 49, 52–53
Tiger Fund, 74
Trade: buy side, 39, 160–73; defined, 5; sell side, 39
Tradepoint, 64, 189, 201, 202, 203, 212, 214–15, 239–40
Traders: age, 126, 158, 178, 212; anonymity of, 17; art of protecting his position, 126; block trading, advent of and, 48–49; bridge or black jack playing, 18; buy side versus sell side, 58–59, 107–10, 115, 160–73; characteristics and traits, 22–23, 25–27, 43, 63, 66, 74–77, 218; "color," 218–19; computer knowledge and edge, *see* Quants; economic growth and, 5; famous pre–1930s, 21; function of, 5; human art of, 10–11, 12; image of, 39, 69–70, 74; impact and influence of, 14, 17; information, importance, 14, 73–74, 81, 109, 111, 123, 160, 165–66, 222–23; local or day, 22, 38–39, 216; math and statistics skills, 55, *see also* Quants; mind-set of, 12–13; money made and compensation,

27–28, 29, 32; new generation, x, 3, 8–10, 40–41, 198, 204, 212, 237, *see also* Buy-side traders; Quants; old generation, x, 9, 10, 29, 30–31, 50, 211, 212, 237; partnership and firm loyalty, 28–30; proprietary, 39–40, 178; red flag for, 178–79; responsibility of, 16–17; rogue, 13; sports, parallel with, 32; styles, 42–43; women, 17, 103–25; workplaces, various types, 39–42; world of, example, 6–7; young, novice, 13. *See also individuals*

Traders magazine, 71–72

Trading: consolidation in the industry, 1970s, 51; description of, 37; emerges as a profession, 51; gambling versus, 16; globalization of, 6–7, 58, 208–9, 238–41; government regulation, 20, 236; growth, 1980s, 56, 57, 69–70; losers versus winners, 13; misconceptions, 13; public or economic good and, 17–18, 30; purpose and value of, 5; stress of, 25–26; Wall Street history, 20. *See also* Computer and technology revolution

Trading floors, 7–9; design, 22; formal, 39; pit, 37, 93

Trading Places (film), 36

Treasury bills, 91–92, 216–17

Tsai, Gerry, 105

Tuchman, Barbara, 211

Turner, Ted, 100

U.K., individual investing in, 230. *See also* London Stock Exchange

Union Bank of Switzerland, 24, 126

Unocal Corporation, 101

Von Clemm, Michael, 6, 31

Wall Street (film), 70

Wall Street Journal, 101–2, 109, 111

Ward, Ken, 106

Wheat, Alan, 158

White Weld, 179

Whitney Group, 27

Wilson, Steve, 212, 215

Wit Capital, 220

Women's Forum, 107

Women traders, 17, 103–25; African American, 107, 119–24; restrictions, 111. *See also individuals*

Workplaces, various types, 39–42. *See also individuals*

World Airways, 53

W. R. Grace, 112, 113

Yago, Glenn, 70

Yassukovich, Stanislas, 30, 71, 128, 129, 139, 179

Zapata Oil, 99